J O H N
MUIR
L I F E
A N D
W O R K

John Muir relaxing on Little Kern River, ca. 1908, probably during a Sierra Club outing. Photograph by Edward Hughes. John Muir Papers, Holt Atherton Library. Copyright 1984 by Muir-Hanna Trust.

J O H N
MUIR
L I F E
A N D
W O R K

EDITED BY SALLY M. MILLER

UNIVERSITY OF NEW MEXICO PRESS

ALBUQUERQUE

Library of Congress Cataloging-in-Publication Data

John Muir, life and work/edited by Sally M. Miller.— 1st ed.
p.   cm.
Rev. versions of papers presented at a conference held in April
1990 at the University of the Pacific.
Includes bibliographical references and index.
ISBN 0-8263-1452-X
1. Muir, John, 1838–1914—Congresses.
2. Muir, John, 1838–1914—Family—Congresses.
3. Naturalists—United States—Biography—Congresses.
4. Conservationists—United States—Biography—Congresses.
I. Miller, Sally M., 1937–
QH31.M9J65   1993
333.7'2'092—dc20
[B]   93-10925
CIP

First paperbound printing, 1994

*To the memory of John Muir and to all those whom he
inspired to walk the path he trod*

On Renewing Muir's Dream

Today on Muir's birthday we
    Muir devotees walk the valley
    of Hetch Hetchy where the
    Ahwahneechees collected grasses
    to weave their baskets when
    Muir was born back in Scotland;
    we hike along the dammed up
    waters of Hetch Hetchy where the
    dreams of Indians and John Muir
    and glacially polished cliffs
    with sugar pines, mountain paint,
    and kitkidizie were all drowned.
    We hike to the foot of Wapama Falls
    to catch a misty glimpse of the
    real power of this inundated valley,
    that other Yosemite the Scotsman
    dreamed of saving and we dream of
    draining if only we can find a way.

Richard F. Fleck
April 21, 1990

CONTENTS

INTRODUCTION:
JOHN MUIR'S LIFE AND LEGACY
RONALD H. LIMBAUGH
3

PART I:
MUIR THE INDIVIDUAL

CHAPTER 1.
"AFFECTIONATELY YOURS, JOHN MUIR"
THE CORRESPONDENCE BETWEEN JOHN MUIR AND
HIS PARENTS, BROTHERS AND SISTERS
KEITH E. KENNEDY
16

CHAPTER 2.
JOHN MUIR AND VERTICAL SAUNTERING
ARTHUR W. EWART
42

PART II:
MUIR AND RELIGION

CHAPTER 3.
GOD AND JOHN MUIR:
A PSYCHOLOGICAL INTERPRETATION OF JOHN MUIR'S JOURNEY
FROM THE CAMPBELLITES TO THE "RANGE OF LIGHT"
MARK STOLL
64

CHAPTER 4.
JOHN MUIR, CHRISTIAN MYSTICISM,
AND THE SPIRITUAL VALUE OF NATURE
DENNIS WILLIAMS
82

PART III:
MUIR AND WILDERNESS

CHAPTER 5.
WHY WILDERNESS? JOHN MUIR'S "DEEP ECOLOGY"
JAMES D. HEFFERNAN
102

CHAPTER 6.
JOHN MUIR AND THE WILDERNESS IDEAL
DON WEISS
118

PART IV:
THE LITERARY MUIR

CHAPTER 7.
JOHN MUIR'S TRANSCENDENTAL IMAGERY
RICHARD F. FLECK
136

CHAPTER 8.
ON THE TOPS OF MOUNTAINS:
JOHN MUIR AND HENRY THOREAU
EDGAR M. CASTELLINI
152

PART V:
MUIR AND THE PHYSICAL SCIENCES

CHAPTER 9.
MUIR AND GEOLOGY
DENNIS R. DEAN
168

CHAPTER 10.
BOTANICAL EXPLORATION OF CALIFORNIA
FROM MENZIES TO MUIR (1786–1900)
WITH SPECIAL EMPHASIS ON THE SIERRA NEVADA
NANCY G. SLACK
194

PART VI:
MUIR'S PLACES

CHAPTER 11.
AFTER YOSEMITE:
JOHN MUIR AND THE SOUTHERN SIERRA
PAUL D. SHEATS
244

CHAPTER 12.
"FEAR NOTHING"
AN INTERPRETATION OF JOHN MUIR'S
WRITINGS ON YELLOWSTONE
BRUCE A. RICHARDSON
266

CHAPTER 13.
JOHN MUIR'S TRAVELS IN AUSTRALASIA, 1903–1904:
THEIR SIGNIFICANCE FOR CONSERVATION
AND ENVIRONMENTAL THOUGHT
C. MICHAEL HALL
286

CHRONOLOGY
310

CONTRIBUTORS
313

INDEX
317

ACKNOWLEDGMENTS

It is my pleasure as editor to acknowledge all of those who made this work possible. This volume originated in a conference held in April, 1990, at the University of the Pacific on the life and work of John Muir, the forty-third annual conference in the series known as the California History Institute. Thereafter, the John Muir Center for Regional Studies gathered together revised versions of the papers presented at the conference.

I wish to thank all of the presenters and authors who made the original conference a success. I also wish to extend my appreciation to the director of the John Muir Center, R. H. Limbaugh, for his support, assistance, and resourcefulness. The work of the Center would not be able to proceed without his efforts, nor those of two able, enthusiastic, and supportive administrators at this institution, Vice President Joseph L. Subbiondo and Dean Robert R. Benedetti of the College of the Pacific. The assistance of Daryl Morrison, Special Collections Librarian, and her staff at the Holt-Atherton Center of the University of the Pacific was of enormous importance to the work on this book; not only is the editor of this volume beholden to Daryl but so are the various contributors. Lastly, and more important of all, it is my pleasure to thank Pamela Altree whose administrative and clerical assistance and good cheer were the basic elements that made this project possible.

J O H N
MUIR
L I F E
A N D
W O R K

Introduction:
John Muir's
Life and Legacy

Ronald H. Limbaugh

As a young man John Muir had little time to contemplate the wonders of nature. The third of eight children born in Scotland to Daniel and Anne (Gilrye) Muir, he was eleven when his family emigrated to central Wisconsin in 1849. His father, a stern Calvinist, kept his sons busy clearing land and farming. John escaped from his routine when he left home in 1860, intending first to pursue a career as an inventor, then taking an interest in medicine.

Muir attended the University of Wisconsin for two years, immersing himself in the natural sciences while also reading Emerson and Thoreau for the first time, encouraged by his men-

3

tors, Professor Ezra Carr and his wife Jeanne. Unable to continue full-time without means of support, he dropped out to teach public school one winter, then worked on his brother-in-law's farm. Before he could resume his studies the Civil War draft intervened. A conscientious objector, in March of 1864 he left for Canada to join his younger brother who had earlier crossed the border to avoid being conscripted. Ironically neither John nor his brother was actually called for service.

With unexpected time on his hands in Canada Muir studied nature, traveling extensively in the lower provinces during the spring and summer of 1864. The need for money, however, cut short this early expedition. For eighteen months he intermittently botanized and worked as a mill hand at a broom factory in Meaford, Ontario, but returned to the United States after the plant burned in March of 1866. For nearly a year he pursued an industrial career, earning praise as foreman in an Indianapolis carriage factory. Then fate intervened. An eye accident in March of 1867 temporarily blinded him and directed his thoughts to full-time nature study. Striking out for South America, he walked to the Gulf of Mexico, but a long illness in Florida changed his plans and turned his interests westward.

Muir arrived by ship in San Francisco in March of 1868, walked to the Sierra Nevada, and began a five-year wilderness sojourn during which he made his year-round home in Yosemite Valley. Employed as sheepherder and lumberman when he needed money for supplies, he investigated the length and breath of the Sierra range. Although overgrazing and imprudent lumbering already began to stir his latent conservation instincts, in this period most of his attention focused on glaciation and its impact on mountain topography. His early correspondence and newspaper articles earned him the respect of eastern intellectuals and scientists such as Ralph Waldo Emerson and Asa Gray, both of whom sought him out during their visits to California.

Encouraged by his friend and mentor Jeanne Carr, in the early 1870s he took up nature writing as a profession. Late in

Introduction

1873 he set up winter quarters in Oakland, beginning a pattern of wintering in the Bay Area to prepare manuscripts based on journal entries made during his summer excursions. With but few exceptions he continued this cycle until 1880. His travels included three explorations of Mount Shasta and the Great Basin, one excursion over the mountains of Southern California and the Coast Range, and his first of seven trips to Alaska. Interspersed with these far-ranging expeditions were numerous shorter trips to the Sierra and its river systems. He financed his travels and modest bachelor lifestyle with revenue from contributions published in the *San Francisco Bulletin, Overland Monthly, Scribners,* and other newspapers and magazines. His published articles and his lectures in the Bay Area and Sacramento attracted the attention of scientists and naturalists across the country. In this period he also inaugurated the first lobbying effort to protect Sierra forests from wasteful lumbering practices.

In the 1880s, family matters ended these annual expeditions. On April 14, 1880 he married Louisa "Louie" Strentzel, daughter of a prominent physician and horticulturalist in the Alhambra Valley near Martinez, California. Quickly learning the fruit business, Muir soon found himself caught up in the full-time management of his father-in-law's vast orchards and properties. After two more trips to Alaska in the early 1880s, he settled down uneasily to home life. Two daughters added to his domestic responsibilities. His writing diminished both in quantity and quality during the decade, with only one lengthy project completed, an illustrated travelogue for which he was editor and principal contributor. It was published as *Picturesque California* in 1887–1888.

Muir's reputation as conservation leader and "father" of national parks dates from the late 1880s. Prompted by the persistent urging of Robert Underwood Johnson, associate editor of *Century Magazine,* and freed from domestic chores by his cooperative wife (who sold part of the Strentzel estate after her father died and turned over the rest to relatives to manage), Muir launched a major writing and lobbying campaign. It culminated in the 1890s with the creation of Yosemite, Sequoia, and General Grant National Parks. Muir also helped stimulate interest in the creation of Mount Rainier National Park in 1899. An attempt to add Kings Canyon to Sequoia Park failed, but he helped found the Sierra Club to coordinate conservation efforts and used its collective influence to prevent a serious threat to Yosemite Park boundaries. In the meantime he revived both his travels and his literary output. In addition to numerous articles in national magazines, he completed his first major book, *The Mountains of California*, in 1894, but it took nine more years to produce the second, *Our National Parks*.

As a conservation leader, he was advisor to the federal Forestry Commission, organized in 1896 to survey the nation's forest resources. Although not an official member, he was a close friend of commission chairman C. S. Sargent, and he traveled with the Commission intermittently during its northern and western surveys. Over the next two years he journeyed with Sargent and with William Canby in a wide-ranging study of forest resources in Canada and Alaska, the South Atlantic, the Midwest, and New England. His seventh and last trip to Alaska was in 1899 as a member of the Harriman Alaska Expedition.

During the Progressive Era Muir led the preservationist wing away from utilitarian conservationists headed by Theodore Roosevelt and Gifford Pinchot. Muir welcomed the opportunity to escort Roosevelt on a three-day camping trip to Yosemite early in 1903. He left soon after on a year-long world tour that took him to the hinterlands of at least sixteen countries in Europe, Asia, North Africa, and the South Pacific. When he returned in the spring of 1904, a series of family health problems and a rising concern over conservation issues sidetracked his writing career. A long series of respiratory problems invalided his youngest daughter, Helen, and forced her to seek the healthier air of the high desert regions in Arizona and southern California. Muir was a dutiful, perhaps overindulgent father, especially after his

Introduction

wife died in August 1905. He made frequent trips to visit and comfort Helen. Out of this southwest travel came his efforts to protect the Petrified Forest and the Grand Canyon.

In between family trips, Muir led a successful campaign to return Yosemite Valley to federal jurisdiction as part of the National Park. He also took up the battle against progressives, encouraged by Pinchot, who wanted to convert Hetch Hetchy Valley in the Yosemite Park into a reservoir for the bustling city of San Francisco. The Hetch Hetchy fight, Muir's biggest and longest wilderness preservation effort, took most of his time and energy after 1907. He and his preservationist allies succeeded in delaying dam authorization for five years.

During the Hetch Hetchy struggle, Muir managed to complete the manuscripts of four popular books: *Stickeen* (1909), *My First Summer in the Sierra* (1911), *The Yosemite* (1912), and *The Story of My Boyhood and Youth* (1913). While the latter two were still at the printers, he broke away for an eight-month tour to the last major portions of the globe he had not yet seen. Beginning with the Amazon River in the summer of 1911, he toured the rest of South America, then crossed the Atlantic to see the baobab trees along the Zambezi River and also Lake Victoria.

The Hetch Hetchy controversy was still boiling when he returned in February of 1912, and he carried on a vigorous fight until President Wilson signed the Raker Act in 1913, allowing San Francisco to build the dam. Muir accepted the loss stoically and turned his attention back to his writing schedule, determined to complete a major Alaska manuscript. He worked until failing health forced him into a Los Angeles hospital late in 1914, where he died December 24 with an unfinished chapter on Alaska at his side.

John Muir missed much of the twentieth century, but he has a larger following today than during his own lifetime. A decade ago he won a statewide poll of California historians who named him the most important figure in California history. Seventy-five years after his death the California legislature honored him

by designating April 21 as John Muir Day, an annual celebration of his life and a time of environmental study and reflection.
Even if the various schools, hospitals, banks, and motels that are
named in his honor do not adequately represent his environmental philosophy, the Muir National Monument in Martinez, the
Muir Woods State Park in Marin County, California, the Muir
Wilderness area in the Sierra, and the National Scenic Trail that
follows the mountain crests from Canada to Mexico, among other
landmarks, all demonstrate the importance of Muir's legacy.

Muir and his work are best known in the Far West, where the
popularity of outdoor recreation, the visibility of the Sierra Club,
and the commercialization of Muir's name all have heightened
public awareness and concern. But his national stature continues
to increase. In the last decade three major biographies have been
published, all based on new research made possible by the opening of Muir's papers that had been virtually closed to scholars for
over a half-century. A recently republished comprehensive bibliography of Muir's published works lists at least 150 reprintings
in a variety of media forms since 1977, when the first edition of
the bibliography was made available.[1] This does not include a
long list of scholarly and popular books and articles about Muir
that have come on the market in recent years. Between 1979
and 1990 at least sixty-seven books and articles on Muir have
appeared, according to the indexes to *America: History and Life,*
a scholarly periodical abstract.

Overseas interest in Muir has also increased in recent years.
To honor their native son, residents of Dunbar, Scotland, have
restored his birthplace and have developed it into a major tourist
attraction. Along the southern coast of the Firth of Forth a 1,700
acre wildlife preserve, one of the most important estuarian habi-
tats bordering the North Sea, has been named in his honor.

As Muir's stature continues to grow, so does the movement
he helped originate. Yet modern environmentalism is a far cry
from the conservation movement as Muir knew it. One reason
is fairly obvious: massive assaults on the global environment—

Introduction

air pollution, urban decay, overpopulation, rain forest destruction, toxic waste disposal, groundwater pollution, the greenhouse effect, red tides—were not anticipated in Muir's day. A second reason was the breakdown of unity among conservation leaders. Even before Muir died the movement split over a fundamental difference in philosophy that can be expressed in two words: utilization and preservation.

Utilitarian conservation was articulated first by Gifford Pinchot while he was chief forester for the Teddy Roosevelt administration, and it was subsequently modified but not radically altered. It is based on the Enlightenment premise that human material development is paramount, progressive, benevolent, and inevitable. From this perspective raw nature has little inherent value because human needs, having priority in the biosphere, require constant utilization of the earth's energy sources whether in animal, vegetable, or mineral form. Thus, in the name of public interest, resources must be used as efficiently as possible to satisfy the widest variety of human wants with the least amount of waste and pollution. Planning, progress, wise and multiple use, efficiency, utility—these are the shibboleths of utilitarian conservation.

John Muir rejected the materialism of the utilitarians if not their anthropocentric assumptions. Linking the philosophical beliefs of romantic primitivism and modern ecology—the bridge between Jean-Jacques Rousseau and Aldo Leopold—Muir had an intuitive grasp of ecological principles but emphasized aesthetics rather than science as the primary reason for preservation.[2] "Man needs beauty as well as bread!" Muir's famous Hetch Hetchy adage best summarizes his preservationist philosophy. To him, pristine wilderness, the sublime expression of ultimate good, restored the human spirit and stimulated man's creative powers.[3] Thus Muir found intellectual and spiritual reasons for saving wild nature: it benefited man in nonmaterial ways.

The contrast between Muir's preservationist rhetoric and

9

Ronald H. Limbaugh

the strident slash-and-burn materialist-progressive ethic of post–
Civil War America has stimulated a reassessment of his role as
cultural iconoclast. But the diversity of modern Muir scholar-
ship, and the frequent clash of opinions, indicate that Muir's
significance in modern intellectual and environmental history
remains unclear. Several modern scholars consider him the god-
father, if not the father, of the modern environmental movement.
They have concluded that in positing an egalitarian universe,
Muir consciously rejected Christianity and the anthropocentric
world view upon which it is based.[4] More recently, "deep"
ecologists, departing from more conventional ecological thinking
that they consider utilitarian and "shallow," have found common ground with Muir and other early environmentalists who
challenged traditional ethics by insisting that all life forms have
inherent worth.[5]

Although Muir has an important role in the development of
modern ecological thinking, the core of his nature philosophy
does not rest on ecological principles. He defended the moral
equality of plants and animals, but, unlike George Marsh, Muir's
contemporary, or Aldo Leopold later, he did not develop a co-
herent and consistent ecological rationale. Despite what some
Muir scholars have implied, Muir's writings are generally barren
of arguments that saving wilderness was essential for land health,
or for biotic diversity, or for habitat sustainability, or for global
equilibrium, or for any other reason that could be considered part
of the basic arsenal of modern ecological science. Instead, the
bedrock of Muir's *weltanschauung* is anthropocentric: humans,
as the highest link in the "Great Chain of Being," have a special responsibility to care for the rest of God's creatures, animal,
vegetable, or mineral.[6] Biblical stewardship theory, not ecological science, gave humans a mandate for understanding and
protecting the natural world. Muir was essentially a nineteenth-
century Christian humanist, a wilderness popularizer who raised
public consciousness with eloquent appeals for selective preservation.[7]

The biocentric undercurrent in modern preservationism has

washed away much of Muir's romantic justification for wilderness.[8] Yet Muir's aesthetic appreciation of nature is by no means obsolete—albeit largely unrecognized as a major influence on modern environmental thinking.[9] Also not well recognized is his emphasis on the recreational values of wilderness—an important component of wilderness management planning today.[10]

The two main divisions of conservation thinking today are not mutually exclusive. Preservationists and utilitarian conservationists have often joined forces to support antipollution legislation and other measures to restore the deteriorating man-made environments of city, farm, and suburb, although they have often disagreed over means and priorities. More profound are differences over issues involving wilderness—the natural environment not yet radically changed by humans. Instead of presuming ultimate development of all natural resources for human benefit, preservationists underscore the intrinsic values of undisturbed natural environments.

Since the publication of *Silent Spring* in the early 1960s the environmental movement has expanded far beyond the scope of earlier efforts to conserve natural resources. Although current environmental thinking probably owes more to Muir than to Pinchot, modern environmentalism is a more broadly based and comprehensive movement than either utilitarian conservation or preservationism.[11] This is hardly surprising; the climax of urban-industrial development—Alvin Toffler's *Second Wave* civilization—was not reached until mid-century, fifty years after the first nationwide conservation efforts. Neither Muir nor Pinchot could anticipate the global impact of modern technology and its deleterious consequences on both natural and man-made environments. Yet for all its complexities, environmentalism today has a bedrock dedication to protecting and preserving the full spectrum of our natural endowment, including those few remaining patches of pristine wilderness that still can uplift and inspire. Popularizing love for wild nature in all its forms is perhaps John Muir's most important legacy.

Ronald H. Limbaugh

NOTES

Earlier versions of this article were published in *The Guide and Index to the Microform Edition of the John Muir Papers* (Alexandria, VA: Chadwyck-Healey Inc., 1986), pp. 17–19; the Portland *Oregonian*, and the *San Francisco Chronicle*, December 22, 24, 1990.

    1. William F. Kimes and Maymie Kimes, *John Muir: a Reading Bibliography*, 2d ed., revised and enlarged(Fresno, Calif.: Panorama West Books, 1986).

    2. A lengthy discussion of the role of aesthetics in the evolution of Western attitudes toward nature, as well as the interplay of science and art in the development of preservationist philosophy, can be found in Eugene C. Hargrove, "The Historical Foundations of American Environmental Attitudes," *Environmental Ethics* 1 (Fall 1979): 209–240. See also Allen Carlson, "Nature and Positive Aesthetics," *Environmental Ethics* 6 (Spring 1984): 5–34.

    3. Recognition and appreciation of the sublime in wild nature continues to reinforce preservationist arguments today. See Kenneth H. Simonsen, "The Value of Wildness," *Environmental Ethics* 3 (Fall 1981): 260–261.

    4. Stephen Fox, *John Muir and His Legacy: The American Conservation Movement* (Boston: Little, Brown, 1981) pp. 360, 373–374.

    5. Bill Devall, "Muir as Deep Ecologist," *Environmental Review* 6 (Spring 1982): 63–86; Luis P. Hinchman and Sandra K. Hinchman, " 'Deep Ecology' and the Revival of Natural Right," *Western Political Quarterly* 42 (September 1989), 203–204.

    6. Arthur O. Lovejoy's classic study is still the best for understanding the impact of Chain theory on Western thought. See *The Great Chain of Being: A Study of the History of an Idea* (New York: Harper Torchbooks, 1936, 1960). For the influence of the Chain theory on Muir, see Ronald H. Limbaugh, "*Stickeen* and the Moral Education of John Muir," *Environmental History Review* 15 (Spring 1991): 29–31.

    7. For a full discussion of Muir's Christian anthropocentrism, see Ronald H. Limbaugh, "The Nature of John Muir's Religion," *Pacific Historian* 29 (Summer/ Fall 1985): 16–27. Instructive in this context is the distinction made between "weak" and "strong" anthropocentrism by Bryan Norton. By Norton's definition, Muir was a "weak" anthropocentrist who identified with human value systems but who also criticized those who exploited nature. Bryan G. Norton, "Environmental Ethics and Weak Anthropocentrism," *Environmental Ethics* 6 (Summer 1984): 131–148.

    8. An incisive analysis of the biocentric view may be found in Paul W. Taylor, "The Ethics of Respect for Nature," *Environmental Ethics* 3 (Fall 1981): 197–218. See also his subsequent article, "In Defense of Biocentrism," *Environmental Ethics* 5 (Fall 1985): 237–243.

    9. J. Baird Callicott in "The Land Aesthetic," *Environmental Review* 7 (Winter 1983): 345–358 credits Aldo Leopold, not Muir, with developing ". . . the first genuinely autonomous natural aesthetic since Kant's in Western philosophical lit-

Introduction

erature." Recently, however, the influence of Muir's aesthetics seems to be rising among young environmental activists. See Michael Cohen, *The Pathless Way: John Muir and American Wilderness* (Madison: University of Wisconsin Press, 1984); Richard Cartwright Austin, "Beauty: A Foundation for Environmental Ethics," *Environmental Ethics* 7 (Fall 1985): 203.

10. Marvin Hinberg, "Wilderness as Playground," *Environmental Ethics* 6 (Fall 1984): 251–263.

11. S. L. Albrecht, "Legacy of the Environmental Movement," *Environment and Behavior* 8 (June 1976): 147–168; Thomas R. Dunlap, "Conservationists and Environmentalists: An Attempt at Definition," *Environmental Review* 4 (1, 1979): 29–31. Contrary to Dunlap's claim, utilitarian conservation did not collapse when the Progressive Movement ended. Pinchot's influence on the New Deal is well documented, and his key concepts still govern much of the thinking in the Forest Service, the Bureau of Land Management, the Corps of Army Engineers, and other federal regulatory agencies. Stephen Fox, *John Muir and His Legacy*, pp. 188–189, 228, 270, 289–290.

PART

I

MUIR

T H E

INDIVIDUAL

1.
"Affectionately Yours, John Muir"

The Correspondence between John Muir and His Parents, Brothers, and Sisters

Keith E. Kennedy

John Muir's biographers have struggled with the complex, multisided personality of their subject. In the preface to her 1945 Pulitzer prize-winning biography *Son of the Wilderness*, Linnie Marsh Wolfe recounts a conversation that she had with Wanda Muir Hanna, the eldest daughter of John Muir. Wanda hoped for a biography that would shed some light on John Muir's human relationships. When Wolfe lamented the fact that she had not known him personally, Wanda told her this was just as well because not even his closest friends saw the same sides of his personality or had the same impression of him.[1] Frederick Turner, author of the 1985 biography *Rediscovering America: John Muir in His Time and Ours*, has written about the need for further research into Muir's complex personality. For example, Turner commends Muir as a worthy subject for a psychobiography. He also suggests that more analysis is needed of such topics as Muir's literary influences, ranch life, relationships with women, and marriage.[2]

The public and familiar Muir persona alone is suggestive of his multidimensional personality; he was an inventor, botanist, geologist, glaciologist, naturalist, adventurer, farmer, author, lobbyist, and a principal founder and first president of the Sierra Club. The purpose of this article, however, is to explore the unfamiliar and personal aspects of Muir's personality. To achieve this goal, the unpublished correspondence between John Muir and his brothers, sisters, and parents have been examined. The objective is to identify the ordinary or extraordinary characteristics of his personality that may be revealed in these letters. Developing an awareness of the inner man can provide a foundation for understanding this unique nineteenth-century American. By seeing John Muir in the unfamiliar roles of a brother and son, we can perhaps gain a more complete picture of his life.

The letters between Muir and his family of origin were selected for several reasons. We expect correspondence among family members to be fundamentally personal and intimate. Never intended for publication, the letters represent the spontaneous and unabridged thoughts of the authors. In addition, Muir's affiliation with his family of origin spanned a longer period than that of any other of his relationships. The correspondence begins in 1860 and ends with Muir's death in 1914. This long stretch of time presents an opportunity to observe changes and furnishes insights into a variety of circumstances. Finally, the quantity, distribution and the bidirectional paths of the letters are adequate for valid historical conclusions.[3]

The only strained relationship John had with any family member was with his father, Daniel Muir. John rebelled against his father's tyrannical, orthodox Calvinism, and his rebellion proved to be a constant source of friction between them. This rift is evident in the unpublished letters. First, it is probably no accident that the fewest surviving letters between John and his family of origin are those between him and his father. The absence of a single letter from John to his father can be attributed to many factors, but one possible reason might be that John simply had very little to say to his father. The letters from his brothers and sisters kept John apprised of his father's activities. Second, Daniel's letters are barren of any trace of love or respect for John. They read more like pastoral epistles to a congregation than familial letters to a son, and their dour and critical tone is unrelenting.

Daniel's first letter to John set the pattern for most of the subsequent letters. John had left home for the first time in 1860 to show his inventions and clocks at the Wisconsin State Agricultural Fair in Madison. He won awards and favorable mention in the local press, and he naturally took pride in his accomplishments. He wrote to his sister Sarah about the "flood of praise" he had received, and he admitted that he liked it.[4] Daniel Muir's tyranny penetrated the afterglow of John's first success in the world beyond the farm. Of the pride John justly felt, his father warned him to "not let the vanities of this life possess your soul. . . . Keep the faith, pray sincerely. . . . Keep humble. Do not let the praise of men puff you up. Nothing but Christ can keep you from sinking. . . . Avoid pride, and the Lord will lift you up."[5] In contrast to the commendations that John heard in the state's capital, this letter must have been like a splash of cold water in the face. (See Appendix A.)

Daniel Muir did not mellow with the passage of time. As the only family member to disapprove of John's chosen career, Daniel showed clearly his disappointment in a letter written fourteen years later. Prompted by a reprint of one of John's *Overland Monthly* articles published in 1874, which appeared in a local newspaper, Daniel wrote to tell John that he wished he had not read it. He warned John that he was not doing God's work and that only God's mercy saved him from his folly, insisting that:

> You cannot warm the heart of the saint of God with your cold icy-topped mountains. O, my dear son, come away from them to the Spirit of God and his holy word. . . . And the best and soonest way of getting quit of the writing and publishing [of] your book is to burn it, and then it will do no more harm either to you or others.[6]

This letter stands in striking contrast to the encouragement that he heard from other family members and from his California friends.

John's negative feelings toward his father are hinted at or verified in letters between him and his siblings. He wrote a letter to his brother Daniel prior to his thousand-mile walk to the Gulf in which he included an informal will. He allocated his sparse possessions among family members, but he specifically left nothing to his father, while in contrast allowing his mother her choice among his items. In John's autobiographic books, he wrote candidly about his father's brutality and tyranny. The essential veracity of his account is attested to by his sister Joanna.

19

Keith E. Kennedy

After reading a copy of his proposed autobiography, she wrote that what he had written was sadly true.[7]

The letters between John and his mother, Anne, portray a mutual warmth and respect that is missing in his father's letters. Individually, the letters disclose little of importance about either writer, but judged in total they reveal a strong, loving, and conventional relationship between mother and son. In most respects, Anne Muir was a traditional mother. She would send John a letter on his birthday, April 21. Also, an instinctive concern for her children's well-being was an underlying impulse in her letters to John. Since she heard or read about some of John's life-threatening escapades, Anne's worry was not unwarranted. Concerned about his "dangerous enterprises," she wrote on more than one occasion how pleased she was to see him settle down after he married in 1880.[8]

John and his mother were kindred spirits with respect to nature. He shared his love of the wilderness with her, sometimes sending her copies of his writings, pressed flowers and ferns, or seeds for her garden.[9] A letter John sent to his mother in 1871, during the period that most of Muir's fans consider as his most formative and happiest years—his 1869–1874 Yosemite stay—reflects his exhilaration. It also demonstrates his distinctive prose style. He writes:

> For the last two or three months I have worked incessantly among the most remote and undiscoverable of the deep cañons of this pierced basin, finding many a mountain page glorious with the writing of God and in characters that any earnest eye could read. . . .
>
> In all my lonely journeys among the most distant and difficult pathless, passless mountains, I never wander, am never lost. Providence guides through every danger and takes me to all truths which I need to learn, and someday I hope to show you my sheaves, my big bound pages of mountain gospel.[10]

His desire to articulate and to share this joy with his mother is significant. In comparison to the barren father-son relationship, the closeness he felt with his mother is striking.

"Affectionately Yours"

Anne Gilrye Muir, John Muir's mother, about 1862. A carte de visite by Plumb & Loomis, Portage, Wisconsin. John Muir Papers, Holt Atherton Library, Copyright 1984 by Muir-Hanna Trust.

Keith E. Kennedy

Most of the reviewed letters are between John and his brothers and sisters. He had two older sisters, Margaret and Sarah. Following John in order of birth were his brothers, David and Daniel, and three younger sisters, Annie and his twin sisters Mary and Joanna. Table 1.1 is arranged to show the quantity and distribution of letters between John and his family, and it also shows the sequence and dates of birth for the siblings. The correspondence between John and his brothers and sisters suggests two underlying themes. As the first-born male, John was expected to play a pivotal part, and indeed, he enlarged that role to an uncommon degree. The second theme is the generosity he extended to his siblings. By the end of his life, John had given major financial help at one time or another to every one of them.

A close inspection of the letters discloses no major disagreements between John and his siblings. The only criticisms of John are vague and good-humored references to his propensity to lecture. Given Muir's role of public advocacy and lobbying, it is not surprising that he sometimes lectured his siblings; however, his moralizing certainly did not get in the way of respectful relations.[11]

John did not shrink from offering counsel. Knowing his twenty-one-year-old twin sisters Mary and Annie were troubled about their destinies in life, he sent a letter to them that contained advice as good for young adults today as it was in 1867. He told them, "You will find that now is the golden time for gathering stores of knowledge. It is improbable that at any other time of life you will have equal opportunities. Make yourselves acquainted with all the leading facts in the world's history and . . . pursue the study of natural science. . . . Your range of pleasure will then grow wider and more varied every day."[12]

Muir placed a high priority on education, including the precedence of education over marital matters. Perhaps his educational and marital attitudes explain his own late marriage, at age forty-two. Even though part of his own education consisted of unconventional study in the "University of the Wilderness," he emphasized the importance of a formal education to his siblings. John advised David not to get married but, rather, to resume his studies at the University of Wisconsin. David did not take his advice, but John persisted in his belief that education should take precedence over early marriages. In a letter to Mary he wrote, "I trust, Mary, that you are diligently employed in the acquisition of knowledge. . . . do not think of marrying for long years to come, is my advice. This note will also do for Anna and Joanna." [13]

John influenced the direction especially of Mary's life. He not only seemed to inspire her to attend college, but he also encouraged her artistic talents. She frequently sought John's counsel on her artistic endeavors and teaching career.[14] Mary adored her older brother, and she once wrote, "But if there is anyone in the world that I should like to please it would be and is you. For no one has done more to help me to be what I am and can do than your own dear self, and I shall go on doing my very best, because it is duty to do so, and because I owe it to you to do so." [15] With John's encouragement, Mary proved to be a skilled artist. Her oil painting of John is displayed at the Muir National Historic Site in Martinez.

John Muir was very generous to his siblings, a pattern which started early and intensified over the years. Though he lived on only shepherd and sawyer wages the first few years in California, he helped subsidize Mary's and Daniel's educations. He sent money to both and made nearly identical pledges to them in 1869; as long as he had money, then it was theirs too.[16] In the same year he sent $700 to help David with his dry goods business It was supposed to be an interest-bearing loan, but John subsequently refused to accept interest.[17]

The breadth and degree of John's financial assistance increased over the years. In 1882, because he had not seen a family member since 1867, he paid for his sisters Sarah and Margaret to travel to Martinez for a five-month visit. His sister Annie had been ill for several years, and he finally persuaded her to visit his

Keith E. Kennedy

An unidentified portrait from John Muir's family
album. Long believed to be Muir's sisters, they are
probably the Galloway sisters, Muir's nieces.
Photograph by S. L. Plumb, Portage, Wisconsin,
ca. 1865. John Muir Papers, Holt Atherton Library.
Copyright 1984 by Muir-Hanna Trust.

family in 1885. She recovered her health after a two-year stay.
In 1893, Joanna's family began to experience financial difficulties, and for the next five years John sent her substantial sums
of money whenever they were required. Knowing that Joanna
would be reluctant to ask for help, he asked Sarah to let him
know whenever Joanna was in need.[18]

His sister Margaret and her husband John Reid experienced
financial difficulties that threatened the loss of their Nebraska
farm in the spring of 1889. For nearly two years John Muir

helped them save their farm from foreclosure, and all the while he encouraged them to start anew in Martinez on his ranch. In February 1891 Margaret and her husband accepted John's invitation; John Reid eventually served as the Martinez ranch's supervisor.[19]

In the spring of 1892, soon after Margaret's resettlement, John's brother David and his family moved to Martinez. David's dry goods business had failed, and John persuaded him to come to Martinez and operate a section of the ranch.[20] Finally, Sarah was persuaded to join the California Muirs in 1900.[21]

Clearly, John held a central position among the brothers and sisters. At times he played the part of counselor; at other times he gave financial help. Finally, as if he were a powerful magnet, John had drawn nearly half of his brothers and sisters to California. Biographer Frederick Turner has surmised that John might have felt a desire to reassert the rank of eldest son, a position he could not have easily filled in Wisconsin so long as he and his father were at odds. If Turner is correct, John must have felt considerable pride in being able to aid and comfort his loved ones.[22]

A surprising revelation in the letters is the degree of John Muir's sentimentality. His family formed the central element of his first twenty-two years, and, in spite of his abusive father, he emerged from the period with fond memories of family life. Surviving evidence indicates an element of sentimentalism in Muir after he left the farm, and the fact that he saved family letters supports that view. This practice started early and remained a habit throughout his life. He received a letter from his three young sisters two months after his initial departure from home. The letter itself is childish and trivial, but more revealing is the fact that John saved the letter for fifty-five years. William Frederic Badè, John's literary executor, found the letter in an envelope with John's holographic notation: "Mary's, Annie's, and Joanna's *first* letters."[23]

Despite the many years of solitary quest in the wilderness and of his apparent rejection of family life, John retained an appreciation for familial benefits. Writing from his beloved Yosemite, he told Sarah that even though he was wandering through "foreign lands," his heart was still at home. His family remained the primary wealth of his soul and formed the fundamental element of his life. "No one reflection gives me so much comfort as the completeness and unity of our family," he wrote in 1870. "We stand united like a family clump of trees. . . . do not consider me absent—lost. I have but gone out a little distance to look at the Lord's gardens."[24] Seven years later, in another letter to Sarah, he expressed dismay that he should be a bachelor doomed to roam outside a family circle. His status seemed anomalous to him because he felt he had a greater fondness for home and domestic life than did either of his brothers. He advised Sarah never to take for granted her own family. John also sensed powerful forces compelling him toward another destiny that, for the time being, kept him outside the family circle. He dismissed his present circumstances with, "But we are governed more than we know and are driven as with whips we know not where."[25]

John also took pride in the family name. During his Canadian travels (March 1864 to April 1866), he befriended some people with the unusual last names of Trout, Jay, Eagle, Rose, and other similarly descriptive names. In a letter to his sisters, he described an evening in which he and his friends started talking about family names. A companion volunteered that "Rose" was a fine name. John writes:

> I said that Muir was better than Trout, Jay, Rose, or Eagle because that though a Jay or Eagle was a fine bird, and a Trout a good fish and a Rose a fine flower, a Scottish Muir or Moor had fine birds, and fine fishes in its streams, and fine wild roses together with almost every other excellence, but above all "the bonnie bloomin heather." We may well be proud of our name.[26]

Muir's letters contain samples of his wit and humor, traits that his biographers have noted. Some early inventions, such as the "early risen" machine and the "loafer's chair," were clearly designed to delight and amuse. A letter to David mentioned another obscure contraption—a guillotine for slicing off gopher's heads. Of all his mechanical achievements, John later noted with pleasure that this invention was the least successful.[27]

This jocular style was a familiar pattern in Muir's family letters. While attending the University of Wisconsin, he poked fun at his first beard, telling his sisters that it was so long and scraggly that a fellow student advised him to burn it off.[28] A letter to Sarah in 1877 humorously commemorated the completion of his first book by bequeathing to her the "old gray quill" he had used. He writes:

> I can hardly remember its origin, but I think it is one that I picked up on the mountains, fallen from the wing of a gray eagle; but, possibly it may be only a pinion feather of some tame old goose, and my love of truth compels me to make this unpoetical statement. . . . The frayed upper end of the pen was produced by nervous gnawing when some interruption in my logic or rhetoric occurred from stupidity or weariness. I gnawed the upper end to send the thoughts below and out at the other.[29]

Sarah treasured the "old gray quill"; she mentioned still having it sixteen years later.[30]

On another occasion, John's impish impulses are reflected in a letter to Mary on a tiny scrap of paper measuring no larger than two by two-and-a-half inches; the number of words, however, fill a typewritten page. Written in 1864, the letter describes his new friends in Canada. John uses their last names, cited earlier, Trout and Jay, to create clever puns and plays on words. Given the unusual dimensions of the letter and its humorous content, it is not surprising to see why Mary chose this letter to be the first of many letters she would treasure from her famous brother. Selected quotations from the letter would not do it justice; therefore, a transcript of the letter appears in Appendix B.[31]

A part of understanding the inner man consists of knowing something about personal beliefs and attitudes. Fortunately, the letters cover a long enough period so that some impressions emerge.

The epochal event of John's generation was the Civil War. Though of the prime age to become involved, he did not serve and so escaped the ravages of this war. His thoughts on the war are contained in two letters to Sarah. The first was written in the fall of 1861 from the University of Wisconsin. The war was popular and in its early stages; he could see the confidence and pomp in the volunteers at nearby Camp Randall. He wrote that the soldiers and their camp were all very impressive, "but how can all the great and showy coverings of war hide its real hideousness?" [32] The other letter was written in the fall of 1862. Circumstances of war had nearly forced the closure of the university, and he blamed it on the "war demon." He found it strange that a country with so many schools and churches could be "desolated by so unsightly a monster." He concludes:

> Leaves have their time to fall, and though indeed there is a kind of melancholy present when they, withered and dead, are plucked from their places and made the sport of the gloomy autumn wind, yet we hardly deplore their fate, because there is nothing unnatural in it. They have done all that their Creator wished them to do, and they should not remain longer in their green vigor. But may the same be said of the slaughtered upon a battle field? [33]

Muir's view on war in general is clear enough from these passages. This tragic war was, however, so pervasive that he could not ignore it. In the early war years, John did not have to worry about conscription because there were so many volunteers. In March, 1863, the inevitable shadow of war fell upon him when wartime drafts were imposed by Congress. Muir himself is silent on the steps he took to stay out of the war. Despite his voluminous writing, Muir comments surprisingly little about the Civil War. His autobiography, *The Story of My Boyhood and Youth* (1913), does not even mention the war. Neither does the family correspondence reveal any details on his methods or motivations for evading the war. If actions speak louder than words, perhaps it is not coincidental that he commenced a two-year stay in Canada in March of 1864. In February, Lincoln had called for a draft of 500,000. Two Muir biographers, Wolfe and Turner, have more or less concluded that he "skedaddled" to Canada to evade this draft.[34]

A recent controversy has developed over the nature of Muir's religious thinking. His biographers differ on the fundamentals of his Christian beliefs. William Frederic Badè, his literary executor and author of *The Life and Letters of John Muir* (1924), believed that Muir held essentially Christian beliefs. Stephen Fox, author of *John Muir and His Legacy* (1981), contends that Muir had completely rejected Christianity. The bulk of the evidence used to support these conclusions exists outside the family letters. The family letters do, however, provide clues.

First, it is significant to note what the letters do *not* contain. He never exchanged any letters with his family that contain the slightest suggestions of nonChristian beliefs. If Muir had abandoned Christianity, he kept it a secret from his closest kin. Conversely, a simple but not inconsequential thread runs throughout the letters. Muir frequently, consistently, and reverently used words such as "Heaven," "Creator," "Lord," "Heavenly Father," "Christian charity," and other commonly recognized Christian words and phrases. It seems unlikely that he could have continued to use such words in private letters if he had rejected all notions of a Christian God. This situation and its conclusion are analogous to one reached by Ronald H. Limbaugh who argues that it is hard to explain how Muir could have dismissed the Bible for his personal library contained four well-worn Bibles, two of which contain Muir's holographic notations.[35]

These observations, however, do not mean that John was uncritical of Christianity. His rejection of his father's Calvinistic orthodoxy is well known. The family letters contain evidence that he also rejected denominational doctrines. A letter to David ridiculed the exclusiveness of communion, and he found silly the debate over the right quantity of water to use in baptismal rites.[36]

John also linked God and nature in ways that were heretofore considered heretical by some Christian thinkers. He recognized how radical his notions would be to orthodox Christians. "I think I might preach nature like an apostle," he wrote to Daniel, "but if I should enter an ordinary ecclesiastical pulpit, I fear I should be found preaching much that was unsanctified and unorthodox."[37] The tone of Muir's nature writing suggests a pantheistic orthodoxy. A letter to David, however, shows that John ascribed nature's miracles to God. He writes:

> I have not been at church a single time since leaving home. Yet this glorious valley might well be called a church, for every lover of the great Creator who comes within the broad overwhelming influences of the place fails not to worship as he never did before. The glory of the Lord is upon all his works; it is written plainly upon all the fields of every clime, and upon every sky, but here in this place of surpassing glory the Lord has written in capitals.[38]

Perhaps John's relationship to his God was simply stated in a letter he sent to Sarah in 1877. Writing about his own simple needs and pleasures, he expressed the connection of God, nature, and himself by writing, "A crust by a brookside out on the mountains with God is more to me than all beyond comparison."[39]

Muir's attitude toward his ranch life in Martinez is disclosed in family letters. His domestic life and farming enterprise began after his marriage to Louie Strentzel on April 14, 1880. For reasons they never disclosed, John and Louie kept their engagement a secret. John's family in Wisconsin did not know of the wedding until after it had occurred. His mother and siblings, however, were glad to see him "settle down." They had seen their son and brother wander in virtual solitude for a dozen years. Furthermore, twenty years had passed since John had left the farm for the wider world. How, they might have wondered, would John adapt to the yoke of domestic life.[40]

Particularly after the birth of Wanda in 1881, John immersed himself in the life of a fruit rancher. In characteristic fashion, John devoted all of his energies into making a success of the ranch. He struggled to achieve financial independence. Although the ranch required his full devotion, he never really adjusted to this new role.

John's uneasiness with ranch responsibilities was communicated to his family in Wisconsin. Mary detected his discomfort and teased him about being a staid homebody surrounded by comforts. "Do you not wish for an opportunity to climb to some mountain top where you have not yet been?" she taunted.[41] John and his siblings had tried for several years to schedule a reunion, but John was unable to commit to one due to his farm obligations. He feared the ranch could not function without his supervision of the numerous workmen. In 1884, John asked David if he knew of a "steady fellow" in Wisconsin who might be interested in the fruit business? The job would be permanent according to John. Three years later he inquired again to see if David knew of some sturdy men who were willing to work. He also asked Margaret to be on the lookout for a good foreman. Given these less-than-subtle hints, maybe it is not ironic that six and seven years later Margaret's and David's families relocated to Martinez and helped relieve John of his burdens. In fact, John Muir began to orchestrate their migration to California many years before.[42]

The siblings' happiness in seeing John settle down diminished as John's feelings of bondage increased. John wrote to David in 1887 that he was nerve shaken, lean as a crow, and burdened with care, work, and worry. Later in the year, he told David that the ranch was becoming an "eternal fountain of work." Perhaps Joanna spoke for the others when she wrote to John and expressed her concern. She had hoped that he would evade the curse of overwork. "It makes our hearts ache," she wrote, "to think of you as tired or worried by the vexatious botherations of ordinary mortals."[43]

Muir's self-imposed exile lasted until 1888. He picked up his pen and began writing that year for *Picturesque California*. His

31

ranch worries did not really lessen, however, until Margaret's and David's families joined him in Martinez in 1891 and 1892. At last, he could relinquish management of the ranch to trusted family members.

The most engaging aspect of the family letters is to see the development and maturation of Muir's passion for nature. The first signs of his genius were in mechanical inventions rather than environmental. It seemed logical to friends, family, and maybe to Muir himself that he could excel as a machinist. Indeed, the purpose of going to the Wisconsin State Fair in 1860 was to show off his inventions and thereby attract some job offers from machine shops. The plan seemed clear enough, and prospects for the future looked bright.

In truth, Muir had doubts about his role in the world. He thought a lot about what he could do to earn his daily bread. In a letter to Sarah, he observed, "A body has an extraordinary amount of long faced sober scheming and thought to get butter and bread for their bodies." [44] After trying and abandoning a brief career as a mechanics apprentice, John enrolled in the University of Wisconsin in 1861. Uncertain of his own interests, he fashioned his own eclectic curriculum. He basically dabbled in whatever interested him, never following a course of instruction leading to a specific degree.

Writing to his sisters in May 1861, Muir reveals for the first time an interest in botany. He mentions the botanical trips of other students but adds that his current schedule did not permit the study of flowers. While ignorant of the botanical sciences, his love of flowers is clear enough. He describes his room to his sisters as follows:

> I like pretty flowers, but I haven't time to study much about them. I've got a fine posy at my nose here in an old ink bottle. And I've got a peppermint plant and a young bramble in an old glass bottle and on the shelf stands my stew pan full of brambles 2 or 3 feet long and slips of gooseberry bushes and wild plum . . . further along you may see my tin cup in the same business.[45]

"Affectionately Yours"

Muir subsequently pursued his interest in botany on his own. As his nascent interest in the plant world unfolded, he started taking field trips to collect and identify botanical specimens. He described to Sarah in 1863 one of his solitary trips, reporting that he had rambled twenty-five miles one day, collecting flowers, weeds, and mosses as he walked through marshes and mud. He loved this adventure and wrote, "It is the most exciting thing in the form of even amusement, much more of study, that I ever knew." [46]

A month later, Muir and two college friends went on a month-long geological and botanical excursion down the Wisconsin River and into Iowa. The trip intensified his interest in nature. Another letter to Sarah exudes this enthusiasm and a passage foreshadows the poetic heights that his prose would reach. He writes:

> Those ravines are the most perfect, the most heavenly plant conservatories I ever saw. Thousand of happy flowers are there, but ferns and mosses are the favored ones. *No human language will ever describe them.* . . . such scenery. . . . and happy hunting and happy finding of dear plant things we never before enjoyed (emphasis added).[47]

Muir did not realize it then, but his own remarkable gift for descriptive language would more than adequately describe nature for legions of new wilderness lovers.

A few more years were to pass before Muir realized the magnitude of his own wilderness rapture. He still had the experiences of Canada, Indianapolis, and the 1,000-mile walk to the Gulf ahead of him. Throughout these experiences, however, he figuratively wandered about in search of his meaning and purpose in life. In the summer of 1869 he found his destiny in Yosemite. A letter written to Sarah shows that his passion for nature was now fully formed and total. His mission is clear; there is no turning back and no regrets:

> A few months will call upon me to decide to what portion of God's glorious star I will next turn. The sweets of home, the

33

smooth waters of civilized life have attractions for me whose power is increased by time and constant rambling, but I am a captive, I am bound. Love of pure unblemished nature seems to overmaster and blur out of sight all other objects and considerations. I know that I could under ordinary circumstances accumulate wealth and obtain a fair position in society, and I am arrived at an age that requires that I should choose some definite course for life. But I am sure that the mind of no truant school boy is more free and disengaged from all the grave plans and purposes and pursuits of ordinary orthodox life than mine.[48]

Muir's public achievements and persona are well known, but this article has concentrated on finding traces of the private, inner man. His family letters have been a window through which we could focus on the intimate sides of his personality. They have reflected the stark contrasts in his relationships with his father and mother; the former was cold and barren and distinguished by a lack of mutual interests, and the latter was warm and loving and cemented by a shared affection for nature. With his siblings, we have seen that he commanded a central, influential position that was founded upon his generous nature and respect for his counsel. The letters showed that he possessed a sense of humor and a streak of sentimentalism, and they have illuminated his inner thoughts on war, religion, and the world of work. Finally, these letters provided the first glimpses of his wilderness rapture. Through an examination of private letters between Muir and those he loved, we have come closer to his inner being.

Table 1.1
Quantity and Path of Correspondence between John Muir and his Parents, Brothers, and Sisters (1860 to 1914)

	Father Daniel Muir (1804–1885)	Mother Anne Muir (1813–1896)	Margaret (Muir) Reid (1834–1910)	Sarah (Muir) Galloway (1836–1932)	David Muir (1840–1916)	Daniel Muir Jr. (1843–?)	Annie Muir (1846–1903)	Mary (Muir) Hand (1846–1928)	Joanna (Muir) Brown (1850–?)	Total
To John Muir (1838–1914)	15	63	51	95	27	11	30	32	65	389
From John Muir		12	4	46	35	24	10	38	13	182
Total	15	75	55	141	62	35	40	70	78	571

The quantity of correspondence was derived by counting the entries shown in the Index of:
The Guide and Index to the Microform Edition of the John Muir Papers, 1858–1957, Holt-Atherton Library, University of the Pacific.
The dates of death of John's brothers and sisters were surprisingly hard to find. The John Muir National Historic Site in Martinez provided the dates shown, but they could not give me the dates for Joanna and Daniel, Jr.

Keith E. Kennedy

APPENDIX A

Letter from Daniel Muir to John Muir*

Hickory Dale, Oct. 14th, 1860.

Dear John:

I am glad you are well in body. I should like to hear of your spiritual health being good. Do not let the vanities of this life possess your soul. Do all to the glory of God, and he will prosper you in that which is good. Keep the faith, pray sincerely. Always aim at the glory of God and good of man. Keep humble. Do not let the praise of men puff you up. Nothing but Christ can keep you from sinking. Take his counsel; then strive to please God in all things. Be always ready to give in your account. If you always look to Jesus as your all and follow His spirit you will be safe. I am glad that God has provided a lodging for you. Strive always to love your neighbor as yourself practically. In order to have friends we must be friendly. Love begeteth love. Be merciful that you may have mercy. Look not at high things but condescend to men of low estate. Practice economy in all you do, in order to be great be [the] servant of all. Avoid pride, and the lord will lift you up. Do not think that God will aid you in anything that is not good, but the fruit of the Spirit is in all goodness. See that all that you do is founded upon scripture. Show to all around you that you are a man of honesty and truth. You have much need to watch and pray, for all eyes are upon you. Being a stranger your present character will be made [to] appear according as you think, speak and do in the eyes of the public. I am praying for you, hoping you will use the grace and live. Pray for me, dear John, that we may meet at God's right hand without spot, and rejoice forever together with all the sanctified.

I will send a trunk with your things by railway, as directed, to the care of your master, Mr. Wirad.

From your Father [Daniel Muir]

*This letter is copied from the William Frederic Badè transcripts. Words in brackets are supplied by Badè where, in his professional opinion, words or dates are missing.

"Affectionately Yours"

APPENDIX B

Letter from John Muir to Mary Muir*

Meaford, [Canada] Oct. 23, [1864]

Dear Sis[ter] Mary:

I am well and hope that this, er, letter will find you ditto as much as possible. Danny and I have a pleasant home and do not work hard or long hours, so of course we are growing fatter and fatter, and perhaps we will soon be as big as Gog and Magog.

Our family here consists of first of all Me, a most good man and big boy. Second, Daniel, who is also mostly big, and three or four trifles funny. Third, Mr. William Trout, an unmarried boy of thirty summers, who, according to a multiplicity of common prognostications, is going to elect a lady mistress of Trout's Hollow some day. (Fourth), Charles Jay, a bird of twenty-five, who is said to coo to a Trout. He is created like a blue-jay, with bristly hair and good-natured and vociferous as any parrot. This Jay and last mentioned Trout are in partnership and are rulers of the two scotch heather Muirs. Fifth, Mary Trout of perhaps more than thirty years, an unmarried lady of great many good qualities. Sixth, Harriet Trout, a very happy and sportive fish who employs herself in giggling and making giggle for hours at a time, is about twenty years of age, 5½ ft. long and will perhaps sometime join affinity to the Jay who whistles and coos and gesticulates so funnily to her.

We all live happily together. Occasionally an extra Trout comes up-stream or a brother Jay alights at our door, but they are not of our family.

I must now bid goodbye. Write soon,

Yours,

John

*This letter is also a copy of a Badè transcript of the original. Bracketed words have been added by Badè.

Keith E. Kennedy

NOTES

1. Linnie Marsh Wolfe, *Son of the Wilderness: The Life of John Muir* (Madison: University of Wisconsin Press, 1945), p. vii.

2. Frederick Turner, "Toward Future Muir Biographies: Problems and Prospects," *The Pacific Historian* 29 (Summer/Fall 1985): 159–166.

3. The University of the Pacific Holt-Atherton Library is the designated repository for the Muir family papers. The information contained in Table 1.1 is derived from the Center's *The Guide and Index to the Microform Edition of the John Muir Papers, 1858–1957.* Table 1.1 is arranged to show the quantity, distribution, and paths of the correspondence. The *Guide and Index* lists over 6,800 letters and other papers that were sent and received by all of the Muir families. The 571 letters reviewed for this paper represent 8.4 percent of the total and are primarily unpublished; perhaps a score have been published in their entirety and maybe a few score more have had fragments published. John Muir saved the bulk of the letters; over two-thirds of the reviewed letters were sent to him.

4. Letter to Sarah (Muir) Galloway, October 1860, John Muir Papers, University of the Pacific. Sarah was the sister closest to John in age. As can be seen in Table 1.1, the greatest number of letters are between John and Sarah. John's letters to Sarah in the years before his marriage are particularly candid and useful in assessing John's life. The letters read for this article were William Frederic Badè's typewritten transcripts, which he used for the preparation of *The Life and Letters of John Muir* (1923). I wish to thank the staff at the Holt-Atherton Library at the University of the Pacific (UOP) for sparing me the chore of reading handwritten letters on microfilm readers. Badè's transcripts are acceptable for content analysis. See the *Guide and Index* for a description of how to use microfilm copies of the Muir papers.

5. Daniel Muir to John Muir, 14 October, 1860, John Muir Papers, UOP. Hereafter, all references to the John Muir Papers at the University of the Pacific will consist of just the author, recipient, and date. This letter is so representative of the letters John received from his father that a full transcript has been attached as Appendix A.

6. Daniel Muir to John Muir, 19 March, 1874.

7. John Muir to Daniel Muir Jr., 1 September, 1867; Joanna Brown to John Muir, 7 October, 1913.

8. Ann Muir to John Muir, 28 February, 1876, 21 February, 1882, 7 May, 1882, and 16 August, 1882.

9. Ann Muir to John Muir, 26 February, 1872, January 1883, and 29 December, 1891.

10. John Muir to Ann Muir, 16 November, 1871.

11. Mary Muir to John Muir, 27 May, 1878; Margaret Reid to John Muir, 22 August, 1887; John Muir to Mary Muir, 20 December, 1880.

12. John Muir to Mary and Annie Muir, 11 February, 1867.

13. David Muir to John Muir, 11 April, 1863; John Muir to Mary Muir, 5 March, 1865.

"Affectionately Yours"

14. Mary Muir to John Muir, 14 April, 1867; John Muir to Mary Muir, 2 May, 1869, 11 September, 1874, 1 January, 1883, and 5 December, 1886.

15. Mary Muir to John Muir, 27 May, 1878.

16. John Muir to Mary Muir, 2 May, 1869, and 24 March, 1870; John Muir to Daniel Muir, Jr., 17 April, 1869, and 4 June, 1871.

17. John Muir to David Muir, 24 September, 1869. The forgiveness of interest is found in John Muir to Louie (Strentzel) Muir, 19 September, 1885.

18. Sarah Galloway to John Muir, October 1882; Margaret Reid to John Muir, 28 March, 1883; Annie Muir to John Muir, 13 November, 1884, and 21 October, 1888. The episode concerning Joanna's family spans many letters. Some of the key letters are Joanna Brown to John Muir, 26 March, 1893, 2 March, 1895, and 1 October, 1896; Sarah Galloway to John Muir, 9 January, 1895, 15 February, 1895, 6 January, 1897, and 11 January, 1898.

19. The evidence for the Margaret and John Reid episode spans many letters, but some key letters are John Muir to David Muir, 20 April, 1889; Margaret Reid to John Muir, dated 9 December, 1889, 1 February, 1890, and 15 February, 1891. The fact of John Reid's ranch supervision duties is taken from Frederick Turner, *Rediscovering America: John Muir in His Time and Ours* (New York: Viking, 1985), p. 276.

20. David Muir to John Muir, 19 March, 1892, and 5 May, 1892; John Muir to David Muir, 8 August, 1893.

21. The reasons for Sarah's move are not explained in the letters. A letter from Sarah Galloway to John Muir, 11 February, 1899, was written from Wisconsin and gave no hint of a migration. The next letter is written from Pacific Grove, California, and it also gives no clue as to the reason for the change. See Sarah Galloway to John Muir, 30 January, 1900. None of the Muir biographies gives an explanation of the migration. The reasons for her move are undoubtedly a mixture. She was widowed in 1884, and the death of their mother in 1896 lessened her ties to Wisconsin. She had visited John in 1883, so she knew from personal experience of the better climate in California. A recurring pattern in the letters originating from Wisconsin was the constant complaints of ill health. Her health must have been a consideration. Finally, with David and Margaret already in California due to John's persuasion, it is safe to infer that John persuaded Sarah to try California as well.

22. Frederick Turner, *Rediscovering America*, p. 319.

23. Annie, Mary, and Joanna Muir to John Muir, 21 October, 1860.

24. John Muir to Sarah Galloway, 24 March, 1870.

25. Ibid., 12 January 1877.

26. John Muir to Mary, Annie, and Joanna Muir, 24 December, 1865.

27. John Muir to David Muir, 20 March, 1870.

28. John Muir to Mary, Annie, and Joanna Muir, May 1861.

29. John Muir to Sarah Galloway, 23 April, 1877.

30. Sarah Galloway to John Muir, 28 March, 1893. The "old gray quill" is on display at the John Muir Historical Site in Martinez, California.

31. John Muir to Mary Muir, 23 October, 1864.

Keith E. Kennedy

32. John Muir to Sarah Galloway, Fall 1861.

33. Ibid., Fall 1862.

34. Frederick Turner, *Rediscovering America*, pp. 109–112.; Linnie Marsh Wolfe, *Son of the Wilderness*, pp. 88–94. Turner was unequivocal in concluding that Muir was a draft dodger. Wolfe was reluctant to assign a clear motivation for Muir's actions. Turner uncovered an ironic sidelight to history. His research of draft records for Muir's Wisconsin congressional district show his name was never called. Thus, even if John did "skedaddle" to Canada as a primary motivation, his action may not have been necessary.

35. Ronald H. Limbaugh, "The Nature of John Muir's Religion," *The Pacific Historian* 29 (Summer/Fall 1985): 19. Much of the information contained in this paragraph is drawn from this essay. The assessments on the family correspondence are, however, my own.

36. John Muir to David Muir, 10 April, 1870.

37. John Muir to Daniel Muir, 17 April, 1869.

38. John Muir to David Muir, 20 March, 1870.

39. John Muir to Sarah Galloway, 29 November, 1877.

40. Sarah Galloway to John Muir, 23 May, 1880; Ann Muir to John Muir, 21 February, 1882.

41. Mary Muir to John Muir, 23 May, 1883.

42. John Muir to David Muir, 30 December, 1884, 26 December, 1887; Margaret Reid to John Muir, 4 July, 1885.

43. John Muir to David Muir, 7 August, 1887, and 26 December, 1887; Joanna Brown to John Muir, 8 December, 1889.

44. John Muir to Sarah Galloway, September 1860.

45. John Muir to Mary and Annie, and Joanna Muir, May 1861.

46. John Muir to Sarah Galloway, 1 June, 1863.

47. Ibid., July 1863.

48. Ibid., 1 August, 1869.

2.
John Muir and Vertical Sauntering

SOMETHING HIDDEN. GO AND FIND IT.
GO AND LOOK BEHIND THE RANGES—
SOMETHING LOST BEHIND THE RANGES.
LOST AND WAITING FOR YOU. GO!

—*KIPLING*

Arthur W. Ewart

Right on the rim of Yosemite Valley, toes actually hanging out over the 3,000-foot drop, John Muir could not "help fearing a little that the rock might split off," as he said. Overwhelmed by his first view of the valley from above, he backed off and ran around shouting, waving his arms and scaring off a bear with his frenzy. He had galloped westward along the rim in search of just such a place where he could look straight down. After drawing back from the lip he cautioned himself, "now don't go out on the verge again." But it was no use. In the face of such scenery "one's body seems to go where it likes with a will over which we seem to have scarce any control," he said. Actually it was a glimpse of the falls that Muir really sought, so he followed Yosemite Creek down to the point where the water plunged over the abyss, and there he took off his boots and crept along the rushing water. The roar of the falls was deafening, but he was not quite able to peer over. He searched for some natural flaw in the smooth granite, hoping to climb still further out and gain a better view. "Scanning it keenly," he said, "I discovered a narrow shelf about three inches wide on the very brink, just wide enough for a rest for one's heels." He had second thoughts. The perch looked a little too "nerve trying," he said. "I therefore concluded not to venture farther." No sooner had he decided against the attempt than he changed his mind again. Recognizing a nearby plant as one quite caustic to the taste, he filled his mouth with the leaves, "hoping they might help to prevent giddiness." His mind thus distracted from thoughts of self-preservation and fear, Muir slipped his heels down onto the narrow shelf and moved slowly out to gain a perfect view of the frothy water on its 1,400-foot descent. Muir was enchanted, transfixed. He let his mind drift, trusting his body to do intuitively what was needed for safety, and he lost all sense of time.[1]

Aside from the many achievements that marked John Muir for immortality, he had another accomplishment less well publicized but equally distinguished. In the last quarter of the nineteenth century, John Muir was the best mountaineer in the United States. He set physical standards in the sport that are difficult to match today, and his mountaineering ethics have come to be appreciated and emulated only recently within the American climbing community.

A climber of legendary endurance, Muir moved with unparalleled finesse on vertical rock and ice. He had a string of mountain summits to his credit equaled by no other in his era. In sheer number of solitary ascents alone, Muir earned his title as the best mountaineer of his times. Yet preeminence as a climber is due him not so much for his physical prowess as for the personal philosophy he developed: a perspective on nature that he brought to the sport of climbing. To fully appreciate Muir the climber it is necessary not only to recount his feats but also to ask what motivated his efforts. No other climber was better at finding and becoming part of the harmony and perfection in the mountains, blending with the rocks, and revering them as teachers of God's design. Muir saw manifestations of God's intent everywhere he looked, and climbing to mountain summits was his way of finding that Spirit.

In the summer of 1869 Muir began a period of active mountaineering that spanned more than twenty-five years, and during that time he became not only an accomplished rock and ice climber, but also an all-round alpinist. With meager provisions—usually just bread, tea, occasionally a little oatmeal, and a couple of blankets—Muir climbed peak after peak, alone most often; sometimes in bone-chilling, subfreezing weather, in the face of formidable storms, and well beyond any hope of rescue. " 'Come higher,' " Muir reported the mountain voices saying to him. "Many still voices . . . are calling, 'Come higher.' "[2]

Vertical Sauntering

Weaned on harsh, demanding farm work in his youth and a lifestyle of puritanical frugality, Muir came to the mountains already armed with a determined will and leathery constitution. As one of his biographers said: "He developed within himself a hard, stubborn core beyond the reach of any external situation." [3] In many ways he led the life of an ascetic, deprived by most standards, but anything more to Muir seemed excessive luxury, appealing to the flesh while impeding the spirit. "Just bread and water and delightful toil is all I need," he said.[4] Refusing to care for himself in a conventional way, he actually enjoyed this life of privation. "There is a weird charm in carrying out such a free and pathless plan," he said of this method.[5] Muir attributed his pure physical drive to inherited qualities, his "Scottish pluck and perseverance." [6] That pluck allowed him to endure extreme hardship, to sleep out in his shirt-sleeves, often to go days without food in arduous situations that would break all but the most rugged souls.

California's Mount Whitney, the highest point in the contiguous United States, is not easily located by sight. It blends in with a number of other surrounding 14,000 foot peaks. On October 15, 1873, when Muir set out alone to climb the mountain, the problem of finding it was compounded by the fact that in Clarence King's *Geological Survey of California,* upon which Muir relied, designation of the highest mountain had been conferred on the wrong peak. When Muir gained the summit he used his own elevation instrument to sight the real Whitney off in the distance. Setting out at once on foot, with no equipment, no blankets or food, he reached a 14,000-foot subpeak just 500 feet below the summit of Whitney as darkness set in. It was extremely cold, Muir was sick, and, well above timberline, he had no wood for a fire. Here he spent a dreadful night and was able to keep warm only by staying in constant motion. "I had to dance all night to keep from freezing," he recalled, "and was feeble and starving the next morning." [7] At daybreak he attempted the summit again but was stopped by that "other self" of which he sometimes spoke. This time it was clearly an audible voice that said "Go back." "I felt as if Someone had caught me by the shoulder and turned me around," he said.[8] He descended and walked all the way down to the town of Independence, a distance of about twenty miles. Replenished from a day of food and rest, he started out again on October 19 and walked up the easy canyon below the mountain. Ascending the east face, he arrived on the top of Whitney by 8 A.M. on the twenty-first, the first person ever to climb the mountain by that route. Despite the fact that he used "small points of stones frozen . . . into the surface," for footholds, the route is not considered technically difficult by today's high standards of rock climbing.[9] Still, that does not diminish the arduousness of the whole experience. Francis Farquhar, historian of the Sierra Nevada, reminds us: "Should someone of the present generation of mountain climbers feel inclined to make light of Muir's exploits, let him endeavor to duplicate it, starting from Independence—not Lone Pine—on foot, with or without sleeping bag and the present-day advantage of concentrated foods." [10]

The 1870s witnessed Muir's most intensive period of mountaineering. He roamed throughout the Sierra from Tahoe, south to Mount Whitney and north again to Mount Shasta. Characteristics of Muir's climbing style emerged in the early period: his reliance on minimal supplies (lacking even a rope, for example), the absence of self-glorification, and his unbridled enthusiasm for every adventure. Unabashed, he climbed talking out loud, whispering to flowers along the way, yelling, and gesticulating when he saw something particularly impressive. Muir had a spiritual love affair with everything wild, and he climbed to intensify his affection. "Who wouldn't be a mountaineer?" he asked. "Up here all the world's prizes seem nothing." [11]

Living and working in Yosemite Valley in the early 1870s, he spent his Sundays scampering around his beloved valley. After he left his work as a sawyer and carpenter in 1871, he was free to "saunter" as he called it, through the mountains in pursuit of his glacial studies, while all the time climbing day after day for long stretches. In 1872, Muir became the first and perhaps only American climber to be featured as a central figure in a work of fiction. The eccentric Therese Yelverton, defrocked European countess and writer, visited Yosemite in search of material for her next book. She became enchanted with Muir. In her book, *Zanita: A Tale of the Yosemite*, he appeared as Kenmuir, a "lithe figure . . . skipping over the rough boulders, poising with the balance of an athlete." [12] Muir was affected by his encounter with Yelverton, slightly embarrassed by the adulation, but not nearly so moved by her as she was by him. And in later years, when he looked back on this year of his life, it was not the flirtation with a countess he recalled most vividly, but his epic climb of Mount Ritter in the Central Sierra.

The next year, 1873, was an especially productive climbing year for Muir. He climbed throughout the Minarets, the beautiful subrange of peaks south of Yosemite; in the fall he completed the Whitney climb by way of what is now appropriately called the Mountaineer's Route. Muir was bursting with enthusiasm for his chosen sport after the Whitney ascent. He wrote to a friend, "I saw no mountains in all this region that appeared at all inaccessible to a mountaineer. Give me a summer and a bunch of matches and a sack of meal and I will climb every one in the region." [13] Muir was caught, captivated by the tonic that comes from adventure on high peaks, and he loved everything to do with the sport, even the hardships. He was coming to grips with himself, using the mountains and climbing as a means to search for himself. In his mid-thirties by this time, Muir was ready to state with certainty the one occupation he would always claim, "I am hopelessly and forever a mountaineer." [14]

Still half wild during this period, Muir resisted domestication, reluctantly coming down from the mountains only at the behest of his friends who implored him to share his knowledge. He relented in 1873, set up temporary residence in Oakland and spent ten months writing. It was his first extended period

Arthur W. Ewart

John Muir with the Sierra Club on the summit of Mt. Whitney, August 11, 1902. Photograph by Marian Hooker. John Muir Papers, Holt Atherton Library. Copyright 1984 by Muir-Hanna Trust.

of confinement in six years, and he barely tolerated it. When he broke out finally in fall of 1874, he shouted "I'm wild once more," and bolted for Yosemite Valley.[15] In November he was on top of Mount Shasta for the first time and after climbing the massive glacier's flanked peak, sat out a four-day storm camped on the side of the mountain. Local residents had given him up for lost. "They thought that poor, crazy mountain climber must be frozen solid and lost below the drifts," he later wrote.[16] In April, 1875, he was again on Shasta, though this particular ascent nearly did cost him his life.

Vertical Sauntering

When the storm "began to declare itself," Muir recalled, he and his companion, Jerome Fay, were still on the summit of Mount Shasta completing a geodetic survey.[17] Fay, an employee of Justin Sisson who was a local hotel owner and majordomo of Shasta, had guided Muir part way up Shasta on the first ascent. Following that climb, Muir had extolled the mountain's virtues to a friend by saying "The extent of its individuality is perfectly wonderful."[18] Surely he and Fay must have also known that the severity of storms on the summits of singular mountains like Shasta was also distinctive. This one came on fast and ferocious, soon engulfing them in high winds and a severe hail shower. Still not alarmed, Muir took time to examine the hail's symmetry: "Six-sided pyramids with rounded base, rich and sumptuous looking, and fashioned with loving care." With the situation rapidly deteriorating, descent that would take them entirely off the mountain seemed out of the question. Muir's thermometer registered below zero, the sky darkened, and lightning flashed simultaneously with ear-shattering thunder.

Muir was determined to walk off the mountain, but Fay was against the idea. Just below the summit, within the old volcanic core, there was then, on April 30th, 1875, as today, a hot, bubbling fumarole pit where mud and steaming gases create a stark contrast to the ice that surrounds the hollow. This was where Fay decided to make his stand. Muir agreed: "We can lie in the mud and steam and sludge, warm at least on one side." This was no easy decision, for they committed themselves to wet clothes, the cardinal sin of mountaineering. They passed the night there. Two feet of snow fell in the first few hours. Their backs scalded in the hot mud as snow drifted over them "augmenting our novel misery," said Muir. When the storm cleared, the temperature dropped even lower, and the two climbers talked to each other to keep from falling asleep and possibly dying. They began to hallucinate, seeing visions brought on by their "dreamy stupor," and each hour passed as if it were a year. Finally day broke, and though it was still bitterly cold, they had to descend. Both climbers gulped down some whiskey left in Fay's flask, proving perhaps that Muir was uninhibited in the mountains if not always discriminate, and they began to stumble down the mountain. Both men had frozen feet and one of Muir's arms was numb, but they called upon "a kind of second life, available only in emergencies." When they finally felt the warmth of the sun it renewed their will once more. Waiting for them as they reached timber line was Sisson who, knowing they were in trouble, had brought horses and provisions. It was the only time Muir ever had to be rescued in the mountains and he was glad for it. He convalesced with the help of the Sisson family, and regained full use of his arm but was slightly hobbled the rest of his life by those frozen feet that never fully recovered.

Muir continued his glacial studies and vertical adventures during his Alaskan trips, the first in 1879. But with his marriage to Louie Strentzel, the arrival of two daughters, and the demands of the family fruit ranch, Muir was sequestered at home in Martinez, California, for much of the 1880s. Finally in 1888, at age fifty, he broke out again, this time for good. He and a group of friends made the seventh recorded ascent of Mount Rainier in Washington. "I did not mean to climb it," he wrote, "but got excited and soon was on top." [19]

Approaching his sixtieth birthday in the mid-1890s, Muir showed no sign of retiring from the mountains. "I must have been born a mountaineer," he said in 1895, following a six-week trip to all his old haunts in the Sierra. "I suppose old age will put an end to scrambling in rocks and ice, but I can still climb as well as ever." [20] Even during his round-the-world tour of 1903–1904, when he was sixty-five, he was skilled enough to romp across the Mueller Glacier on Mount Cook in New Zealand, obviously enjoying himself, delighting in his continued agility. "In jumping on the boulder-clad snout," he wrote, "I found my feet had not lost their cunning." [21]

John Muir's climbing grit and unprecedented number of climbs during the era is impressive, but the ideas behind his achievements are still the most fascinating aspect of his mountaineering. When the focus is on Muir's thoughts, the philosopher-scientist-mountaineer is truly seen and the reason for his vertical quest becomes clear. Influenced by a background in the classics, the scriptures, and humanism, his driving force was essentially spiritual. One of America's foremost wilderness philosophers, with his own unique blend of mysticism, transcendentalism, pantheism, and mainstream Christianity, he was the only one to practice his philosophy on granite walls where even solid rock spoke to him. "Religion is on all the rocks," he said.[22] This inspiration brought an added dimension to Muir's exploits, and it is impossible to know the climber without understanding his spiritual preoccupation. When Muir looked at ice and rock, he saw something most of us miss. From the tiniest granite crystal to the most exalted, singular mountain monoliths, he heard and saw a "Beauty," as he called it, that led him on, pulling him up into the world of vertical sauntering.

John Muir sensed more than silent, stoic beauty when he saw mountains; he felt brilliant, ebullient life bursting forth from the rock and ice. This vision affected all aspects of Muir's climbing and elevated his efforts from the realm of simple sport to spiritual quest. Mountains were not imposing barriers of inhospitable character, fraught with dangers, purposefully protected from assault by natural embattlements. Rather, they were gentle and had a message to convey to those who could intuitively sense their value. "If I want the Sierra Mountain feeling on my back," said Muir, "I stand with my back to them as I would to a fire."[23] Mountains and vertical cliffs were friendly and inviting to Muir, and he couldn't wait to make their acquaintance. "When I reached Yosemite, all the rocks seemed talkative and more telling and lovable than ever," he said. "I love them with a love intensified by long and close companionship."[24]

Muir felt a "Spirit" speak in every whisper of wind on each summit, in movements of shadows cast across rock, in the intimate touch of cloud against rock, and in the piercing report of ice breaking away from the cliff. Nowhere was this relationship to the environment more obvious than in Muir's special cathedral, Yosemite Valley. "No temple made with hands can compare with Yosemite. Every rock in its walls seems to glow with life," he said.[25] The life he perceived in each crystal was a smaller, but no less magnificent, expression of the Spirit he felt in the entire mountain range. When he designated the Sierras as the "Range of Light," he was not acclaiming the illumination of the afternoon alpenglow but recognizing the inspirational qualities of the whole range: an element of preternatural wisdom apparent to those who sought the "good tidings" of the mountains. Intoxicated with this Beauty, Muir was swept into a dynamic interplay of physical environment and personal revelation, and he began to identify closely with the mountains and all their features.

"This I may say, is the first time I have been at church in California," said Muir after his climb of Cathedral Peak in the Sierra in the summer of 1869.[26] Several weeks earlier, when he first saw the peak he had hoped not to conquer it but to "climb to it to say my prayers and hear the stone sermons." Unbeknownst to Muir, his ascent of Cathedral Peak was the most difficult rock climb anyone had done in America.[27] Had he known what he was about to achieve in one of his first Yosemite climbs, he might have provided more of a literary drum roll, but as it was at the time, he stated simply, "Left camp at daybreak and made direct for Cathedral Peak, which I reached at noon, having loitered by the way to study the fine trees." Climbing by himself with no onlookers, no media to record the feat, Muir missed this opportunity for glory. Did he not know this was 1869 and he was in California, a land preoccupied with the heroic imperative, a place where people were chopping down the tallest, damming the wildest, building the biggest, extracting the most, and boasting of virility everywhere? Quite out of step for his time, Muir sensed only his diminutiveness, and awed by his reverence for everything wild, he felt no more important than all that was around him. Muir presented a counterimage for the Californians quite unlike that of the heroic conqueror. He became, according to Kevin Starr, all that the mountains themselves promised: "simplicity, strength, joy, and affirmation," and he ultimately "upgraded the entire Californian relationship to the mountains." [28] Muir's confident steps toward Cathedral Peak were also some of his first steps toward becoming one of the most important figures in California history.

That a religious zeal permeated Muir's philosophy and his every move in the mountains should come as no surprise. Muir grew up hiding any book he read but the Bible from his harsh Calvinist father, but he memorized the entire Old Testament and much of the New. He never lost his love of the Bible for its beautiful prose or for its examples of life's ethical proprieties. Few people lived a more Christian life than did Muir who, ultimately came to peace with himself, and rejected his father's God and embraced a more benevolent deity, thereafter designated as "Nature" or "Beauty" or "Spirit" in his writings. Influenced by his courses at the University of Wisconsin, his botany and geology classes, and especially by his friendship with Jeanne Carr, wife of one of his professors, Muir was introduced to another world. Lyrical spokesmen for nature like Wordsworth and fellow Scotsman Robert Burns, coupled with the transcendentalists Thoreau and Emerson, convinced Muir that his particular vision of the world was not at odds with Christianity, and that in fact, as he concluded, nature and the Bible "harmonize beautifully." [29] Later, in the midst of his Yosemite love affair he stated with confidence, "Christianity and mountainanity are streams from the same fountain." [30] America's foremost apostle of nature, Muir was on his own errand unto the wilderness, lending poignancy to his father's criticism.

Ultimately Muir's religion, a kind of wilderness egalitarianism, had a significant effect on how he practiced his sport of mountaineering, for he never sought to conquer the peaks, only to merge with them as equals. To a friend on the eve of her first visit to Yosemite he wrote, "You'll find me as rough as the rocks and about the same color—granite."[31] What a sight he must have been for visitors to Yosemite as he returned from one of his mountain sojourns wearing his tattered clothes, his hair tangled, his face purposefully blackened to prevent burn, and forever skinny, having gone for days eating only bread, looking for all the world like some feral man. If there is a singlemost important feature that separated John Muir from other climbers, it was his humility derived from his religion and his belief in the interdependence of all life. He had no wish to set himself apart, as some sovereign entity who could prove himself stronger than the mountains. Forever self-effacing, he never indulged in self-importance, he never bragged, and he certainly never left any physical evidence of his feats. "I have never left my name on any mountain, rock, or tree in any wilderness," he wrote in 1903.[32] Always respecting his Scots/Christian injunction against displays of vanity, indeed, Muir felt no pride in climbing a mountain, only joy and a sense that he was a little closer to the "Spirit" he sought on high peaks.

A final quality that separated Muir from other climbers once again was not his physical stamina, nor his technical finesse, but a sharply defined "soul life," an intuition, a virtual sixth sense he developed in climbing. "The life of a mountaineer seems to be particularly favorable to development of soul life," he explained.[33] Speaking to him through his "other self," this sense saved him in perilous situations, as on his first attempt of Mount Whitney, for example, and it always enabled him to climb beyond the point where others, bound by logic or reason, were stopped. This quality marked him off from more cerebral or purely physical climbers. Never was this characteristic more in evidence than on his ascent of Mount Ritter.

If a mountaineer truly presses himself to excel, sooner or later he will be faced with a seemingly insoluble and perilous situation high on a vertical face. Having exhausted his repertoire of physical and mental solutions to the difficulty mild panic may set in, which only makes the predicament worse. Better climbers can keep this mental chaos at bay, but not for long. Logic is a poor partner at this point; reasoning fails the climber. In Muir's case, when this happened to him, he was on the face of Mount Ritter in the Sierra, and he recalled that his mind "seemed to fill with a stifling smoke." [34] By himself as usual, with no rope, his arms and legs spreadeagled on the rock and unable to move up or down, Muir was sure he was going to fall. Suddenly, inexplicably, he became "possessed of a new sense. The other self . . . call it what you will—came forward and assumed control . . . and my limbs moved with a positiveness and precision with which I seemed to have nothing at all to do." The danger passed, he continued on to the summit. Remaining on top almost until sunset, he was spellbound the entire time, his body reverberated from the new-found "energy" that acutely heightened his senses.

In this episode, contemporary climbers see all the elements of a classic, epic climb: a first ascent, scaled on an unclimbed route, accomplished by a small, minimally equipped party; seemingly insurmountable danger skirted with the help of an intuitive sense. Finally, the climb ends on the summit with the climber in an altered state, experiencing a lucidity of mind and tranquility of mood. This serenity is intoxicating, and will not let the climber leave the mountain top. Muir's ascent of Ritter had all these elements. There was no finer climb for him. [35]

More than once Muir came uncomfortably close to death in the mountains before escaping unharmed. On a number of occasions he was either lucky or had Someone watching over him. He made mistakes as does every mountaineer. Sometimes his judgement was poor, other times he was simply caught in reverie while nature was busy enveloping him in severity. Never for a moment did be forget that he was mortal, but his religion removed the fear of dying in the mountains. "Death is stingless indeed," he said, "and as beautiful as life itself." [36] He even dreamt about his death several times. Once, what would have been a nightmare for most was accepted with equanimity by Muir. "I dreamed I stood on the edge of a precipice shaken by an earthquake. The rock started to fall. I said, 'Let us die calmly. This is a noble death.'"[37] Another time, dreaming he fell from a cliff, he sensed himself "rushing through the air." Startled awake, he was both shaken and ecstatic, and he shouted "Where could a mountaineer find a more glorious death."[38] Muir never wanted to die while climbing, but he accepted that possibility as the price for getting that much closer to the Beauty he knew was most conspicuous in high places.

S. Hall Young, Alaskan missionary, friend and occasional climbing partner of John Muir, was not quite as blasé about his own mortality as was Muir. Faced with the imminent possibility of his death on Glenora Peak, high above the Stickeen River in Alaska, Young found himself reviewing his life, thinking of his pregnant wife, and wondering how long the fall would last before he hit the glacier below.[39]

This occurred after Muir, on his first trip by steam ship to Alaska, met Young who was in the company of some renowned missionaries. When the steamer tied up for the day at Glenora, the Captain told all the passengers to amuse themselves. Muir came to life. "I saw Muir's eyes light up across the table," said Young. The evangelist was in a fix, however, having to defer to his superiors who, as he remembered "had a special mission to suppress all my self-destructive proclivities toward dangerous adventure, and especially to protect me from 'that wild Muir' and his harebrained schemes of mountain climbing." With the enticement of an 8,000-foot peak, ten miles away, Muir had a goal for the day and was impatient. Young, using a little "guile," devised a way to elude his elders for the day, and soon he and Muir were off.

The climb went fairly well with Muir stopping to talk to flowers in a "curious mixture of scientific lingo and baby talk," Young said. He marveled at Muir's climbing ability and swore that Muir had some sort of negative gravity machine strapped to his back. Still, Young managed to keep up with him until a fall, where the venture took a sharp turn from lighthearted to serious.

Vertical Sauntering

Muir was climbing sightly ahead of Young and had reached the summit unaware of his partner's predicament. Backtracking, he came upon Young and was startled. "My God!" he cried when he saw him. Young had tried to launch himself across a small gap, but slipped and made a desperate lunge for the other side. The fall dislocated both of Young's shoulders, and though he landed on a small ledge, he was gradually slipping off. When Muir spotted him he instantly reassured Young. "Hold fast. I'm going to get you out of this." Unable to reach Young from his advanced position, Muir crossed behind the peak and arrived just above his partner.

By that time, Young was almost over the edge and, with the pain in his shoulder almost unbearable, had nearly given up. Muir crept down to him, holding onto the rock with one hand, reached down, and grabbed Young by the belt with the other hand. With Young's feet providing some grip on the rock, Muir pulled the fallen climber up and out over the sheer drop. "My head swung down, my impotent arms dangling," remembered Young. Muir pulled him up close, caught his collar with his teeth, and managed to bring him to rest on a small ledge where they were both temporarily safe.

What followed was a nightmare for the two as they were still a thousand feet above the glacier, with no rope, as always, and ten miles from the ship once they got off the vertical rock. The temperature was quite cold, the sun was just setting, and neither had a coat. Standing on that small ledge, Muir worked on Young's shoulders and was able to get the right arm back into its socket, restoring partial use. The left arm, however, was much worse, with the head of the bone thrust up into Young's armpit: it could not be reset. The two began a night-long descent. Muir would lower himself and then Young would slip down on top of him. Young's worst arm was in a sling, and the other, his right, offered some support, though it popped out three more times during their struggle to reach the ship.

When they reached the glacier below, the ten remaining miles seemed impossible, but the pair labored on, Muir "always cheery, full of talk," said Young. He cracked jokes while working tirelessly, lowering Young down the gravel slopes and throwing water in his face when Young was about to faint. By daylight they were back at the ship to find the grim, senior missionaries staring down at them from the deck.

The catalog of John Muir's mountaineering exploits continues, each story revealing a little more about this consummate climber and each adding to a well-deserved legend. Norman Foerster in his work *Nature in American Literature* wrote of Muir: "Never, perhaps, had there been such a complete mountaineer and glacier climber as he, unsurpassed alike in skill, in knowledge, in passionate enjoyment." [40] Muir was the first well-known climber in America to realize that the object of the sport was not *what* you climbed, but *how* you climbed: means were more important than ends, finesse more important than force. Climbing was part of Muir's religion, not mere egotistical diversion; he simply brought body and spirit to the vertical world—not mounds of equipment, rock hammers, or bolts to be driven into the rock. It has taken American climbers 100 years to understand what Muir was talking about when he said "It is astonishing how high and far we can climb in the mountains that we love and how little we require food and clothing." [41] Climbing demands a certain humility in the face of the superiority of Nature, and an acknowledgment that brute strength and advanced equipment will only take one so far in the mountains. There is a proper way to climb, the image of the rugged individualist making his own rules in the wilderness notwithstanding, and Muir knew this a century before the ethical craze hit the American climbing scene in the early 1970s. Suddenly then—exposing their puritan roots—American climbers became consumed with moral imperatives about the proper way to climb and imposed injunctions against harming the rock with excessive equipment.

Muir was a climbing purist, the founding father of "clean climbing" in this country, and the best climber of his era. The virtues he brought to the sport—intellect, determination, perse-

Vertical Sauntering

The Reverend S. Hall Young, Muir's traveling companion on his first two Alaska expeditions, at Child's Glacier in 1910. Photograph by Lawrence Martin. John Muir Papers, Holt Atherton Library. Copyright 1984 by Muir-Hanna Trust.

verance, spirituality, and the desire to understand divine manifestations—made him the sport's foremost Renaissance man. We can confer this title upon him not simply by looking at his ideas or by recounting his feats, but by studying the juncture between his ideas and his actions. No armchair transcendentalist, no cloistered seminarian, he was out in the world searching for God and showing the way for others, intensely involved in both spiritual pursuit and civic responsibility. The success of the Sierra Club is testimony to his efforts in the latter, and his own words leave little doubt that he achieved his vision quest. "When the glorious summits are gained, the weariness all vanishes in a moment as the vast landscapes of white mountains are beheld reposing in the sky, every peak with its broad flowing folds of white, glowing in God's sunshine, serene and silent, devout like a human being. This is true transportation."[42]

It is painful to think of John Muir, on the night of December 24, 1914, dying in that hospital bed rather than among his

Arthur W. Ewart

friends, the mountains. There is stark contrast between the image of the young, powerful climber earlier in his life and the coughing, lonely figure close to death still trying to spread the Word, his notes for his next book at hand. But Muir survives in the power of his mountaineering legacy, and the virtues he possessed as a climber were not simply means for scaling icy peaks or granite cliffs but also guidelines for living.

> **"The mountains are calling and I must go."** [43]
> John Muir

NOTES

1. Details of this account on the rim of Yosemite Valley, and Muir's words, are taken from John Muir, *My First Summer in the Sierra* (1911; reprinted, Boston: Houghton Mifflin, 1979), pp. 115–121.

2. Ibid., p. 86.

3. Stephen Fox, *John Muir and His Legacy: The American Conservation Movement* (Boston: Little, Brown, 1981), p. 34.

4. Muir, *First Summer*, p. 78.

5. John Muir, quoted in William Frederic Badè, *The Life and Letters of John Muir*, 2 Vols. (Boston: Houghton Mifflin, 1924), I, p. 311.

6. John Muir, letter to Mrs. Daniel Muir, 16 November, 1871, in Ibid., p. 315.

7. John Muir, *John of the Mountains: The Unpublished Journals of John Muir*, ed. Linnie Marsh Wolfe (1938; reprinted, Madison: University of Wisconsin Press, 1979), p. 187.

8. John Muir quoted in Linnie Marsh Wolfe, *Son of the Wilderness: The Life of John Muir* (1945; reprinted, Madison: University of Wisconsin Press, 1979), p. 169.

9. John Muir, correspondence to *San Francisco Bulletin*, reprinted in Robert Engberg, *John Muir: Summering in the Sierra* (Madison: University of Wisconsin Press, 1984), p. 110.

10. Francis Farquhar, "The Story of Mt. Whitney," *Sierra Club Bulletin* (1935): 85. Steve Roper credits Muir with the first ascent: Roper, *Climber's Guide to the High Sierra* (San Francisco: Sierra Club Books, 1976), p. 368.

11. Muir, *First Summer*, p. 53.

12. Therese Yelverton Longsworth, *Zanita: A Tale of the Yosemite* (New York: Hurd and Houghton, 1872), pp. 5–8.

13. John Muir, letter to Jeanne Carr, 13 October, 1874, in Badè, *Life and Letters*, I, pp. 393–394.

14. Ibid., 7 October, 1874, p. 28.

Vertical Sauntering

15. Muir, quoted in Wolfe, *Son of the Wilderness*, p. 176.

16. John Muir, letter to J. B. McChesney, 9 November, 1874, in Badè, *Life and Letters*, II, p. 35.

17. Details of the Shasta climb and Muir's quotes, unless otherwise noted, are found in John Muir, *Steep Trails*, edited by William Frederic Badè (New York: Houghton Mifflin, 1918), pp. 57–81.

18. Muir, letter to Jeanne Carr, 1 November 1874, in Badè, *Life and Letters*, II, p. 31.

19. Muir, quoted in Badè, *Life and Letters*, II, pp. 219–220.

20. Ibid., pp. 290–291.

21. Muir, quoted in Wolfe, *Son of the Wilderness*, p. 299.

22. Ibid., p. 144.

23. John Muir, letter to John and Maggie Reid, 13 January. 1869, p. 8.

24. Muir, *Steep Trails*, pp. 19–20.

25. John Muir, *The Yosemite* (1912; reprinted, San Francisco: Sierra Club Books, 1989), p. 34.

26. Details of the Cathedral Peak climb, as well as Muir's quotes, are taken from *First Summer*, pp. 198, 247–250.

27. For this determination, I have relied upon the judgment of Steve Roper, *The Climber's Guide to the High Sierra*, p. 13. Roper also credits Muir with the first ascent of Cathedral Peak (p. 334).

28. Kevin Starr, *Americans and the California Dream* (New York: Oxford University Press, 1973), p. 184.

29. John Muir, letter to Jeanne Carr, 21 January, 1866. In John Muir, *Letters to a Friend*, (1915, reprinted, Dunwoody. Norman S. Burg, 1973), p. 1.

30. John Muir, letter to J. B. McChesney, 10 January, 1883, in Badè, *Life and Letters*, I, p. 378.

31. John Muir, letter to Emily Pelton, 2 April, 1872, in *Muir, Letters to a Friend*, I, p. 325.

32. Muir, quoted in Badè, *Life and Letters*, I, p. 396.

33. Muir, *John of the Mountains*, p. 77.

34. Details of the Ritter climb, as well as Muir's quotes, are found in Muir, *The Mountains of California* (1894; reprinted, New York: Dorset Press, 1988), pp. 52–74.

35. That Muir made the first ascent of Ritter is cited in Roper, *Climber's Guide to the High Sierra*, p. 336.

36. John Muir, *Thousand Mile Walk* (Boston: Houghton Mifflin, 1915), p. 71.

37. Muir, *John of the Mountains*, p. 125.

38. Muir, *First Summer*, p. 121.

39. Details of the Glenora Peak climb and quotes from Young are found in S. Young Hall, *Alaska Days with John Muir* (New York: Fleming Revell Company, 1912), pp. 11–56. Muir was somewhat embarrassed by the publicity from this and other glamorized accounts of the climb, and wrote his own version. Still, the essential facts remained unchanged.

Arthur W. Ewart

40. Norman Foerster, *Nature in American Literature* (New York: Russell and Russell, 1958), p. 243.

41. Muir, *John of the Mountains*, p. 69.

42. Ibid., p. 329.

43. John Muir, letter to Sarah Galloway, 3 September, 1873, in Badè, *Life and Letters*, I, p. 385.

PART
II
MUIR
AND
RELIGION

3.
God and John Muir

A Psychological Interpretation of John Muir's Journey from the Campbellites to the "Range of Light"

Mark Stoll

When, on December 5, 1871, readers of the New York *Tribune*, the leading newspaper of its day, turned to an article entitled "Yosemite Glaciers," they found themselves reading descriptions of nature like none they had seen before. It was the first attempt of the author, John Muir, to write for publication, and it was also the beginning of a long, affectionate relationship between Muir and his readers. Decades after the appearance of some of his articles, readers would still write him to thank him belatedly for the enjoyment he had given them.

More than anyone else, he massed public sentiment behind the preservation of America's forests and mountains but in all that has been written about Muir, what drove him to become a preservationist has never been satisfactorily answered. The answer to this question must explain why he departed from his strict Scottish evangelical background for a religious view of nature so pronounced as to lead some to believe that he had abandoned Christianity altogether.

Emerging from the religious revivals in Europe and America in the 1820s and 1830s, Protestantism experienced during Muir's youth the shocks of the rapid advances of science, the scrutiny of higher criticism, and the defection of the romantics and transcendentalists. Muir's thought combined those elements—evangelical Protestantism, science, romanticism, and transcendentalism—in a way that was unique and, through his writings, widely influential. The resulting amalgam in Muir's life was forged in the fiery religion and strict discipline of his father, Daniel Muir, whose specter haunted Muir's entire life. From a close examination of the individuals who peopled his life, the kind of events that filled it, and the modes of thought that enlivened it, a psychological understanding of John Muir emerges that helps show why he turned onto the paths he trod.[1]

Daniel Muir was born in 1804 to Scottish parents and orphaned in infancy. Settling in Dunbar, Scotland, he married Anne Gilrye in 1833 following the deaths of his first wife and child, and became a prosperous merchant and grain dealer. John Muir, their third child and first son, was born in 1838. Scotland at the time was a land of tremendous religious schism and controversy. Those sects that rejected orthodox Calvinism and that emphasized free grace to the repentant and a religion of the heart had attracted Daniel after his religious conversion at age fourteen. He searched in several congregations for the right combination of holiness and zeal until the Campbellites came to Dunbar in the 1840s. Ancestor to the present-day Disciples of Christ and Churches of Christ, this sect was founded by two Scottish immigrants in Ohio, Thomas Campbell and his son Alexander, in the years after 1807. Their rational, simple, straightforward approach to doctrine and Biblical interpretation appealed to frontiersmen and Scotsmen alike, and the sect spread rapidly from an axis centered in the Ohio valley.

Inspired by the Campbellite desire to recreate the primitive Church, Daniel Muir practiced a hard and humorless religion. Every evening at family worship Daniel prayed long and fervently; he was a strict disciplinarian and required John to memorize Bible verses or hymns daily or face a whipping. After a while Daniel stopped playing the violin he had built as a teenager and shaped his wife, by nature a fun-loving and boisterous woman, to keep her lighter side to herself and to practice such small pleasures as knitting and needlepoint (when not strictly necessary) only when her husband would not see her. Anne's role in the family was ambiguous. In her husband's absence, she either encouraged or at least did not oppose carefree activities in the household of which Daniel would not have approved. At other times, she seemed an obedient Christian wife, either accommodating or acquiescing in her subordinate place within the biblically-ordained patriarchal family.

Very strick childhood.

God And John Muir

The only known portrait of John Muir's father
Daniel, copied from a painting by Muir's sister
Mary. Published in Linne Marsh Wolfe, *Son of
the Wilderness* (1945). John Muir Papers, Holt
Atherton Library. Copyright 1984 by
Muir-Hanna Trust.

When Daniel heard from Campbellite leaders of religious
freedom and cheap land in America, he made the decision to
move and settled among a community of Campbellites in Wisconsin. In the comparative isolation of the frontier, deprived
of the buffers provided by the network of kith and kin, and
surrounded by many fellow Campbellites, Daniel's propensities toward religion and discipline (and profit) were exacerbated.
While his children, often including the girls, labored to clear
the forest and raise the crops, Daniel retired to his study to read
the Bible. The Disciples of Christ had no regular clergy but
relied on "preaching elders," usually self-taught, like Daniel.

Very popular as a preacher, he traveled around the countryside to whichever churches would hear him.

At home he was a tyrant and allowed no stopping of work, even for sickness, and his children were afraid to rest in the shade or to get a drink of water. Only once, when John had pneumonia, did Daniel allow him to stay in bed, although no doctor was called, for "God and hard work were by far the best doctors."[2] For any infraction, major or minor, real or imagined, the punishment was a severe whipping. The family kept their small pleasures out of his sight, and John spent his free Sunday afternoons enjoying nature and the changing seasons.

Daniel had forbidden all books as frivolous or impious except for religious or practical ones. John Muir's intellectual horizons suddenly opened up at age fifteen when two neighbor boys with whom he was working recited to him their favorite poets —Byron, Poe, Wordsworth, Milton. He discovered that many neighbors had small libraries in their homes, and he secretly but avidly began to read the romantic poets as well as the travels of Mungo Park and Alexander von Humboldt, novels, biographies, natural history, mathematics, and philosophy. Here began Muir's lifelong love of poetry. The romantics attracted him with their love of nature, mountains and wilderness, and their rejection of a too utilitarian view of nature in favor of an investment of nature with human moods and emotions.

Around the same time, Muir began to rise hours before breakfast in order to enjoy some free time. In the summer he read, and in the darkness of winter he invented and built an astonishing array of devices: wooden clocks, thermometers, pyrometers, hygrometers, a barometer, a combination lock— all without any formal training or knowledge beyond simple mathematics. His father was clearly impressed but refrained from praising John, which he feared would encourage the sin of pride. The neighbors were far more effusive, and in 1860, in spite of his father's pointed refusal of money or blessing, Muir took his inventions to the state fair at Madison, where he hoped to win the attention of an inventor or machine shop with whom he could work. He won renown rather than a permanent job, but to his joy, the struggling young University of Wisconsin gladly accepted him.

The knowledge Muir acquired during his short time at the university would be invaluable to him in later life. Away from his father's tyranny, he threw himself with great delight into his studies at the university. His New England-educated professors had been students of Ralph Waldo Emerson and Louis Agassiz, the geologist who first hypothesized the Ice Age. Dr. Ezra Slocum Carr taught science. Muir's fascination with glaciation dated from Carr's introduction of Agassiz's works and his class field trips to see local evidence of glaciation. His classics teacher had Muir read Wordsworth, Thoreau, and Emerson, and acquainted him with the transcendentalist regard for nature. In imitation of Emerson, he began to keep a journal, the first of great stacks of journals he would accumulate by the time of his death. Finally, one of Muir's fellow students introduced him to one of his life's loves, botany.

Muir's exposure to geology and botany brought him face to face with science that could not be harmonized with a literal reading of the Bible, but exposure to liberal Christianity showed him a way to reconcile religion and science. Carr's wife, Jeanne, introduced him to the thought of William Ellery Channing, with his positive view of a loving God and indwelling divinity. Muir also accepted Agassiz's precept that "a physical fact is as sacred as a moral principle." [3] Toward Darwin he was not so charitable; he accepted evolution but rejected "Darwin's mean ungodly word 'struggle'" [4] in favor of a principle of divine guidance. At this point, Muir still held actively to his Christian beliefs and an evangelical concern for the state of everyone else's soul. When the Civil War broke out he went to the newly established army encampment and gave moral talks to the soldiers. In 1863 he was elected president of the local Young Men's Christian Association, at that time a club where young men met to study the Bible and put Christian belief into practice.

Muir left Wisconsin before finishing his studies and lived

in Canada until 1866. He took with him books by Humboldt, who powerfully influenced Muir's thought, both as a life model and as a theorist of cosmic unity amidst the complexity of phenomena. Without intellectual stimulation, lonely, approaching thirty, unmarried, and with no prospects, Muir wrote to the Carrs in 1865, the start of a long friendship with Mrs. Carr. She became a sort of mother/mentor figure for Muir, while at the same time, a friend of Emerson and possibly an intellectually frustrated housewife, she seemed to live vicariously through Muir and constantly encouraged his ambitions.

Intent on a life as an inventor, Muir in 1866 went to Indianapolis, a railroad and industrial center located in the midst of a great deciduous forest where he could botanize. He found a job in a major machine shop, and the impressed owners were on the verge of making him a partner when a file slipped and pierced Muir's right eye. His sight quickly drained out of the one eye, and the other went into "sympathetic" blindness.

This was the central, pivotal event in Muir's life. Plunged into despair, depression, and literal darkness, Muir experienced something of a conversion as his sight slowly returned, and he came away from the accident inspired with a new sense of purpose. When a doctor first told him his sight would return, he wrote Mrs. Carr, "Now had I arisen from the grave."[5] Convalescing in bed with a brochure on Yosemite valley in his lap, he mused about the industrial accident that nearly robbed him of the ability to investigate the glory of God's creation. When the shop owners came to offer him a partnership in the firm, he declined. In a letter to Mrs Carr he explained, "God has to nearly kill us sometimes, to teach us lessons."[6] Much later he remembered,

> As soon as I got out into Heaven's light I started on another long excursion, making haste with all my heart to store my mind with the Lord's beauty and thus be ready to any fate, light or dark. And it was from this time that my long continuous wanderings may be said to have fairly commenced. I bade adieu to all my mechanical

God And John Muir

inventions, determined to devote the rest of my life to the study of the inventions of God.[7]

This brush with blindness called Muir to a higher purpose, beyond any thing defined in terms of wealth or human utility. Ever after aware of the preciousness of sight, Muir referred to God and nature in terms of light and dubbed the Sierras the "Range of Light."

When he was sufficiently recovered, Muir set out to live a fantasy he had conceived while wandering in Canada: he would be a new Humboldt. First he made a farewell trip to Wisconsin, where he met with the constant criticism and disapproval of his father. As Muir was about to leave, Daniel asked him for money for room and board for the time he had stayed. Muir complied but told him he could be sure it would be a long time before he returned. They did not see each other until nearly twenty years later, just before Daniel's death in 1885.

Returning to Indianapolis, Muir set out by foot for the Gulf Coast with a vague intention of continuing on to South America in imitation of Humboldt. During his trip he had plenty of time to think and write in his journal, and he developed the principles that would guide him the rest of his life. The main intellectual influences of his life appeared in his journals and publications from then on: from the university he acquired a scientific appreciation for the workings and wonders of nature; from Humboldt a sense of the ecological interconnectedness of everything; from the transcendentalists and romantics beliefs in nature's connection with higher impulses and powers, and in a near pantheistic immanence; from liberal Christianity a feeling for a benign God of love; and from evangelical Christianity a desire to preach salvation to the nations, albeit not a heavenly but a wilderness salvation.[8]

A severe malarial fever in Florida kept Muir from getting any closer to South America than Cuba. With the encouragement of Mrs. Carr, now in Berkeley with her husband, he headed instead to the Yosemite Valley in California. He spent the next years climbing mountains and exploring the Sierra range. Mrs. Carr sent a parade of important visitors his way, and Muir did not fail to make an impression on each: biologists, philosophers, professors, painters, scientists. The inspiration and rapture in his steady stream of letters to Mrs. Carr caused her to encourage him to write for publication. His success at writing brought him fame and embroiled him in the controversial movement to preserve the wilderness. In the 1880s his marriage and ten-year stint as family man and fruit grower brought a temporary lull in his activity. Then he returned to the fight to establish and defend national parks. In 1892 he founded the Sierra Club, and he later befriended Presidents Roosevelt and Taft. By the time he died of double pneumonia in 1914, he had become something of a national treasure.

This bare biography of John Muir has concentrated on his childhood and sketched in the foundations upon which he based his life and thought. Across all of Muir's life and works lay the shadow of one man, without whom both Muir's boundless drive and departure from the religious mainstream are nearly inconceivable: his father, Daniel. Psychologists have developed a model that does much to illuminate the workings of the father-son relationship. This model describes the relationship in light of three processes: the son's identification with the father; the father's counter-identification with the son; and the father's competition with his teenage son.[9] Applied to Daniel and John Muir, it highlights and brings into perspective many of the motivations, emotions, and tensions of their relationship and their lives.

Boys identify with their fathers, and in doing so emulate not only attitudes, values, roles, gestures, and emotional reactions but problem-solving strategies, thinking processes, and vocabulary as well. Thus, in many sundry ways John Muir's life paralleled Daniel's. Daniel found God at age fourteen; Muir discovered the world of poetry and books at age fifteen. Daniel took his family to homestead in Wisconsin, sold the improved land and homesteaded again; as a family man during the 1880s

God And John Muir

Muir owned and ran a fruit ranch and won a reputation as a sharp haggler who always got the best prices for his produce.

The strongest similarity between Muir and his father is that each rejected an orthodox religion and preached the Gospel according to his own lights—for Daniel the Campbellite Gospel, for Muir the Gospel of Nature. Both father and son were only too happy to abandon mundane tasks to dedicate themselves to higher, holy causes. Daniel did well as a merchant in Dunbar and a farmer in Wisconsin but eventually abandoned all work to devote himself to his religion. Inventing brought Muir escape from the farm, notoriety, and the beginnings of worldly success, but he abandoned this career to study "the inventions of God;" later, after a decade as a responsible family man, he heeded the call a second time to lead the cause of wilderness.

Scottish preachers have long been popular in the United States for their serious demeanor and "Thus saith the Lord" declamatory style.[10] Although Daniel's sermons are lost to history, this style easily accords with his character and religion. Similarly, especially during the Hetch Hetchy dam controversy, Muir's increasingly strident rhetoric grew to resemble this style, inspiring his friend, Congressman William Kent, to make the remark, "With him, it is me and God and the rock where God put it."[11] Muir liked to describe himself in biblical terms, a John the Baptist preaching the wilderness gospel. The sight of Muir, long beard flowing in the breeze, descending from the Sierras caused visitors to recall images of prophets returning from the wilderness. Interestingly enough, just as the biblical Daniel, prophet of the Old Testament God of Wrath, was succeeded by John, prophet of the New Testament God of Love, so was the wrathful Daniel Muir succeeded by the loving John Muir.

The process of a son's identification with his father proceeds very well with nurturing, supportive, and sufficiently masculine fathers. Boys reject as models undemonstrative, frustrating, critical fathers. This is not an unfair description of Daniel, and many incidents could be cited to show how strongly Muir rejected his example. For instance, John Muir's affection and compassion for children and animals may have roots in his rejection of the model offered by his punishing father and his identification instead with fellow victims of the whip. Muir could never bring himself to strike children or animals. He once wrote, "When the rod is falling on the flesh of a child, and, what may oftentimes be worse, heart-breaking scolding falling on its tender little heart, it makes the whole family seem far from the Kingdom of Heaven." [12] As a university student, Muir taught school for a while and caused parents to complain that "he don't half whip." [13] Muir saw animals overworked on his parents' farm, and Daniel once drove a horse to death. As an adult, Muir fired on the spot any hand abusing an animal on his ranch. Ranch ownership was perhaps too close to his father's life and values to be comfortable to Muir. He never seemed happy there, and a possibly asthmatic cough constantly bothered him; allergies are sometimes psychosomatic, and conceivably his cough could be related psychologically to the pneumonia that excused him from farm work as a boy.

As John Muir rejected Daniel's harsher aspects, he also rejected his father's concepts of God and nature. Daniel subscribed to the contemporary view, based on the Bible and strengthened by the teachings of the Enlightenment and the necessities of frontier life, that God made nature for man's dominion and use. John Muir broke from this view and developed a conception of the value in itself of all creation and the ecological interconnectedness of all things. God made nature for man's use, yes, but also for his spirit. A walk into the wilderness was a religious activity, for there one immersed oneself in the glory of God's immaculate handiwork. The study of nature was also a religious experience, for there the scientist read the manuscripts of God as surely as he read them in the Bible. Muir's distaste for an understanding of wilderness in terms of its "usefulness" later led him inexorably into conflict with the scientific-management school of conservation.

A father's idea of God the Father and conception of Him

God And John Muir

either as benevolent and merciful, or stern and judgmental, influence the way he governs his family.[14] The wrathful, punishing aspects of evangelical fatherhood such as Daniel's reflected the stern image of God found in the Old Testament and in certain sections of the New Testament. In the Bible, divine wrath often took the form of natural disasters—floods, earthquakes, storms. When John Muir rejected the wrathful, punishing model of fatherhood, he also rejected the same concept of God and with it, the identification of natural disasters with divine fury. For Muir, the God of love was revealed in all nature, even storms and earthquakes.

Daniel's preaching emphasized sin and damnation at least as much as joy and salvation, for hatred of sin and fear of damnation could move a potential convert to repentance. John Muir remembered burning a pile of brush and waste wood during his Wisconsin boyhood. He and his brothers enjoyed the spectacle of the flames until his father turned the fire into a lesson on the horrible flames of hell awaiting every unrepentant sinner. As an adult, Muir reversed Daniel's emphasis and spoke much less of sin and damnation than the promises of salvation that the wilderness offered. In Muir's wilderness catechism, sin was a product of the man-made environment of the city. Cutting oneself off from nature could cut oneself off from God. But rarely did Muir discuss sin, concentrating instead on the promise of renewal, both spiritual and physical, that nature held for humanity.

Within our psychological model, the son identifies with his father as a second process unfolds: the father's counteridentification with his son. Here the father sees in his present situation his son's probable general future situation, while the son's present behavior may remind the father of his own past. Perhaps difficulties he now sees in the son he once overcame successfully, sometimes after a struggle that may now be unconsciously reactivated. Counteridentification may thus motivate the father to counteract these disturbing behaviors in his son and to attempt at the same time to stifle the same tendencies in himself.

Seen in this light, Daniel's overactive concern for his children's souls was simply a reflection of his concern for his own. "Strange to say," wrote John Muir, "father carefully taught us to consider ourselves very poor worms of the dust, conceived in sin, etc., and devoutly believed that quenching every spark of pride and self-confidence was a sacred duty, without realizing that in so doing he might at the same time be quenching everything else. Praise he considered most venomous. . . ."[15] Daniel was simply applying evangelical theology to family government: a hatred of sinful flesh that reflected a basic tenet of Protestantism; and the evangelical morphology of conversion, whereby the conviction of one's worthlessness and helplessness without God preceded a conversion experience. Thereafter, the convert attempts to suppress all sin and sinful thoughts in himself and to achieve Christian perfection in this life.[16] John Muir internalized hatred of sin as self-criticism and low self-esteem, which manifested themselves in his lonely avocations of botanizing and mountain climbing, and in his youthful lack of grooming habits, which drew comments even by the slack standards of frontier Madison. So self-effacing could he be that some of his early letters lack date or signature.

Anxious to raise obedient and pure-minded Christian children, Daniel controlled, restricted, and punished them. Psychologists have noted that such childraising methods impede the masculinity of sons.[17] Indeed, Muir was quite shy and did not "court" girls as a youth, or as far as is known for certain, until he married at age 42. During his Yosemite days his friends thought that he was a woman hater or a confirmed bachelor. His botanist's fascination with flowers brought the occasional questioning remark about the manliness of the pursuit.[18]

As adolescent boys become men, the third process in father-son relations begins as sons and fathers see each other as competitors and rivals. One of the striking aspects of John Muir's adolescence is how much he tried to outdo his father. He constantly competed with the hired farmworkers, who were older, larger, and stronger, to do the most farmwork. He split rails so

God And John Muir

John Muir, ca. 1875, photographed in San Francisco by Carleton E. Watkins. This is his second oldest portrait, taken after he had completed most of his Yosemite studies and was developing a career as a popular nature writer. John Muir Papers, Holt Atherton Library. Copyright 1984 by Muir-Hanna Trust.

much better than Daniel that the latter gave over the entire job to his son. The father had made his violin, but his son constructed so many wondrous inventions that the whole township came to admire them. As Daniel inspected his son's creations, perhaps he felt a pride of counteridentification mingled with the envy of competition, and envy won out. Even in their more spiritual adult callings, no matter how much Daniel preached to whomever would hear, it was Muir whose preaching stirred the nation.

John Muir's competition with his father continued until Daniel's death, and Muir in some ways succeeded in sharing his place, or even replacing him, in the responsibilities as head of his household. Beginning with his withdrawal from work to study his Bible when John Muir was a teenager, Daniel slowly began to abdicate his role as head of the household. In his old age, he lived apart from his wife and stayed with a daughter in Kansas City, from which one might infer a certain marital estrangement. Meanwhile, John Muir sent his mother letters, copies of his publications, pressed flowers and plants, and seeds for her garden. These actions seem more appropriate for a suitor in competition for her affections (and contrast with his much more restrained later courtship and marriage). John Muir also gave advice and significant financial help to every one of his siblings at one time or another, even convincing three of them to move to California and live close to him. Daniel performed increasingly poorly the role the nineteenth century expected of him as husband and father, and John Muir stepped into his place.[19]

One result of Muir's strained relationship with his father was his lifelong attraction to mother figures. It was his mother who gave to him her love of flowers and nature and who enjoyed reading her son's articles and books. Muir's first biographer noted a scarcity of letters to men, which he attributed to the fact that men are less apt to keep letters than women. However, the contrasting rich correspondence to the women in his life, particularly older women, seems to point to something else: Muir's

God And John Muir

dependence on mother figures for encouragement and support. One of these, Mrs. Carr, whom he even addressed as "mother" in some of his letters, was as responsible as anyone for the course of his later life.

Muir published his autobiography in 1913, when he was seventy-five. He expressed the resentment and hostility he still bore toward his father in many stories of the latter's harshness and cruelty, which contrasted with the rare but affectionate mention of his mother. But any man's feelings toward his father constitute a complex mixture; Muir always claimed that Daniel had a good heart and to some degree admired him and identified with him. But so driven was Daniel in his pursuit of godliness that he drove his son away from him, his life model, and his religion, into a wilderness suffused with the divine light of a loving, accepting Deity. That Muir was thus reborn, not from a life of sin to submission to the God of the Bible, but from a life of repression to revelation of the God of Nature, has left us the rich and inspiring legacy of his wilderness gospel.

NOTES

1. The following biography of Muir is drawn from his autobiography, *The Story of My Boyhood and Youth* (Boston: Houghton Mifflin, 1913); from Ronald H. Limbaugh and Kirsten E. Lewis, eds., *The John Muir Papers* (Cambridge, U.K.: Chadwyck-Healy, 1986); and from several biographies: William Frederic Badè, *The Life and Letters of John Muir*, 2 vols. (Boston: Houghton Mifflin, 1924); Linnie Marsh Wolfe, *Son of the Wilderness: The Life of John Muir* (New York: Knopf, 1945); Stephen Fox, *The American Conservation Movement: John Muir and His Legacy* (Madison: University of Wisconsin Press, 1985); and Frederick Turner, *Rediscovering America: John Muir in His Time and Ours* (New York: Viking, 1985).

2. John Muir, *Story of My Boyhood*, p. 224.

3. Quoted in Badè, *Life and Letters*, I, p. 146.

4. Ibid., p. 380.

5. Quoted in Wolfe, *Son of the Wilderness*, p. 104.

6. Ibid., p. 105.

7. Quoted in Badè, *Life and Letters*, I, p. 155.

8. In this paragraph, I wish to correct two misperceptions. First, I have found no positive evidence of Stephen Fox's assertion that Muir ever rejected Chris-

Mark Stoll

tianity outright. In fact, his emphasis on divine immanence and deemphasis of Jesus were quite consonant with liberal religious trends of the day. Second, Muir's ecological and religious ideas were less original and more mainstream than Michael P. Cohen recognizes. In his otherwise excellent biography, *The Pathless Way: John Muir and American Wilderness* (Madison: University of Wisconsin Press, 1984), Cohen sees Muir as a kind of Western Taoist, an interpretation that removes Muir from his historical context.

9. Norma Radin develops this model in "The Role of the Father in Cognitive, Academic, and Intellectual Development," in Michael E. Lamb, ed., *The Role of the Father in Child Development* (New York: Wiley, 1976). There are many possible ways to approach a father-son relationship. This model recommends itself for a variety of reasons: it is empirical and lacks elaborate theory or esoteric jargon; it intuitively makes sense; it is very suggestive; and it makes clear certain themes that ran through Muir's life.

10. David Read, "The Scottish Tradition of Preaching," in Duncan B. Forrester and Douglas M. Murray, eds., *Studies in the History of Worship in Scotland* (Edinburgh: T.& T. Clark, 1984).

11. Quoted in Fox, *The American Conservation Movement*, p. 144.

12. Quoted in Badè, *Life and Letters*, I, p. 57.

13. Ibid., p. 86.

14. See John Nash, "Historical and Social Changes in the Perception of the Role of the Father," in Lamb, *The Role of the Father.*

15. Muir, *Story of My Boyhood*, p. 263.

16. Actually, the exact content of Campbellite theology in general or Daniel's in particular is problematic. Campbellites had a very broad definition of what a Christian was and hoped thereby to unite the warring denominations. But their abandonment of such Calvinist doctrines as innate depravity did not imply a belief in the innate goodness of man, as Daniel's viewpoint shows. Alexander Campbell, himself a product of a strict Calvinistic upbringing, wrote in 1835 that man, although "not under an invincible necessity to sin," nevertheless was "greatly prone to evil, [and] easily seduced into transgression," "*Christian System*," p. 49, quoted in A. T. DeGroot, *Disciple Thought: A History* (Fort Worth: Texas Christian University, 1965), p. 69. The Muir family forms an example of the evangelical family type that Philip Greven describes in *The Protestant Temperament: Patterns of Child-Rearing, Religious Experience, and the Self in Early America* (Chicago: University of Chicago Press, 1977), Part II. In this type of family, children are taught to love and fear both parents and God. The role of the father is authoritarian, whereas the mother is loving. The parents try to separate the family from the sinful world, often resorting to migration and uprootedness to escape bad influences, such as friends and grandparents. Within this authoritarian and repressive family government, disobedience is sinful, and tenderness and indulgence are guarded against; children must be controlled, their will broken, to prevent license and self-destruction. Simple pleasures might be the gateways to lust and sensuality and must be minimized. Children often rebel during their youth, but the self-

God And John Muir

confidence, self-assurance, and self-approval they achieve tend to make them feel unhappy, anxious, and guilty, and often lead them to return to the fold. Also, suppression of aggressive masculine traits (many of which contradict such Christian commandments as turning the other cheek, loving one's enemy, and submitting to the will of God) may impede masculinity and promote latent homosexuality, it is argued. Seen theologically, the destruction of self-worth and self-righteousness that occurs in Greven's evangelical family is a necessary aspect of the process of conversion, for it prepares the convert to submit totally to and rely completely upon God and to deny his own will in perfect obedience.

17. See Henry B. Biller, "The Father and Personality Development: Paternal Deprivation and Sex Role Development," in Lamb, *The Role of the Father.* See also Biller, *Father, Child, and Sex Role: Paternal Determinants of Personality Development* (Lexington, Mass.: Heath, 1971).

18. Michael L. Smith, in Chapter 4 of *Pacific Visions: California Scientists and the Environment, 1850–1915* (New Haven, Conn.: Yale University Press, 1987), discusses Muir's domestication of landscape (the mountain as "hospitable," a "home") and the genderization of science in the nineteenth century. The public tended to feminize and marginalize the life sciences to which Muir was most attracted and masculinize the hard sciences.

19. This paragraph is based on a question to the author by Ron Limbaugh at a session of the John Muir Conference at the University of the Pacific, Stockton, California, April 18–22, 1990. Limbaugh wondered if Muir in his relationships with his siblings had replaced his father. See also Keith Kennedy's essay in this volume.

4.
John Muir,

Christian Mysticism, and the Spiritual Value of Nature

Dennis Williams

Since Lynn White, Jr., asserted that Christianity was responsible, in part, for the modern environmental crisis, students of environmental history and philosophy have sought, if inadvertently, to replace Christianity with another, more ecologically sensitive, world view.[1] Throughout the 1960s and 1970s, the years in which the field of environmental history emerged, many environmental advocates, professionals, and amateurs alike, identified the religious philosophies of Asia as the religions of ecology. Likewise, John Muir, a posthumous ecological guru to many environmentalists, with his religious vision of the environment, became the subject of revisionist biographical interpretations attempting to find some legitimizing oriental strand woven into Muir's philosophy.[2] When one reads Muir's journals and letters from his early adult years, his mysticism is apparent. Yet, it is not a mysticism like that of Buddhism or Taoism, as some biographers have asserted; rather, it carries a strong Christian tone. In fact, as I will attempt to demonstrate, Muir's preservationist ideology emerged as a natural outflow of his mystical Christianity.

In order to test this assertion, we must first reconstruct Muir's conception of God and examine it in light of both Eastern and Christian constructs. If Muir's God was in fact the Christian one, we must determine how Muir's mystical Christianity affected his perception of the relationships between organisms in the natural realm. Was mankind the lord of creation? Were organisms in fact struggling within Darwin's law of survival of the fittest? What purpose did creation fill in Muir's universe? Why was it worth preserving untrammeled? The years between 1866, when Muir left Indiana for the Gulf of Mexico, and 1873,

Dennis Williams

when he left Yosemite to begin his writing career, encompass probably the most formative period in the development of Muir's philosophy. Freed from many social and cultural strictures during this period, Muir questioned the dominant Christian world view of his time, culled the beliefs proven untenable by his observations, and adopted those he found valid. His journals and letters from this period, filled with philosophical analysis of his observations and personal introspection, are the most revealing sources of Muir's mystical vision. In them, we find answers to our questions.

Scholars have seldom questioned Muir's Christianity prior to the day he set out for the Gulf of Mexico. As a young man, he evangelized his friends.[3] His peers elected him president of the Young Men's Christian Association at the University of Wisconsin. He preached piety to the Union volunteers camped in the fairgrounds at Madison. His family, like most rural families, may have feared the corrupting influence of the city, but they believed that their son and brother had faith in God and knew right from wrong. For example, his father, in what some would consider an uncharacteristically affectionate letter written just as John was enrolling in the University of Wisconsin, advised him to choose a course of study that would advance God's will and mentioned that he was glad to know that John was "attending upon the means of grace regularly."[4]

Questions regarding Muir's religious beliefs emerged when modern scholars studied the thoughts recorded in the journals Muir wrote along the trail to the Gulf of Mexico. Michael Cohen, for instance, understood Muir to have renounced Christianity as a viable social order in favor of a faith in Nature.[5] Muir did, in fact, struggle with the value of the anthropocentric doctrines of nineteenth-century Christianity. He assumed, as did a number of scientists and Christian theologians in his day and previously, that nature reflected the mind of God. Nineteenth-century Christians, like practitioners of most theistic religions, asserted that their doctrines reflected the mind of God. As Muir

The Spiritual Value of Nature

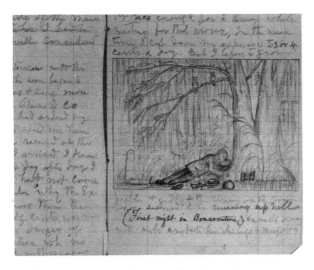

Muir's autobiographical sketch of his first night in
Florida's Bonaventure Cemetery, safe from marauding
guerilla bands during Reconstruction. From the Thousand
Mile Walk journal. John Muir Papers, Holt Atherton
Library. Copyright 1984 by Muir-Hanna Trust.

studied nature and reflected on what he believed it revealed
about its creator, he found that some long-held Christian beliefs
did not reflect the gospel he found in the natural realm.

Muir fought his first serious battle with the accepted doctrines of Christianity while sleeping among the graves of Bonaventure Cemetery in Savannah, Georgia. There Muir questioned the doctrines of life and death, but more importantly, the
concept of an anthropomorphic deity. Muir asserted, with the
type of grandiose generalization that would later become a well-
known component of his literary style, that the English-speaking
segment of Western civilization idolatrously worshipped

a civilized and law abiding gentleman, in favor of a Republican
form of government or a limited monarchy, [who] believes in the
literature and language of England and is a warm supporter of the
English constitution. And all the well gotten sabbath schools and
missionary societies, and in all respects is so purely a manufac-
tured article as any puppet of a half-penny theatre.[6]

85

Dennis Williams

From this passage, some students of Muir's career have concluded that Muir rejected the Christian god. Those seeking an other-than-Christian Muir, after invoking this passage, go on to mold Muir into a transcendentalist, a Taoist, or a Buddhist. However, a careful reading of Muir seems to indicate that he renounced only an anthropomorphic concept of God that he believed to be as idolatrous as the anthropomorphic Hindu gods or, as Muir put it, "the idol institutions of the Hinduos [sic]." [7]

Certainly, many oriental faiths assert that ultimate reality exists nonanthropomorphically. The monistic achievement of Nirvana by the Buddhist is definitely nonanthropomorphic. I suspect, however, that Muir may have found the veneration of the Buddha somewhat idolatrous even had he understood its monistic symbolism. The primeval forces of Taoism, the yin and the yang, take no anthropomorphic form. Likewise, transcendentalism, informed by Buddhism and born of Christianity, asserted the primacy of the spirit and denied an anthropomorphic god. Yet, the "New Views" of transcendentalism did not receive their pneumatic emphasis primarily from Buddhism.

Following Jesus' assertion that under the new dispensation God would be worshiped in spirit, Christian thinkers throughout history, especially those interested in reforming what they believed to be an apostatized church, have emphasized a spiritual concept of God. Many sought to move as far as possible away from the anthropomorphic Old Testament construct. For instance, Robert Barclay, the seventeenth-century Society of Friends theologian, addressed the centrality of the notion that God is spirit to Christianity when he wrote: "Without the Spirit, the Christian faith could no more subsist than this planet could continue to exist without the sun." [8] Thus, all that Muir's statement at Bonaventure Cemetery indicated is that he questioned the validity of describing the Christian god in anthropomorphic terms, not that he questioned the existence of the Christian god.

Muir's positive assertions about his understanding of deity are more revealing and definitive. Throughout this early period,

86

The Spiritual Value of Nature

Muir described God as being both immanent and transcendent.[9] Fresh from the Florida wetlands on his way to California, he wrote, "Swamps are peopled by plants of purest beauty and grow in darkest chambers with the presence of God."[10] In Yosemite too, Muir perceived God to be separate from Nature but within it. Even though he had questioned the anthropomorphic concept of deity in Georgia, Muir's concept of God still contained some anthropomorphic characterizations. He welcomed Jeanne Carr to California during the winter of 1868–1969, writing

> I am glad indeed that you are here to heed for yourself these glorious lessons of sky and plain and mountain. . . . I thought when in the Yosemite valley last spring that the Lord had written things there that you would be allowed to see sometime.[11]

In fact, as Muir experienced his deity in the Sierras, he understood God to be not a "divine principle," an "It," resident in all things, as did the transcendentalists, nor a wrathful transcendent entity, like the popular depiction of the Calvinist Christian God derived from Jonathan Edwards's Puritan sermons, but a close, friendly, and masculine personality. He wrote, "How human is God when we come to know Him by Himself."[12] He found God to be "living and working, working like a human being, by human methods and though always unsearchable and infinite yet writing passages that we can understand and coming within the range of our sympathies."[13] Again, striking a balance between transcendence and immanence, Muir wrote, "God's spirit is felt brooding," an allusion to Genesis 1.2 in which the writer used language evoking a vision of the creator settling on the early stages of creation like a hen incubating eggs, "with boundless eternal love over all making every lifecell rejoice."[14]

Whereas the monism of Buddhism stresses ultimate reality in terms of nonbeing, and the reality of Taoism is utterly immanent, Muir's God closely resembled the mysterious Christian god, who is both separate from his creation and yet so omnipresent that he is everywhere. In fact, Muir's conception of God resembled that of Christian mystics like the Quakers and other Christian enthusiasts. Robert Barclay, following Christian scriptures, which define Christ as the life that is the light of men,[15] identified the Spirit of God as light and indicated that Friends urged people to "believe in the light, and to obey it, so they may come to know Christ in them."[16] Writing of his life since the carriage factory accident that nearly cost him the sight in one eye and did blind him for a short period, Muir declared "I died to light, I lived again, and God who is Light has led me tenderly from light to light to the shoreless ocean of rayless beamless Spirit Light that bathes these holy mountains."[17]

That Muir found God most perceptible in nature, not church buildings, is well documented. Muir found American Protestant Christianity stifled by its affirmation of *sola scriptura*. As new Protestant groups sought to be considered orthodox by those around them, they developed doctrines that placed more value on traditional interpretations of ancient, scriptural revelations than on continuing revelations of God to humanity in the present.[18] Muir, unlike the vast majority of Protestants he seemed to have encountered, believed that truth was more important than alleged orthodoxy. For Muir, if, in experience, God revealed himself as somewhat unlike his appearance in scripture, then one should trust the more recent revelation.

However, Muir did not go so far as to renounce Christian scripture; instead, he found that nature and scripture complemented each other. Muir was not unique in envisioning a reciprocal relationship between natural revelation and scriptural revelation; in fact, it was a concept that ran throughout Old Testament revelation and was a component of Jesus' parabolic sermons and of Paul's Gospel to the Romans found in his epistle to Christians in that city.[19] Though oriental religions rely heavily on natural revelation, Muir's lack of exposure to them and his intense exposure to Christian scripture and creed tend to mitigate against the argument that this aspect of his vision of nature originated from oriental sources.

The Spiritual Value of Nature

One of several Bibles in John Muir's personal library collection, with an inscription showing it was presented to him while he was still under his father's wing at the Hickory Hill farm in Wisconsin. John Muir Papers, Holt Atherton Library.

Muir exemplified his mysticism in the journal entries and letters describing his spiritual discoveries in the Sierra around Yosemite. He wrote in the high country, "Here we may see God in very truth on account of the simplicity of the manifestations and the calm thought causing solitude."[20] In the valley, he confessed to his brother David,

> I have not been at church a single time since leaving home. Yet this glorious valley might well be called a church for every lover of the great Creator who comes within the broad overwhelming influences of the place fail not to worship as they never did before.[21]

Muir wrote Jeanne Carr in the summer of 1870:

> I have spent every Sabbath for the last two months in the spirit world, screaming among the peaks and outside meadows like a negro methodist preacher in revival time, and every intervening

clump of days in trying to fix down and assimilate my shapeless harvests of revealed glory into the common earth of my existence, and I am rich . . . . [22]

Muir believed that he experienced God directly, that he had a relationship with Him. His assertion that he enjoyed a personal relationship with God fit within traditional Christian dogma. While Muir took it to levels that would have made more conservative elements of the faith uncomfortable, he was still well within the mainstream.[23]

Christianity had been from its beginning a highly mystical faith. Over time, rank and file adherents to the faith and church leaders found comfort in the safety of doctrinal prescriptions that maintained a semblance of creedal homogeneity. Mysticism, which tended toward emotional subjectivity and at times organizational divisiveness, declined in its overt phenomenal forms. Intercessory and confessional prayer became the standard mystical act of most Christians. At times, however, especially during periods of economic or social upheaval, mystics arose who claimed or exhibited special communion with God. Often, these individuals became, to the less mystical Christians around them, religious symbols themselves.[24] After the Reformation, a number of sectarian Protestant groups, most with charismatic, mystical leaders, especially in the United States, emerged almost each generation claiming that organized Christianity had gone astray and that true believers needed to return to a more mystical practice such as they perceived the early church to have possessed. Muir, like his Disciples of Christ father, fit into this branch of Christian tradition.[25]

Muir was not nearly as unorthodox as others have interpreted him. He held a number of traditional Christian beliefs. Two related doctrines that distinctly influenced his vision of humanity's relationship with nature were those of human depravity and original sin. Throughout his writings, Muir appears to have accepted the Christian tenet that mankind was depraved. This doctrine asserts that mankind is naturally inclined to rebel against the will of its creator. Muir believed that mankind's aspi-

The Spiritual Value of Nature

ration to be like God, the sin behind the fall myth, placed the human outside the spiritual community of the Garden of Eden. Separated from easy communion with God, mankind continued to assert its original position before the fall as ruler over creation, an assertion Muir came to see as quite heretical. He concluded that humanity's callous approach to the environment was the result of sin. Writing of a fellow shepherd's lack of enthusiasm for a fern thicket, Muir explained, tongue in cheek perhaps, that "such souls I suppose are simply asleep, covered and smoothered [sic] into insensibility beneath a non-conducting incrustation of dirty sin."[26]

Muir broadened this traditional, individualistic perspective on sin by asserting that civilization and culture were both a result of sin and the agents that transmitted the effects of original sin to mankind. He lamented to J. B. McChesney in 1871, "Man as he came from the hand of his Maker was poetic in both mind and body, but the gross heathenism of civilization has generally destroyed nature, and poetry, and all that is spiritual."[27] He wrote that even the great philosophers and ministers are "so ground and pressed by the mills of *culture* that God cannot play a single tune upon them."[28] Muir's solution to this problem was to get people out into nature, away from civilization and culture, so that they could experience the Spirit of God directly as it worked in creation, to have them baptized in the "shoreless ocean of rayless beamless Spirit Light that bathes these holy mountains," as he himself had been.[29]

For Muir, an effectual part of nature's value resided in its purity. Muir asserted that, except for man, "absolute, unmistakable purity is over all creations of the Lord." Nature still enjoyed the same status it held with God prior to mankind's fall. It was, in Muir's words, "beautiful in the eyes of God" and "part of God's family, unfallen, undepraved, and cared for by the same species of tenderness and love as is bestowed on angels in heaven or saints on earth." Nature was untouched by the "diabolical consequences of Eve and the apple."[30]

Muir's belief that God was presently perceptible in the

Dennis Williams

world around him, reinforced by his apparent commitment to the teachings of Christianity, led him to interpret the relationship between organisms in the natural world from a Christian perspective that appears naive from the modern, scientific standpoint and at odds with the amoral nature implied by Darwinism. In Muir's eyes, since nature was spiritually pure, it functioned according to the perfect will of God. For him, the logical conclusion of such an assumption was that nature operated according to the law of love. This is where Muir's world view appears most Christian, most ecological, and most unbelievable unless one has the faith to accept the underlying premise. He proposed, within the bounds of his theistic universe, something like what James Lovelock, in the bounds of an atheistic universe, called the Gaia hypothesis.

Lovelock, an English physicist, described the ideal planetary organism that he termed Gaia, which is a theoretical construct thinly veiling his view of the Earth. Gaia is a single self-regulating entity. When operating properly, all its parts serve the good of the whole. When some component creates a systemic imbalance, Gaia responds to bring the system back into a healthy equilibrium. Mankind, a collective species, is one component within the total Gaian biosystem. Humans possess the intellectual and technological ability to significantly alter the environment around them. Likewise, due to the interrelationship of all the components of Gaia, humans are directly affected by the ecosystem's overall health and its responses to systemic imbalances. Thus, Lovelock encouraged his readers to accept his enlightened and somewhat mystical vision of ecological responsibility and create policies that would direct technology and development toward enhancing the health of the Gaian organism.[31]

Similarly, Muir believed that "man forms but a small portion of the great unit of creation and bears and snakes have rights as well as he," that "God's creation is unchangeably pure[,] unfallable [sic][, and] undepravable. The world is one word of God and his angels[,] his men[,] and his beasts together form one pure globe of primary fountain life." [32] Here Muir's inconsistent view of the spiritual state of mankind is apparent, but his point, of course, was that each part of nature, inextricably connected to the rest, operated symbiotically, for the good of the whole. Though Muir believed that the finite reality of mankind's existence precluded one from fully understanding the intricacies of all the affinities and repellents within nature, he wrote, "All that is God-made is related and oned [sic] by forces inescapable as all comprehending gravitation." [33] A good example of the effects this belief had on Muir's vision of the Sierra is found in a journal entry written in Tuolumne Canyon. Muir observed—or, more probably, projected his a priori beliefs onto his subject—that nature, "proclaim[s] with one accord the doctrine of love as the law of the rocky realms." [34] To Muir's ear, the robins sang, " 'fear not, only joy and love is here.' " Seeing a water ouzel playing in a waterfall, Muir wrote, "We may miss the meaning of the loud resounding torrent but the still small voice—only Love is in it." [35] Ultimately, in 1873, Muir proclaimed to his sister Margaret that:

> whatever we can read in all the world is contained in that sentence of boundless meaning, "God is Love." This is the sum and substance of all that the sunshine utters, and all that is spoken by the calms and storms of the mountains, and by what we call terrible earthquakes and furious torrents, and wild beating tone of the ocean.[36]

The "law of love," as manifest in Christian scripture, entails an individual to be patient, kind, selfless, humble, forgiving, righteous, and persevering toward God, one's neighbor, and one's enemy.[37] If, in fact, Muir's assertion that nature operated within such a system were true, then nature would be invaluable as an evangel and teacher, pointing mankind to God and teaching the fallen species God's will. This was one of the most significant values Muir saw in Nature.

Muir saw himself in a spiritual partnership with nature. He

frequently characterized himself, and nature, as John the Baptist. In one instance, he wrote:

> We seem to imagine that since Herod beheaded John the Baptist there is no longer any voice crying in the Wilderness. But no one in the wilderness can possibly make such a mistake. No wilderness in the world is so desolate as to be without God's ministers. The love of God covers all the earth as the sky covers it and fills every pore. And this love has voices heard by all who have ears to hear. Everything breaks into songs of Divine Love just as banks of snow, cold and silent, burst forth in songful cascading water. Yosemite creek is at once one of the most sublime and sweetest voiced evangels of the Wilderness of the Sierra.[38]

This became the underlying motivation for Muir's preservationist activity. Wilderness, which for Muir meant nature uncorrupted by human civilization, had to be saved because it was one of the last pure places where an individual with open eyes and a clean heart could experience the sense of community that the first man and woman had experienced before the fall. Muir believed that in the wilderness God still walked perceptibly among the inhabitants of his garden, who submitted to one another under the law of love. If it was destroyed, not only would many conscious and sentient creatures suffer and die, but mankind might lose the last great prophet.

Muir initially saw his role as pointing people to the wilderness so that it could teach them how to love and help them see God. People could follow nature's lead, they could "consciously, peaceful[ly], thoughtfully, faithfully [await] God's will."[39] However, as mankind's destruction continued to encroach on the wilderness throughout the Gilded Age, his mission took on a new responsibility. He had to help save the "temples of God" so that future generations might have the opportunity to do as he had admonished: "Go to the mountains," where one could hear "God himself preaching" in the waterfalls, see God revealed in the confident stability of the mountain goats, and delight in "inventions" like the pine seed, which Muir described as "a one

The Spiritual Value of Nature

winged bird with one feather and which in all its life takes but one flight," that made "the creator smile when he happened to hit upon [it] and first gave it a try." If the wilderness was preserved for others to contemplate the law that governed it and experience the God who continued to create it, they could say as did Muir, the Christian mystic of the Sierras, "I never found the devil in the Sierras nor any evil, but God in clearness and the religion of Jesus Christ." [40]

An example of how Christian mysticism influenced Muir's preservationist ideology may serve to illustrate the value of this approach in interpreting certain seemingly inconsistent attitudes Muir possessed. Muir, a founder of the Sierra Club, worked actively to ensure that the Sierra, especially Yosemite, would be protected from development. Muir's idea of scenic protection, however, was not identical to our contemporary, ecologically driven ideals. Alfred Runte points out, as did Richard Orsi before him, that Muir courted the Southern Pacific Railroad for the political help it could provide in influencing legislators to support the Sierra Club viewpoint. [41] They imply that Muir worked with Edward Henry Harriman and agents of the Southern Pacific Company for politically expedient reasons. Muir would gain park protection and Harriman's railroad would profit from the tourist riding their rails. Such an interpretation is of course accurate to a degree but implies that Muir compromised his principles and sold out to the developers, as some of his critics asserted at the time. However, Muir may have been more ideologically consistent than it appears. He believed that some development, for the sake of providing visitors to Yosemite an opportunity to perhaps see God, was worth the certain amount of change that it might cause. For instance, in January of 1905, in the heat of the Yosemite Recession Campaign, Muir received a letter from R. B. Marshall, a California forestry activist, warning him that commissioners investigating the conditions in Yosemite National Park had discovered a railroad interested in putting a train into the park. Marshall opposed it and requested Muir to use his notoriety to attempt to influence policy makers against such activity. Muir wrote Robert Underwood Johnson, his close friend and influential assistant editor of *Century Magazine*, requesting him to check into the matter. Muir was ultimately opposed to such a scheme because he feared overdevelopment or too much scenic confusion. However, on the back of Marshall's letter, Muir scribbled,

> An electric car spinning through the groves and around the margins of the meadows and big talus slopes would seem convenient and cheap enabling the quick going tourist to *do* the valley cheaper and faster than ever and hurting or confusing the scenery hardly more than the present stages and saddle trains.[42]

From Muir's religious perspective, the scenery of the Yosemite Valley, though no longer wilderness by his own definition, had spiritual value for those who experienced it. If not overdeveloped, "quick going" tourists might catch a glimpse of the revelation Muir found in nature. If they were influenced, even slightly, toward behaving more in line with the will of God, then Muir believed that he and nature had accomplished their purpose.

John Muir was neither a Buddhist nor a Taoist nor even a transcendentalist. His God was a unique, personal being, the creator and loving father of the world, both immanently still creating and managing it, and transcendentally separate from it. Unlike the transcendentalists, at least as they have been traditionally interpreted by historians, Muir believed that humanity was totally depraved in his present state but that mankind could reach its full potential by following the will of God, which was displayed in nature more clearly than in scripture. Muir believed that wilderness had to be protected from the "encrusting dirty sin" of civilization so that mankind, desperately in need of its message, could find its proper place in the scheme of creation. Muir's Christian mysticism tempered his view of nature's value to man and directed his conservation efforts throughout the early Progressive Era.

The Spiritual Value of Nature

NOTES

1. Lynn White, Jr., "The Historical Roots of Our Environmental Crisis," *Science* 155 (10 March 1967); 1203–1207, reprinted in Ian G. Barbour, ed., *Western Man and Environmental Ethics: Attitudes toward Nature and Technology*, (Reading, Mass.: Addison-Wesley, 1973), pp. 21–30.

2. See Stephen Fox, *John Muir and His Legacy: The American Conservation Movement* (Boston: Little, Brown, 1981); Michael Cohen, *The Pathless Way: John Muir and American Wilderness* (Madison: University of Wisconsin Press, 1984); and Bill Devall, "John Muir as Deep Ecologist," *Environmental Review* 6 (Spring 1982): 63–86. Notable exceptions to the "other-than-Christian" Muir interpretations include Ronald Limbaugh's "The Nature of John Muir's Religion," *The Pacific Historian* 29, nos. 2–3: 16–29, in which Limbaugh asserted that Muir was a Christian humanist, and Richard Cartwright Austin's *Baptized Into Wilderness: A Christian Perspective on John Muir* (Atlanta: John Knox Press, 1987), in which Austin asserted that although Muir did not hold to traditional Christian doctrine, he was a "prophet of God."

3. See John Muir to Bradley Brown, 1856, *The John Muir Papers Microfilm edition*. Edited by Ronald Limbaugh and Kristin Lewis (hereafter *John Muir Papers*), University of the Pacific.

4. Daniel Muir to John Muir, 15 January, 1861, *John Muir Papers.*

5. Michael Cohen, *The Pathless Way*, pp. 25–27.

6. Florida to Cuba Journal, *John Muir Papers.*

7. Florida to Cuba Journal, *John Muir Papers.*

8. Robert Barclay, *Barclay's Apology in Modern English*, edited by Dean Freiday (n.p.: The Hemlock Press, 1967), p. 32.

9. Throughout this paper, I will use "God" to indicate Muir's deity because he both capitalized the term in his journals and he appeared to be referring to a distinct being imbued with personality and possessing a name, which Muir called "God" after the manner of English-speaking members of Judeo-Christian society.

10. Crossing the Panama Isthmus Journal, *John Muir Papers.*

11. John Muir to Jeanne Carr, 24 February [1869], *John Muir Papers.*

12. Yosemite Journal, *John Muir Papers.*

13. Note fragment on philosophy and religion, *John Muir Papers.*

14. *John Muir Papers.* For a new, more detailed study of the relationship between theological exegesis of Genesis and Muir's religious environmentalism, see J. Baird Callicott's "Genesis and John Muir" *Revision* 12, no. 3 (Winter 1990): 31–47.

15. John 1.1–10.

16. Barclay, *Barclay's Apology*, pp. 410–411.

17. John Muir to Kate N. Daggett, 30 December, 1872, *John Muir Papers.*

18. David Lovejoy, in his *Religious Enthusiasm in the New World* (Cambridge: Harvard University Press, 1985), provided a fine analysis of this evolution of religious sects from enthusiasm, which he defined as a religious philosophy that

Dennis Williams

incorporated direct revelation from God to individuals into present practice, to orthodoxy, which tended to discount direct revelation and emphasize the value of past revelation, especially scriptures. Lovejoy's analysis of the Plymouth separatists' transition to Puritan-defined orthodoxy during the seventeenth century is typical of the evolution of sectarian groups throughout the history of Christianity and other theistic, scriptural faiths.

19. John Muir to Jeanne Carr, 21 January, 1866, *John Muir Papers*. In Romans 2. 13–15 NEB (New English Version), Paul, a Christian evangelist to the Gentiles, wrote "It is not by hearing the law, but by doing it, that men will be justified before God. When Gentiles who do not possess the law carry out its precepts by the light of nature . . . they display the effect of the law inscribed on their hearts."

20. Sierra Journal, Summer of 1869, vol. 2, *John Muir Papers*.

21. John Muir to David Muir, 20 March [1870?], *John Muir Papers*.

22. John Muir to Jeanne Carr, 29 July [1870], *John Muir Papers*.

23. Muir expressed his perception of his relationship with God clearly in two letters; one to his brother David Muir on March 20, 1870, and one to a friend, Kate N. Daggett, on December 30, 1872, *John Muir Papers*.

24. Peter Brown, "The Rise and Function of the Holy Man in Late Antiquity," in Peter Brown, ed., *The Making of Late Antiquity* (Cambridge/London: Harvard University Press, 1978), pp. 80–101; John Howe, "The Awesome Hermit," *Numen* 30, no. 1: pp. 106–119, see especially pp. 112–113.

25. Martin Marty, *Pilgrims in Their Own Land: 500 Years of Religion in America* (Boston: Little, Brown, 1984), pp. 169–224.

26. Sierra Journal, Summer of 1869, vol. 2, *John Muir Papers*.

27. John Muir to J. B. McChesney, 19 September, 1871, *John Muir Papers*.

28. John Muir to Charles Warren Stoddard, 2 February, 1872, *John Muir Papers*.

29. John Muir to Kate N. Daggett, 30 December, 1872, *John Muir Papers*.

30. Muir defined the symbiotic relationship of creatures like alligators, "hideous and cruel" in the eyes of mankind, to the rest of creation and God in the Journal of his trip to the Gulf. Florida and Cuba Trip Journal, *John Muir Papers*.

31. See James Lovelock, *Gaia: A New Look at Life on Earth* (Oxford: Oxford University Press, 1979, 1987).

32. Note fragment on bears, *John Muir Papers*.

33. "Illilouette", *John Muir Papers*.

34. Yosemite Notebook, *John Muir Papers*.

35. Sierra Journal, Summer of 1869, vol. 3 and vol. 2 respectively, *John Muir Papers*.

36. John Muir to Maggie Lauder [Margaret Muir Reid], 1 March, 1873, *John Muir Papers*.

37. I Corinthians 13. 4–7; Luke 10. 25–28, 6.27.

38. Yosemite, etc. Notebook [Pt. II], 1872–1874, *John Muir Papers*.

39. Sierra Journal, Summer of 1869, vol. 3, *John Muir Papers*.

40. Tuolumne Journal, September–October 1872, *John Muir Papers*.

41. Alfred Runte, *Yosemite: The Embattled Wilderness* (Lincoln: University of

The Spiritual Value of Nature

Nebraska Press, 1990), pp. 54–55. For a more detailed examination of this topic see Richard J. Orsi, " 'Wilderness Saint' and 'Robber Baron': The Anomalous Partnership of John Muir and the Southern Pacific Company for Preservation of Yosemite National Park," *Pacific Historian* 29 (Summer/Fall 1985): 136–156, on which Runte relied heavily.

42. R. B. Marshall to John Muir, 27 January, 1905, *John Muir Papers.*

PART III

MUIR AND WILDERNESS

5.
Why Wilderness?

John Muir's "Deep Ecology"

James D. Heffernan

This century has witnessed environmental destruction to an unprecedented degree. We are threatened by pollution of the earth's most important resources, its water and its air. Children now living may see the virtual disappearance of wild nature in many parts of the world, especially the tropical rain forests. This situation has led one author to speak of the "end" of nature.[1] A vocal environmental movement has arisen to try and stop the human destruction of wild nature. But, because humans must be the ones convinced to support the preservation of wilderness, this invites the questions: Why? What makes wilderness worth preserving? In what sense is wilderness valuable or worthwhile?

In the literature of environmental ethics, two types of answers are given. One is the human-centered answer that points out that human beings will suffer a great loss if wild nature is not preserved. But a second answer goes deeper and cuts to the quick, reflecting on the attitudes that have given rise to the disregard of the environment. This is the answer of biocentrism that urges humans to shed the arrogant attitude called "humanism" that considers humans alone as deserving of moral consideration. Biocentrism often cites Aldo Leopold as its inspiration and his famous "land ethic" as its moral principle: "A thing is right when it tends to preserve the integrity, stability, and beauty of the biotic community. It is wrong when it tends otherwise."[2] Biocentrism invites us to recognize that human-centered ethics is as cramped in its ethical vision as is egoism, self-centered ethics. Egoism is the view according to which only I have moral value. It fails to acknowledge the value of others in the human community. Humanism, by analogy, is the view that only humans have moral value. It fails to acknowledge the value of others in the biotic community, the community of life.

James D. Heffernan

This difference between a human-centered environmental ethic and a biocentered ethic has also been referred to as a difference between "shallow ecology" and "deep ecology." Deep ecology as an environmental attitude is contrasted with shallow ecology by the philosopher Arne Naess.[3] Shallow ecology, according to Naess, places pollution and resource depletion at the top of its list of environmental concerns. It focuses exclusively on human needs now and in the future. Deep ecology, on the other hand, advocates overcoming the human-centeredness of shallow ecology and promotes what Naess calls "biospherical egalitarianism." This would involve extending our moral concern beyond human beings to all forms of life.

The purpose of this essay is to bring together the elements of John Muir's philosophy of wilderness preservation and to emphasize one which is often overlooked by his biographers and other interpreters: his recognition that wild things are worthwhile in themselves. This is what I will call John Muir's "deep ecology."

Let us then raise the question afresh: why is wilderness worthwhile? According to John Muir, several answers can be given to this question. First of all, a thing may be worthwhile because it has utility or is useful for some human purpose. For example, as Muir noted in *Our National Parks*, the wood of the sugar pine is useful for making "shakes."[4] Redwood makes good lumber. Mountain meadows make good pasture land. In each of these cases the entity is worthwhile because it serves a human purpose. To care about nature because it is a valuable natural resource is to recognize nature's utility. Indeed, in his campaign to preserve the forests of the west in the 1890s Muir invoked the protection of watershed as one important reason.[5]

But Muir vehemently transcended this perspective and opposed those for whom wilderness has *only* utility value: "No dogma taught by the present civilization seems to form so insuperable an obstacle in the way of a right understanding of the relations which culture sustains to wildness as that which regards

Why Wilderness?

A page from Muir's 1879 Alaska journal, showing his interest in minute creatures as well as broad landscapes. John Muir Papers, Holt Atherton, Library. Copyright 1984 by Muir-Hanna Trust.

the world as made especially for the uses of man."[6] Connected with this view is the "barbarous notion . . . almost universally entertained by civilized man, that there is in all the manufactures of Nature something essentially coarse which can and must be eradicated by human culture."[7] Wild things on this account are without value until "improved" by human artifice. Muir notes:

> To such properly trimmed people, the sheep, for example, is an easy problem—food and clothing for 'us,' eating grass and daisies white by divine appointment for this predestined purpose, on perceiving the demand for wool that would be occasioned by the eating of the apple in the Garden of Eden.
>
> In the same pleasant plan, whales are storehouses of oil for us, to help out the stars in lighting our dark ways until the discovery of the Pennsylvania oil wells. Among plants, hemp, to say nothing of the cereals, is a case of evident destination for ships' rigging, wrapping packages, and hanging the wicked. Cotton is another plain case of clothing. Iron was made for hammers and ploughs, and lead for bullets; all intended for us. And so of other small handfuls of insignificant things.[8]

James D. Heffernan

According to Muir this conviction is "not supported by all the facts." There are numerous creatures that do not seem well-fitted to serve human purposes:

> But if we should ask these profound expositors of God's intentions, how about those man-eating animals—lions, tigers, alligators—which smack their lips over raw man? Or about those myriads of noxious insects that destroy labor and drink his blood? Doubtless man was intended for food and drink for all these? Oh, no! These are unresolvable difficulties connected with Eden's apple and the Devil.[9]

Another problem with this utilitarian view of wilderness and wild things is that it ignores their value in another sense. Thus, in this second sense something may be worthwhile or valuable because it is a source of worthwhile experiences, because contemplating it or experiencing it is of inherent value. For example, a sunset or a landscape is worth experiencing or contemplating. John Muir's description of his experience at Horseshoe Bend on the Merced River conveys this kind of value especially well:

> The whole landscape showed design, like man's noblest sculptures. How wonderful the power of its beauty! Gazing awe-stricken, I might have left everything for it. Glad, endless work would then be mine tracing the forces that have brought forth its features, its rocks and plants and animals and glorious weather. Beauty beyond thought everywhere, beneath, above, made and being made forever.[10]

In this sense, Nature's objects of contemplation are worthwhile in themselves. In his campaign to preserve Hetch Hetchy Valley, Muir was acknowledging the value of wild lands in this sense when he remarked that people need "beauty as well as bread, places to play in and pray in, where Nature may heal and cheer and give strength to body and soul alike."[11] Muir hailed the establishment of National Parks as a sign that this aspect of wilderness was finally being recognized. These parks are, Muir notes, "fountains of life."[12] Wilderness is valuable because of

Why Wilderness?

the rewarding experiences it provides. In his notebooks of 1873 he wrote:

> No sane man in the hands of Nature can doubt the doubleness of his life. Soul and body receive separate nourishment and separate exercise, and speedily reach a stage of development wherein each is easily known apart from the other. Living artificially, we seldom see much of our real selves. Our torpid souls are hopelessly entangled with our torpid bodies, and not only is there a confused mingling of our own souls with our own bodies, but we hardly possess a separate existence from our neighbors.[13]

A thoughtful person, however, might reflect that all this talk of wildness as a source of worthwhile experiences is a kind of ruse. After all, those who use the wilderness for contemplation are finding utility in nature somewhat similar to those who use it as a source of lumber or for water storage. Indeed, at least one of Muir's biographers characterizes the difference between Muir and his opponents as a difference between an "aesthetic-utilitarian" approach and a "strictly utilitarian" approach to wilderness.[14] This way of characterizing the disagreement between Muir and his opponents suggests that the debate is simply over which human purposes wilderness ought to serve: spiritual or material. This is appropriate in one respect; Muir did in fact disagree with the utilitarians about which purpose wilderness ought to serve. But in other respects, it is misleading. The person who contemplates the grandeur of a landscape or the awesome power of a waterfall is in a sense using it, but this sort of use is very different from that involved in cultivation or development.

Cultivation tends to remove wild things from nature's uses and set them to human purposes. In *Steep Trails* Muir notes:

> Every cultivated apple is crab, not improved, but *cooked*, variously softened, spiced, and rendered pulpy and foodful, but as utterly unfit for the uses of nature as a meadowlark killed and plucked and roasted.[15]

James D. Heffernan

To contemplate wild things does not interfere (in any direct or intentional way) with their pursuit of their own ends or with the accomplishment of nature's purposes.

To recognize that wilderness and wild things have their own ends is to begin to see that they are worthwhile in the third sense, worthwhile in their own right, not for the sake of something else but for their own sakes. Human life, the life of any human being, the happiness, satisfaction, or well-being or any human being all are worthwhile in themselves. In this regard, such questions as "Why is it valuable?" or "What is it good for?" tend to appear pointless. John Muir came to recognize that wild things also were worthwhile in themselves. As he often put it, they are "good for themselves." He remarked in *Steep Trails:* "I have never yet happened upon a trace of evidence that seemed to show that any one animal was ever made for another as much as it was made for itself." [16]

This claim that organisms are made for themselves recurs frequently in Muir's reflections. Consider his remarks on poison oak:

> Poison oak or poison ivy (*Rhus diversiloba*), both as a bush and a scrambler up trees and rocks, is common throughout the foothill region up to a height of at least three thousand feet above the sea. It is somewhat troublesome to most travelers, inflaming the skin and eyes, but blends harmoniously with its companion plants, and many a charming flower leans confidingly upon it for protection and shade. . . . Like most other things not apparently useful to man, it has few friends, and the blind question, "Why was that made?" goes on and on with never a guess that first of all it might have been made for itself. [17]

It is interesting to note that Muir's own conscience apparently evolved in this regard. In *Our National Parks* [18] he relates two occasions when he killed rattlesnakes. At first he thought "rattlesnakes should be killed wherever found." While walking in the San Joaquin Valley, he came upon a coiled rattler and stamped it to death. He felt, he said, "degraded by the killing

Why Wilderness?

business." He resolved then to kill only in self-defense. The second episode occurred while he was living in Yosemite Valley. He found a rattlesnake living in his cabin, and, fearing for the safety of visitors, especially children, he killed the snake. After that he went out of his way to avoid killing snakes.

In his most mature phase Muir recognized that rattlesnakes have value in the third sense: they are good for themselves, worthwhile for their own sakes:

> Poor creatures, loved only by their Maker, they are timid and bashful, as mountaineers know, and though perhaps not possessed of much of that charity that suffers long and is kind, seldom, either by mistake or by mishap, do harm to any one. Certainly they cause not the hundredth part of the pain and death that follow the footsteps of the admired Rocky Mountain trapper. Nevertheless, again and again, in season and out of season, the question comes up, "What are rattlesnakes good for?" As if nothing that does not obviously make for the benefit of man has any right to exist; as if our ways were God's ways. Long ago, an Indian to whom a French traveler put this old question replied that their tails were good for toothache, and their heads for fever. Anyhow, they are all, head and tail, good for themselves, and we need not begrudge them their share of life.[19]

Elsewhere, again in opposition to the utilitarians, Muir argues that "Nature's object in making animals and plants might possibly be first of all the happiness of each one of them, not the creation of all for the happiness of one." He finds it arrogant of human beings to value themselves as "more than a small part of the one great unit of creation." Moreover, he maintains, if the universe would be somehow incomplete without human beings, "it would also be incomplete without the smallest transmicroscopic creature that dwells beyond our conceitful eyes and knowledge."[20]

Hence, it would seem, Muir's most considered answer to the question "Why wilderness?" would lie in his conviction that wilderness and wild things are good for themselves. This then could be considered to be John Muir's "deep ecology," his conviction about the fundamental shift of perspective required for wilderness preservation to make sense. The shift is analogous to the attainment of moral maturity. When a person recognizes that other human beings deserve care, she has transcended egoism or self-centeredness. When she recognizes that wilderness and wild things deserve care, she has transcended from mere humanism or human-centeredness, the notion that only humans deserve moral consideration.

One problem that the thoughtful person might raise with regard to Muir's conviction that "Nature's object in making animals and plants might possibly be first of all the happiness of each one of them" is that, although it is clear that human beings may be happy (or unhappy), it is not clear that nonhuman animals and plants can be happy (or unhappy), except in a metaphorical sense. What a person who raises this objection probably has in mind, when speaking of happiness, is the feeling of pleasure or satisfaction that only sentient creatures can enjoy. Since it is difficult to argue that insects, trees, or flowers are sentient, it is difficult in turn to see how they could sensibly be said to be happy.

This focus on sentience, the capacity to feel pleasure and pain, is the basis of the so-called "animal rights" or "animal liberation" movement.[21] According to this view the question to ask, when contemplating whether a thing deserves moral respect, is not, Can it think or reason? but can it feel? In at least one passage Muir suggests that plants, even matter itself, may be sentient. It occurs in the previously cited section of *A Thousand-Mile Walk*, perhaps as an attempt to counter the objection we are considering:

> Plants are credited with but dim and uncertain sensation, and minerals with positively none at all. But why may not even a mineral arrangement of matter be endowed with sensation of a kind that we in our blind exclusive perfection can have no manner of communication with?[22]

110

Why Wilderness?

This is a very common way to handle the claim that things that have no feelings are not worthwhile in themselves. It is the response of panpsychism. It is to agree that nonsentient creatures are not worthwhile in themselves, and then to attempt to argue that plants or even "mineral arrangements of matter" are in fact sentient.

However, this maneuver is implausible. Perhaps it is because the capacity to feel pleasure or pain is so intimately connected with the capacity to express it that we must rely on thinly supported claims of "Possibly" or "How do we know?" to argue that creatures that have no obvious expressive capacities nonetheless have feelings. Hence, Muir, I think, did not finally adopt this panpsychist view that all living things are sentient, nor, as I shall argue later, did he agree with the animal rights view that moral respect for animals implies that we may not use them for food or in any other way.

Although the happiness of insects and trees may be only a metaphor, if happiness is construed as a feeling, but it is not merely a metaphor if happiness is construed simply as well-being or as flourishing. It is easy to recognize that all sorts of creatures, insects and trees, as well as flowers and animals, have something we may call well-being, are capable of flourishing, without granting that they are sentient. Moreover, in Muir's view, the well-being of all these creatures is worthwhile in themselves. The evidence of adaptation shows Nature equally concerned for the well-being of each of her creatures. In *Steep Trails* Muir reflects:

> Nature is a good mother, and sees well to the clothing of her many bairns—birds with smoothly imbricated feathers, beetles with shining jackets, and bears with shaggy furs. In the tropical south, where the sun warms like a fire, they are allowed to go thinly clad; but in the snowy northland she takes care to clothe warmly. The squirrel has socks and mittens, and a tail broad enough for a blanket; the grouse is densely feathered down to the ends of his toes; and the wild sheep, besides his undergarment of

James D. Heffernan

A Muir sketch from his 1881 Alaska journal. John Muir Papers, Holt Atherton Library. Copyright 1984 by Muir-Hanna Trust.

fine wool, has a thick overcoat of hair that sheds off both the snow and the rain. Other provisions and adaptations in the dresses of animals, relating less to climate than to the more mechanical circumstances of life, are made with the same consummate skill that characterizes all the love-work of Nature.[23]

This claim that Nature is concerned with the well-being or "happiness" of all creatures, however, seems not to fit well with the idea, spawned by Darwin, that Nature is "red in tooth and claw." Plants and animals prey upon one another for sustenance. Muir even argued that it is right. In this, I take it, he parts company with the animal rights view:

Plants, animals, and stars are all kept in place, bridled along appointed ways, *with* one another, and *through the midst* of one another—killing and being killed, eating and being eaten, in harmonious proportions and quantities. And it is right that we should thus reciprocally make use of one another, rob, cook, and consume, to the utmost of our healthy abilities and desires.[24]

But, he adds:

Why Wilderness?

The consumption of one another in its various modifications is a kind of culture varying with the degree of directness with which it is carried out, but we should be careful not to ascribe to such culture any improving qualities upon those on whom it is brought to bear. The water-ouzel plucks moss from the river-bank to build its nest, but it does not improve the moss by plucking it. We pluck feathers from birds, and less directly wool from wild sheep, for the manufacture of clothing and cradle-nests, without improving the wool for the sheep, or the feathers for the bird that wore them. When a hawk pounces upon a linnet and proceeds to pull out its feathers, preparatory to making a meal, the hawk may be said to be cultivating the linnet, and he certainly does effect an improvement as far as hawk food is concerned; but what of the songster? He ceases to be a linnet as soon as he is snatched from the woodland choir; and when, hawklike, we snatch the wild sheep from its native rock, and, instead of eating and wearing it at once, carry it home, and breed the hair out of its wool and the bones out of its body, it ceases to be a sheep.[25]

That we depend on other creatures for our own well-being does not argue, Muir claims, that they are worthwhile only insofar as they serve our well-being or insofar as they satisfy human desires:

From the dust of the earth, from the common elementary fund, the Creator made *Homo sapiens*. From the same material he has made every other creature, however noxious and insignificant to us. They are earth-born companions and our fellow mortals.[26]

Nor should it be thought that Muir was committed to the view that, for example, the life of a rattlesnake is just as important as the life of a human being. This view is as incorrect as the view that the life of a rattlesnake has no importance whatsoever. Insofar as our survival depends on it, we may take the lives of other creatures. But this does not mean their lives do not matter nor that we may take their lives to satisfy any human desire whatever.

Another problem with Muir's view may be his tendency to personify what many would take to be impersonal forces. For example, the adaptation of creatures to their environment Muir takes as evidence of Nature's (or God's) love of creatures. Nowadays many would talk more comfortably of adaptation as simply the result of natural selection. But we must recall that Muir believed that the world was the work of God and so did most of his opponents, the so-called "utilitarians." The evidence of adaptation, as Muir correctly saw, does not support the view that the world was made or came about for the sake of human beings. Adaptation, if it suggests anything, implies that each organism exists for its own sake. Whether one sees this as the manifestation of God's love, as Muir did, or as the result of impersonal forces, it would seem the crucial point remains: every organism is good for itself.

It seems then that we have answered our opening question, "Why should wilderness be preserved?" The answer is the same as to the question: "Why should human life be preserved?" It is because they are worthwhile in themselves. Wilderness and human life may have utility and may also be sources of worthwhile experiences but as valuable as each may be in these respects, we should not overlook their worthwhileness in their own right:

> [N]o matter, therefore, what may be the note which any creature forms in the song of existence, it is made first for itself, then more and more remotely for all the world and worlds.[27]

In line with Muir's recognition of three senses in which wilderness is valuable, we may distinguish three types of environmental concerns. The first, our acknowledging nature's utility value will *conserve* natural resources so that they will continue to supply the material needs of human beings. The second, our acknowledging nature's value as a source of spiritual refreshment will *preserve* wild places so that human beings may have places of beauty to contemplate. The third type, representing Muir's most mature insights, acknowledges that wilderness and wild things are good for themselves. It is only the third that

Why Wilderness?

reflects what was referred to above as "deep ecology." This type of concern will be expressed mainly in letting things be, letting them go their own ways. One may wonder if this last attitude is genuinely possible in an over-populated world, whether human concerns will not always overwhelm in sheer quantity and urgency the needs of the nonhuman world. But we certainly will not meet these needs if we do not recognize them. This is the apology, then, offered for this deep ecological attitude: we cannot benefit wild things unless we recognize they are "good for themselves." This has an analogy in human affairs: only when we recognize that others have needs are we able to attempt to meet them.

NOTES

1. Bill McKibben, "The End of Nature," *The New Yorker* 65 (September 11, 1989), pp. 47–105.

2. Aldo Leopold, *A Sand County Almanac and Sketches Here and There* (New York: Oxford University Press, 1968), pp. 224–225. For some discussion of Leopold's principle see James Heffernan, "The Land Ethic: A Critical Appraisal," *Environmental Ethics* 4 (Fall 1982): 235–247.

3. My use of the term "deep ecology" is similar to the principal tenet of the view expressed by Arne Naess in an article entitled "The Shallow and the Deep, Long-Range Ecology Movement," *Inquiry* 16 (1973): 95–100. This philosophical view has been elaborated in the book *Deep Ecology: Living as If Nature Mattered* by Bill Devall and George Sessions (Layton, Utah: Gibbs M. Smith, 1985).

4. John Muir, *Our National Parks* (Boston: Houghton Mifflin, 1901), pp. 353–356.

5. See Muir, *Our National Parks*, chapter x, "The American Forests."

6. John Muir, *Steep Trails* (Boston: Houghton Mifflin, 1918), pp. 11–12.

7. Muir, *Steep Trails*, p. 4.

8. John Muir, *A Thousand-Mile Walk to the Gulf* (Boston: Houghton Mifflin, 1916), pp. 137–138.

9. Muir, *A Thousand-Mile Walk to the Gulf*, p. 138.

10. John Muir, *My First Summer in the Sierra* (Sellanraa, Dunwoody, GA: Norman S. Berg, 1972), pp. 18–19.

11. John Muir, *The Yosemite* (Garden City, NY: Anchor Books, 1962), p. 198.

12. Muir, *Our National Parks*, p. 1.

13. John Muir, *John of the Mountains: The Unpublished Journals of John Muir*, ed. Linnie Marsh Wolfe (Boston: Houghton Mifflin, 1938), p. 77.

James D. Heffernan

14. Linnie Marsh Wolfe, *Son of the Wilderness: The Life of John Muir* (New York: Knopf, 1945), p. 276.

15. Muir, *Steep Trails*, pp. 15–16.

16. Muir, *Steep Trails*, p. 12.

17. Muir, *My First Summer in the Sierra*, pp. 34–35.

18. Muir, *Our National Parks*, pp. 206–208.

19. Muir, *Our National Parks*, pp. 57–58.

20. Muir, *A Thousand-Mile Walk*, pp. 138–139.

21. For a thorough discussion of this view, see Peter Singer, *Animal Liberation: A New Ethics for Our Treatment of Animals* (New York: Avon Books, 1975).

22. Muir, *A Thousand-Mile Walk*, p. 140.

23. Muir, *Steep Trails*, pp. 5–6.

24. Muir, *Steep Trails*, p. 13.

25. Muir, *Steep Trails*, pp. 13–14.

26. Muir, *A Thousand-Mile Walk*, p. 139.

27. Muir, *Steep Trails*, p. 12.

6.
John Muir and the
Wilderness Ideal

Don Weiss

On October 7, 1874, John Muir wrote to his mentor Jeanne Carr, "I care to live only to entice people to look at Nature's loveliness."[1] In an article on Yellowstone, later incorporated as a chapter of *Our National Parks*, he called on people to, "Climb the mountains and get their good tidings."[2] Why was he so anxious to draw the population of America's cities out of their houses and into the unspoiled beauty of the forests and mountains of the American West?

A common answer is that he wanted to develop a political constituency for the preservation of natural areas for the benefit of the public. But this explanation ignores the significance of the biblical language in his writings, the context of his earliest calls to experience Nature, and the philosophical speculations found in his journals and personal letters.

The utilitarian interpretation also fails to explain the diverse ways people approach nature—their modes of travel, dress, camping habits, and general behavior—all the clues to what immersion in Nature means to the people who follow Muir's advice and go to the mountains.

There is another explanation. Muir may have meant exactly what he said—he wanted people to hear Nature's "good tidings," which were written in wild places in a language that "no mortal power can ever speak."[3] In other words, he wanted people to experience the kind of mystical transport analyzed by William James in *The Varieties of Religious Experience*. It is also precisely the kind of experience sought in many other religious traditions, especially the various schools of Buddhism. Mahayana Buddhism in particular, the variety dominant in Tibet and Japan, is noted for using the contemplation of nature as part of spiritual discipline. Kukai (also known as Kobo Daishi), the great ninth-century Japanese theorist, is especially important for the way he combined meditation in and on nature with other Buddhist practices.

It is clear from an examination of Muir's life and writings that, by the phrase Nature's "good tidings" he meant what, in other religious traditions, goes by other names such as conversion experience, *satori*, or spirit quest. His rhetoric was Christian, in conformance with his background and his understanding of his audience. But his message was universal.

Muir's reference to "good tidings" is far from being the only religious rhetoric he used. He once compared himself to John the Baptist. "Heaven knows John Baptist was not more eager to get all his fellow sinners into the Jordan than I to baptize all of mine in the beauty of God's mountains." [4] When writing of his first journey to Yosemite, he said, "We were new creatures, born again." [5] In a letter to Jeanne Carr, written from Yosemite in the summer of 1870, he said of his Sundays, "I have spent every Sabbath of the last two months in the spirit world, screaming among the peaks and outside meadows like a negro Methodist in revival time." [6]

This religious language is neither accident nor rhetorical flourish. Though Muir, as is well known, rejected the specific content of his father's religious convictions, he clearly approved of zealous belief. When his father died, Muir wrote: "He belonged to almost every Protestant denomination in turn, going from one to the other, not in search of a better creed, for he was never particular as to the niceties of creeds, but ever in search of a warmer and more active zeal among its members." [7] This may be contrasted to Muir's description of those tourists who exhibited "blank, fleshy apathy." [8]

Muir made frequent references to conversion-type experiences in Nature, all related to his own. His whole life was changed by the accident that nearly blinded him. It was that experience of temporarily losing the visible world that convinced

John Muir and the Wilderness Ideal

him to devote himself to a life in Nature. His journals, especially during his early years in Yosemite, are peppered with references to conversion experiences nearly identical to those enumerated by William James in *The Varieties of Religious Experience*. In addition to the instances already quoted, he wrote the following, originally as a journal entry on June 6, 1869:

> We are now in the mountains and they are in us, kindling enthusiasm, making every nerve quiver, filling every pore and cell of us. Our flesh-and-bone tabernacle seems transparent as glass to the beauty about us, as if truly an inseparable part of it, thrilling with the air and trees, streams and rocks, in the waves of sun—a part of all nature, neither old nor young, sick nor well, but immortal. Just now I can hardly conceive of any bodily condition dependent on food or breath any more than the ground or the sky. How glorious a conversion.[9]

Such accounts of deepening conversion after an initial, profound change in life orientation are common to the basic conversion experience. Kukai, the great Japanese interpreter of Mahayana Buddhism, wrote that, after his own initial conversion experience, "From that time on, I despised fame and wealth and longed for a life in the midst of nature." [10] In a passage closely paralleling this excerpt from Muir, and also reflecting much of the glorious storm rhetoric of Muir's *Stickeen* and "A Wind-Storm in the Forests," the great Puritan preacher Jonathan Edwards spoke of his own deepening appreciation of the divine aspect of Nature:

> My sense of divine things gradually increased, and became more and more lively, and had more of that inward sweetness. The appearance of everything was altered; there seemed to be, as it were, a calm, sweet cast, or appearance of divine glory, in almost everything. God's excellency, his wisdom, his purity and love, seemed to appear in everything; in the sun, moon, and stars; in the clouds and blue sky; in the grass, flowers, and trees; in the water and all nature; which used to greatly fix my mind. And scarce anything, among all the works of nature, was so sweet to me as thunder and lightning; formerly nothing had been so terrible to me. Before, I

Don Weiss

used to be uncommonly terrified with thunder, and to be struck
with terror when I saw a thunderstorm rising; but now, on the
contrary, it rejoices me.[11]

Edwards, in fact is the great American Protestant interpreter
of the conversion experience, and his ideas about Beauty and
Nature are very close to those expressed later by Muir. Edwards
saw the beauty of the natural world as one of the proofs of the
omnipresence of God, so he considered the appreciation of that
beauty as proof of the genuineness of a purported conversion
experience. In the passage above, he is clearly stating that his
conversion experience allowed him at last to experience the
beauty that had previously seemed frightening to him.

Looking at Muir's experience in Nature as a conversion experience adds a new dimension to the first quote above, "I care
to live only to entice people to look on Nature's loveliness."
Clearly what he was attempting was the conversion of thousands
to his own way of perceiving the world, just like the "negro
Methodist in revival time" image he used in one of his letters to
Jeanne Carr.[12]

He began with Jeanne Carr. In his letters to her from
Yosemite in 1869 through 1872, we find repeated references to
his desire for her to experience what he already had:

Feb. 24, 1869 I am glad, indeed, that you are here to read for yourself these glorious lessons of sky and plain and mountains, which
no mortal power can ever speak.[13]
1870 I am rich, rich beyond measure, not in rectangular blocks
of sifted knowledge or in thin sheets of beauty hung picture-like
about "the walls of memory," but in unselected atmospheres of terrestrial glory diffused evenly throughout my whole substance. . . .
Would that you could share my mountain enjoyments![14]
May 31, 1872 Midnight O Mrs Carr, that you could be here to
mingle in this night moon glory![15]

Obviously, the purpose of these early letters was not utilitarian. He was not yet trying to create a lobby for forest protection.
Muir only became a "preservationist" later, when he realized the
threats to the land that he had come to consider "holy ground."[16]

John Muir and the Wilderness Ideal

Jeanne Carr was not the only person drawn to the Sierra by Muir's proselytizing, merely the first. In 1901 he wrote:

> Thousands of tired, nerve-shaken, over-civilized people are beginning to find out that going to the mountains is going home. . . . Briskly venturing and roaming, some are washing off sins and cobweb cares of the devil's spinning in all-day storms on mountains; sauntering in rosiny pinewoods and gentian meadows, brushing through chaparral, bending down and parting sweet, flowery sprays; tracing rivers to their sources, getting in touch with the nerves of Mother Earth; jumping from rock to rock, feeling the life of them, learning the songs of them, panting in whole-souled exercise, and rejoicing in deep, long-drawn breaths of pure wildness.[17]

Note the words he used. "Sins . . . of the devil's spinning. . . . getting in touch with the nerves of Mother Earth . . . jumping from rock to rock, feeling the life of them." This is far beyond the tame speculations of Emerson, writing in *Nature*, "When I behold a rich landscape, it is less to my purpose to recite correctly the order and superposition of the strata than to know why all thought of multitude is lost in a tranquil sense of unity." [18] Even Emerson's famous transparent eyeball metaphor, though it seems pointed in the same direction, still maintains the stance that the human is an observer. In Muir's writings, the mountaineer, in addition to observing, is always a participant. This is the viewpoint that flows through Muir's writings as he called on the thousands to follow him, leaping "from rock to rock," and feeling "the nerves of Mother Earth."

Almost a century after the publication of *Our National Parks*, these thousands are millions, and many of them follow Muir's advice by hiking the trail named for him. The John Muir Trail begins in Yosemite Valley and leads over high passes, across "gentian meadows," 211 miles to the storm-wracked summit of Mt. Whitney.

In the summer of 1989, in an effort to see how Muir's mountain philosophy looked on the ground, I hiked this trail. As I went along, struggling with my pack, battling voracious mos-

Don Weiss

Hiking the John Muir Trail above Cathedral Peak, Yosemite National Park.
Photograph by Don Weiss.

quitoes, exalting in the views, I interviewed dozens of day-hikers and backpackers plus rangers, wranglers, and horseback riding "dudes" in an effort to understand how people act and react when they go to the mountains and try to get their good tidings.

My initial reaction was surprise at the tremendous diversity of people and their behaviors and motivations. Some seemed to be on a Faustian journey, pitting themselves against the trail. Several backpackers carried loads of over 100 pounds so they would not have to pause along the way, go off-trail a few miles and get more supplies. One man, a math teacher from Los Angeles, described this as a way of doing a "Pure Trip."

Others seemed interested mostly in the fish they might catch. I found this a somewhat unnatural preoccupation as nearly all the lakes and streams along the John Muir Trail were barren of fish until stocked with trout in the late nineteenth or early twentieth century. The trout were definitely an example of human intervention in the natural ecosystem. Yet one study of users of the John Muir Wilderness (which surrounds much of the trail) found that 6 percent went there primarily to fish and 43 percent went at least in part to fish.[19]

Muir was ambivalent about fishing in the mountains. He criticized tourists in Yosemite, "seeking pleasure in the pain of fishes struggling for their lives, while God himself is preaching his sublimest water and stone sermons!"[20] Later, in *Our National Parks*, he softened, seeing a higher purpose in fishing. "Catching trout with a bit of bent wire is a rather trivial business, but fortunately people fish better than they know. In most cases it is the man who is caught. Trout fishing regarded as bait for catching men, for the saving of both body and soul, is important, and deserves all the expense and care bestowed on it."[21] Fish to save your soul, he says.

Those who traveled the trail on horseback seemed to provide the greatest contrast to the backpackers with whom I initially felt most at home. The horsemen carried fresh mangos, cold

Don Weiss

beer, and cast-iron grills to barbecue their steaks. The horses damaged fragile meadows, and their droppings covered delicate wildflower scents under an odiferous blanket. Yet is was these horsemen who provided the clue that led me to a deeper understanding of the unity of purpose that characterized most of the people I met, whether fishermen, backpackers, horsemen, or would-be supermen.

Horsemen in the Sierra wear Stetson hats. School teachers from San Diego, computer programmers from the Silicon Valley, teenagers from Orange County all felt their trip would lack something if they were not dressed like cowboys. And why cowboys? Why this American icon, the archetypal American Hero?

Because they wanted to *be* heroes. They could play heroes, psychically, by donning the costume of a hero and entering the realm of a heroic journey, a Wilderness. Similarly, the Faustian hikers emphasized the nature of their quest by erecting barriers, challenging obstacles, enlarging difficulties, and generally emphasizing in their own minds the dangers of the trip. They were following the ideas of the Inuit shaman Igjugaijik, "The only true wisdom lives far from mankind, out in the great loneliness, and can be reached only through suffering. Privation and suffering alone open the mind of man to all that is hidden to others." [22]

The backpackers' preoccupation with bears, that great symbol of Wild Nature, is part of this, but it is exhibited in many other ways: overly heavy packs, defying the dangers of lightning on high mountain peaks, or pushing to complete the trail in record time. [23]

Once I knew to look for evidence of this behavior, playing at the heroic quest, I found it clearly in all kinds of travelers, including myself. I have been a devotee of standard backpacker ethics. I "commune" with Nature. I "take only pictures, leave only footprints." I pack out my trash, don't move rocks, and rarely build fires. Yet Muir, by his own repeated statements, burned ancient Whitebark pine wood to keep himself warm dur-

John Muir and the Wilderness Ideal

ing bivouacs on icy peaks, and he loved a roaring fire. He wrote, "There is scarce a human being in existence that would not shout with excitement on seeing the silver fir in campfire sunshine." [24] Or recall that famous time when Roosevelt and Muir were camping at Glacier Point:

> When the dark was well advanced, Muir rose up quietly and set fire to a tall dead pine in the meadow. Soon the tree was a roaring tower of flame. "Hurrah!" yelled the President. "That's a candle it took five hundred years to make. Hurrah for Yosemite!" [25]

Or again, on a trip to Mt. Shasta with the famous botanists Asa Gray and Sir Joseph Hooker:

> At night, Mr. Muir would make immense fires to display the beauties of the silver fir, which in the glow . . . assumed the appearance of enormous pagodas of filigree silver. Mr. Muir would wave his arms and shout: "Look at the glory! Look at the glory!" [26]

What's happening here is a transformation and liberation. The transformation is of civilized humans into wild, feeling, unthinking primitives, and the liberation is from civilization wrought by fire, though such fires are now shunned in the name of a man who used fire for that purpose.

It seems that having a fire in the mountains at night was, for Muir, an intensification of the basic experience of Man in Nature, which should, he felt, lead to a conversion experience like his own. This use of fire seems designed, in part, to achieve a suppression of rational thought, allowing the feeling portion of the brain to take charge. When he spoke of running down a talus slope to hear the song of the rocks, he was talking about exactly this kind of transformation because, as any mountaineer can testify, you cannot run down a talus slope if you have to stop and think about each leap. Your "other self" must take over, as Muir described in his account of his first ascent of Mt. Ritter.

This sort of cessation of rational thought has been the subject of endless speculation for thousands of years. The Chinese speak of yang and yin, the one rational, the other intuitive. Hindu phi-

127

losophy talks of Shiva and Shakti. Mahayana Buddhism teaches the existence of a Wisdom Mind, whose knowledge cannot be properly expressed in language.

Such knowledge, in all religious traditions, can be considered variations on a theme. Anthropologist I. M. Lewis talks about "Ecstatic Religion" as a separate category[27] found in all religious and cultural traditions, sometimes within the mainstream, sometimes at the fringes. It is a way of accessing certain nonrational kinds of knowledge. Such knowledge is that achieved in the conversion experience, in an ecstatic trance, in Zen *satori* or on a Native American Spirit Quest.

The milieu and process of this sort of quest is nearly identical everywhere. The adept separates himself from society, becomes immersed in Nature, undergoes physical privation, and is transformed through a vision, a numinous experience, an epiphany. Muir wanted to play John the Baptist to the urban hordes of turn-of-the-century Americans. He wanted them to go on spirit journeys, even if they began as fishermen torturing trout in Yosemite Valley. Because he knew that even if their trip started as play acting at being a hero, in a hero's Stetson hat, conversion might follow.

The physiological nature of the sort of conversion experience I am describing has been the subject of brain wave studies by Arthur J. Deikman. He found that when the part of the brain that normally processes language and rational thought is in a resting state, generally the left hemisphere in most right handed persons, it will generate slow frequency alpha and theta waves. Tests on experienced Zen meditators found that they had the ability to turn off this rational thought part of the brain more or less at will, thus initiating what is termed "the receptive mode of consciousness," and generating exactly these wave patterns.[28] This seems to be precisely what Muir alluded to on his Ritter climb, the "something else" that takes over:

> When this final danger flashed upon me, I became nerve-shaken for the first time since setting foot on the mountains, and my mind

seemed to fill with a stifling smoke. But this terrible eclipse lasted only for a moment, when life blazed forth again with preternatural clearness. I seemed suddenly to be possessed of a new sense. The other self, bygone experiences, Instinct, or Guardian Angel—call it what you will—came forward and assumed control. . . . I found a way without effort, and soon stood upon the topmost crag in the blessed light.[29]

This is a perfect description of the "intuitive" part of the brain taking over, here in a physical mode rather than that of religious perception, though the two seem closely linked.

The interpretation of this "right brain" experience, this "receptive mode of consciousness" is especially difficult precisely because it is experienced in a part of the brain that does not process language. Thus, this kind of experience is always filtered through the sieve of language and accustomed rational thought processes, assuming a different appearance in different individuals of different cultures. This is precisely why William James warned against dismissing written descriptions of ecstatic religious experiences. He understood that there was something about the experience that defied precise description, though in his time brain function studies were still decades away.

It is always a struggle to express this sort of experience in words. Kukai founded his monastic headquarters in an uninhabited mountain range so that all his followers could be instructed in the methods of meditation in a natural setting. To an admirer, asking him to come down from his mountain retreat, he wrote a poem ending:

I have never tired of watching the pine trees and the rocks at Mt. Koya;
The limpid stream of the mountain is the source of my inexhaustible joy. . . .
Discipline in the woods alone lets us soon enter the eternal Realm.[30]

Muir felt the same way. Recall his words to Jeanne Carr on learning of her arrival in California, within reach of Yosemite.

Don Weiss

Storm clouds over Diamond Mesa on the John Muir Trail. Photograph by Don Weiss.

"I am glad, indeed, that you are here to read for yourself these glorious lessons of sky and plain and mountain, which no mortal power can ever speak." [31] This is a clear statement that, in his deepening "conversion in Nature," he had come to a wisdom that was not capable of accurate expression in words. It could only be expressed in the song of a mountain stream, the flow of a meadow from use to use, from beauty to beauty. It was the kind of knowledge that Joseph Campbell described when he speaks of the "meaning" of nonlexical things:

> What is the "meaning" of a tree? of a butterfly? of the birth of a child? or of the universe? What is the "meaning" of the song of a rushing stream? Such wonders simply *are*. They are antecedent to meaning, though "meanings" may be read into them.[32]

John Muir and the Wilderness Ideal

Joseph Campbell's studies of the hero's journey provide insight into much of what the wilderness is all about. In fact, it is useful to consider the concept of "wilderness" itself as an archetype of the collective unconscious, as Jung termed it, as the milieu of the testing portion of the hero's journey. Looked at this way, much of the diverse behavior of the backpackers, Faustian or otherwise, and horsepackers, in or out of Stetsons, becomes more readily understandable.

What makes a "place" a "wilderness?" Surely not the presence or absence of "structures" or even the substantiality of the "imprint of man," to paraphrase the Wilderness Act. There are, after all, structures throughout the wilderness in the form of bridges, trails, and signs. The imprint of Man is ubiquitous over the surface of the Earth, and most especially in popular "wilderness areas" like those along the John Muir Trail. "Wilderness," rather, is a word that speaks to the relationship between the place and the person. If the individual is engaged in some level of a hero's journey, consciously or not, intensely or peripherally, then, to that individual, the surroundings can become a wilderness, a place of testing.

This Muir understood. This is what he preached. The "good tidings" of the mountains were the unspoken, unspeakable message he heard when in a "receptive mode of consciousness." He called on all people to hear the songs of the rocks since "songs" are music, another "right brain" mode of understanding. He called on everyone to experience the earth through their feet, their eyes, their sense of taste:

> A fine place for feasting if only one be poor enough. One is speedily absorbed into the spiritual values of things. The body vanishes and the freed soul goes abroad. . . .
> Only in the roar of storms do these mighty solitudes find voice at all commensurate with their grandeur.[33]
> Whether these picture-sheets are to vanish like fallen leaves or go to friends like letters, matters not much; for little can they tell to those who have not themselves seen similar wildness, and like a language have learned it. No pain here, no dull empty hours, no

131

Don Weiss

Eichorn Pinnacle, Cathedral Peak, Yosemite National Park. Photograph by Don Weiss.

fear of the past, no fear of the future . . . the whole body seems to feel beauty when exposed to it as it feels the campfire or the sunshine, entering not by the eyes alone, but equally through all one's flesh like radiant heat, making a passionate ecstatic pleasure-glow not explainable.[34]

What has been described here is what may be called "the wilderness ideal" though this term has not been defined in this

132

John Muir and the Wilderness Ideal

text. I could have said, equally, "the mountains' good tidings." In either case, what I am speaking of, what Muir wrote about, is that message beyond words, the meaning accessible only to the nonrational, "receptive consciousness" part of the brain, accessible by immersion in "nature's loveliness." It is something I experienced along the John Muir Trail, something available, perhaps, to anyone who follows Muir's advice to, "Climb the mountains and get their good tidings."

NOTES

1. John Muir, *Letters to a Friend, Written to Mrs. Ezra S. Carr 1866–1879* (Boston: Houghton Mifflin, 1915), p. 169.
2. John Muir, *Our National Parks* (Madison: University of Wisconsin Press, 1981), p. 56.
3. Muir, *Letters to a Friend*, pp. 85–86.
4. John Muir, *John of the Mountains: The Unpublished Journals of John Muir*, ed. Linnie Marsh Wolfe (Madison: University of Wisconsin Press, 1979), p. 86.
5. William Frederic Badè, ed., *The Life and Letters of John Muir* (Boston: Houghton Mifflin, 1924), I, p. 179.
6. Muir, *Letters to a Friend*, pp. 85–86.
7. Badè, *Life and Letters*, I, pp. 9–10.
8. Muir, *Letters to a Friend*, p. 80.
9. John Muir, *My First Summer in the Sierra* (Boston: Houghton Mifflin, 1911), pp. 15–16.
10. Quoted in Oliver Statler, *Japanese Pilgrimage* (New York: Morrow, 1983), p. 67.
11. Quoted in William James, *The Varieties of Religious Experience* (New York: Modern Library, 1929), p. 243.
12. Muir, *Letters to a Friend* pp. 85–86.
13. Ibid., p. 49.
14. Ibid., pp. 86–87.
15. Ibid., p. 119.
16. See Linda H. Graber, *Wilderness as Sacred Space* (Washington, D.C.: Association of American Geographers, 1976).
17. Muir, *Our National Parks*, pp. 1–2.
18. Ralph Waldo Emerson, *Nature* (Boston: James Munroe and Co., 1836), p. 83.
19. U.S. Forest Service, *John Muir Wilderness Management Plan, Inyo and Sierra National Forests*, 1978, p. 9.
20. Muir, *My First Summer in the Sierra*, p. 190.
21. Muir, *Our National Parks*, p. 212.

Don Weiss

22. Joseph Campbell, *Myths to Live By* (New York: Viking, 1972), p. 205.

23. It has been run in three and a half days and moonlit nights.

24. Muir, *John of the Mountains*, p. 219.

25. Linnie Wolfe Marsh, *Son of the Wilderness: The Life of John Muir* (New York: Knopf, 1945), p. 291.

26. Ibid., p. 194.

27. I. M. Lewis, *Ecstatic Religion* (New York: Penguin, 1971).

28. Arthur J. Deikman, "Bimodal consciousness and the mystic experience," Richard Woods, ed., in *Understanding Mysticism* (Garden City, New York: Image Books, 1980), pp. 261–269.

29. John Muir, "A Near View of the High Sierra," in *The Mountains of California* (New York: The Century Co., 1903), pp.64–65.

30. Yoshito S. Haketa, *Kukai, Major Works* (New York: Columbia University Press, 1972), p. 52.

31. Muir, *Letters to a Friend*, p. 49.

32. Joseph Campbell, *Flight of the Wild Gander: Exploration in the Mythological Dimension* (New York: Viking, 1969).

33. Wolfe, *John of the Mountains*, p. 93.

34. Muir, *My First Summer in the Sierra*, p. 131.

PART
IV
T H E
LITERARY
MUIR

7.
John Muir's Transcendental Imagery

THE WILDEST STORMS ARE AEOLIAN MUSIC
TO THE HEALTHY EAR.

—*JOHN MUIR (UNPUBLISHED APHORISM)*

Richard F. Fleck

As others have already shown, John Muir came under the influence of New England transcendentalism at least as early as his Madison years at the home of Ezra and Jeanne Carr whose library contained the writings of Ralph Waldo Emerson and Henry David Thoreau. He met Ralph Waldo Emerson (whom he called brother to the sequoia) in Yosemite in 1871. We know from the Reverend Samuel Hall Young (*Alaska Days with John Muir*, 1916) that Muir carried with him a volume of Henry David Thoreau (probably an 1864 edition of *The Maine Woods*) on his first trip to Alaska in 1879, and throughout his published writings and letters Muir often refers to Emerson and Thoreau. Muir turned to Thoreau as his literary mentor once he immersed himself in a career as a writer describing his experiences in the wilds of the Sierra and Alaska. His 1906 set of the writings of Henry D. Thoreau as well as his volumes of Emerson's writings are heavily emended, underscored, and indexed on the blank pages at the back with extensive commentary.

My purpose here is not to trace any further transcendental influences per se so much as to explore the literary results of selected unpublished and published writings from 1874 until his death in 1914. One of the richest attributes of John Muir's literary style is his imagery. His wellcrafted images are not mere imitations of Emerson or Thoreau for they reflect experiences in the wild beyond the ken of these two earlier New England masters. An example is the following remarkable passage from *John of the Mountains*, which incorporates New England transcendentalism:

> But it is after both the body and soul of a mountaineer have worked hard, and enjoyed hard, that they are most palpably separate. Our weary limbs, lying at rest on the pine needles, make no attempt to

Richard F. Fleck

follow after or sympathize with the nimble spirit that, apparently
glad of the opportunity, wanders alone down gorges, along beetling cliffs, or away among the peaks and glaciers of the farthest
landscapes, or into realms that eye hath not seen, nor ear heard;
and when at length we are ready to return home to our flesh-and-
bone tabernacle, we scarcely for a moment or two know in what
direction to seek for it.[1]

John Muir's desire to express his thoughts in highly com-
pressed and aphoristic fashion developed early in his writing
career. Because he carried scraps of paper with him on his forest and alpine treks, he was able to record, spontaneously, in
compact, abbreviated fashion, his thoughts and observations.
Usually by the sparks of an evening campfire high in the Sierra,
Muir jotted down pithy reflections of the day. By one such campfire in 1874, for example, he wrote, "It is imposs[ible] to describe
the intense impressiveness of wild fl[owe]rs in night around a
campfire with all the world beside sunk in darkness."[2]

Muir probably began writing his aphoristic notes around
1874; he wrote more aphorisms in 1875, between 1879 and 1880,
and a fair number between 1890 and 1899. His largest outpour-
ing occurred after 1900 when he seriously began to consider
collecting and publishing these bits of campfire chat (which remain unpublished to this day). As nearly as can be inferred from
the John Muir Papers, his method of composition seems fairly
clear. After composing the aphorisms at trailside or campfire
in pencil, Muir eventually transferred his holograph notes to
typescript. Once typed, Muir went over the typescript most as-
siduously, penciling in further revisions and emendations and—
most often—striking and condensing. It should be noted that a
few of these unpublished pieces were completely composed in
the Scribble Den at Martinez where they were sparked not by
campfires but by the thoughts of other writers.

Let us turn to some of his campfire compositions that partake
of transcendentalism. He writes, "Outdoors is the place to store
up spiritual influences. However aimless our walks appear to
be, always some particular object consciously or unconsciously

John Muir's Transcendental Imagery

guides our steps, while we are alert and wide-awake to find what Nature has in store for us."[3] These "spiritual influences" served not only to heighten Muir's sense of the natural world but also his artistic sense in the recording of his observations and thoughts. As an example, note the following unpublished note composed in the field: "There is always heard, even on the stillest days, a kind of fine aeolian harp music in the air. This is always heard—a sort of world harp, giving out immortal unceasing melody, in unison with all the stars of the sky, for this is still the morning of creation and the sound of work in world-making is eternal."[4] Unlike Thoreau's aeolian harp image of *Walden* (generated by the sound of wind in telegraph wires), Muir's aeolian harp is of nature's making, perhaps wind in the sugar pine needles or the upper branches of redwood trees. This music attests to the creator at work creating "unceasing melodies." In one last unpublished composition Muir expresses the transcendental ideal—the idea that the universe is permeated with the spirit of universal intelligence:

> Science never saw a ghost, nor does it ever look for any, but it sees everywhere the traces of a universal intelligence. The more we know of it the less we associate it with any goblin of our imagination. We discover that the only spirit that haunts the world is the universal intelligence which has created it in harmony with all nature.[5]

An important point Muir picked up in his early reading of Ralph Waldo Emerson's "Nature" (1836) was that nature's language writ in stone or tree or ice as emblematic of spirit. Emerson writes:

> It is not words only that are emblematic; it is things which are emblematic. Every natural fact is a symbol of some spiritual fact. Every appearance in nature corresponds to some state of the mind, and that state of the mind can only be described by presenting that natural appearance as its picture.[6]

In order for the poet-philosopher to read spirit he must interpret the hieroglyphic language of nature. Such an interpretation be-

Richard F. Fleck

Ralph Waldo Emerson, ca. 1875. From a trimmed carte de visite, probably sent to Muir by Emerson after his 1871 Yosemite visit. John Muir Papers, Holt Atherton Library.

John Muir's Transcendental Imagery

came Muir's life's work not only as a scientist but also as an artist. His most successful art (or for that matter science) is characterized by insight into the inner workings or interrelationships of living natural objects to one another and to the universal intelligence or spirit. When his descriptive language operates on these relational levels, he transcends far above and beyond the travel literature and natural history so popular in his day because he truly engages the reader's mind. At the same time, his power of description forcefully recreates the genius of place, be it the upper slopes of Mount Ritter, the fiords of Alaska, or the dank redwood forests of California.

Though *My First Summer in the Sierra* was not completed as a book until 1911, it was based on an 1869 log he kept while working as a shepherd during his first summer out West. Once young John Muir beheld the mountains of eternal snow and light with ribbons of water tumbling out of subalpine meadows, he sensed or rather knew that everything was alive with forceful spiritual energies. He writes, "I gazed and gazed and longed and admired until the dusty sheep and packs were far out of sight, made hurried notes and a sketch, though there was no need of either, for the colors and lines and expression of this divine landscape countenance are so burned into mind and heart they surely can never grow dim.[7] Though he did not as yet understand the hieroglyphic language of "a spiry wall of pines," he sensed that "every tree harmoniously related to every other."[8] He became aware of a language of song sung by Hazel Creek and by the trees, and it was so powerful for him that he felt it was irresponsible to sleep and be unaware of the world around him.

As he and fellow shepherds proceeded higher into the mountains, Muir at last beheld the lower end of Yosemite Valley, which he calls "a grand page of mountain manuscript that I would gladly give my life to be able to read."[9] Amazingly, however, within hours he began to be able to read this mountain manuscript. Just two days later he writes, "Night is coming on, the gray rock waves are growing dim in the twilight. How raw and

141

Richard F. Fleck

young this region appears! *Had the ice sheet that swept over it vanished but yesterday, its traces on the more resisting portions about our camp could hardly be more distinct than they now are.*" [10] (Emphasis is mine.) His reading of this mountain manuscript with all of its glacial innuendo became the basis of "Studies in the Sierra," a series of seven articles about the glacial formation of Yosemite Valley written in San Francisco in 1872 at the home of John and Mary Swett and published in *The Overland Monthly.*

Nature so enlivened the spirit of John Muir that, in true Thoreauvian fashion, he wanted to wake up the world because he "feels inclined to shout lustily on rising in the morning like a crowing cock." [11] And like Thoreau, especially in *Walden,* Muir was energized by the coming of dawn. On Thoreau's birthday, 14 July, 1869 he writes: "How death like is sleep in this mountain air, and quick the awakening into newness of life! A calm dawn, yellow and purple, then floods of sungold, making everything tingle and glow." [12] On July 20th he perched himself on the summit of North Dome where he vowed self-denial and renunciation with eternal toil "to learn any lesson in the divine manuscript." [13] All the trees of the valley below consorted to sing for him a divine song while the cliffs of living rock gave sermons to even the deafest ears, he believed.

By the time the reader gets to August of Muir's first summer in the Sierra, he can readily see that Muir's intuitive responses to Nature not only gave him insight into geology but also inspired him to create a commensurate language. After returning to the greener, wetter eastern side of the Sierra on August 21st, Muir records that "reading these grand mountain manuscripts displayed through every vicissitude of heat and cold, calm and storm, upheaving volcanoes and down-grinding glaciers, we see that everything in Nature called destruction must be creation— a change from beauty to beauty." [14] Here Muir came close to the Navajo Mountain Chant that exclaims "In beauty it is finished." In the Sierra, landscapes transcend to countenances, clouds to new worlds, lupines to stars in the mist, waterfalls to psalms,

142

fresh rain on the land to skin, and dew to manna. Such images are a result of John Muir's hieroglyphic ciphering.

After Muir's stay in San Francisco, where he launched his writing career, he returned to his beloved Sierra but with street-deadened feet. Just before his fall described in "A Geologist's Winter Walk" and ensuing self-mortification, Muir quickly became absorbed by the spiritual energies and language of the mountains. He writes:

> when I passed Mirror Lake, I scarcely noticed it, for I was absorbed in the great Tissiack—her crown a mile away in the hushed azure; her purple granite drapery flowing in soft and graceful folds down to my feet, embroidered gloriously around with deep, shadowy forest. I have gazed on Tissiack a thousand times—in days of solemn storms, and when her form shone divine with the jewelry of winter, or was veiled in living clouds; and I have heard her voice of winds, and snowy, tuneful waters when floods were falling; yet never did her soul reveal itself more impressively than now.[15]

It is a pity that Muir did not take the time to describe the nature of Tissiack's (Half Dome's) revelation; he was too much in a hurry to climb higher to glacial country. It is shortly thereafter that he slipped and somersaulted off a ledge. He knocked himself unconscious. Awakening, he scolded himself for his carelessness and punished himself that evening by not providing himself with plushy boughs for comfort. But the next day brought him fully back to his old self—the Muir open to the emblems and language of the Creator. He saw a "water fall fair as a spirit" and heard God's voice in the rocky temples fully infused with love. In Tenaya Canyon he envisioned the ancient *mer de glace* coming together from the separate glaciers of Mounts Lyell, Dana, and Cathedral Peak.

In the fall of 1872, when John Muir sensed the coming of winter, which would close out the high country to all exploration until the next summer, he could not resist one last venture to the high Sierra "aflame with autumn colors, brown and purple and gold, ripe in the mellow sunshine; contrasting brightly with the deep, cobalt blue of the sky, and the black and grapy, and pure, spiritual white of the rocks and glaciers." [16] He encountered two artists (William Keith and Benoni Irwin) who wished to paint alpine scenery from a location that did not offer an overly vast panorama. After guiding them to a perfect spot, Muir went on to climb Mount Ritter, a place where, as Stephen Fox contends, he achieved a psychic integration with the mountains of California. Before arriving at Ritter's base Muir spent the night at 11,000 feet where he was treated to "one of the most impressive of all the terrestrial manifestations of God"—alpine glow that kindled all the mountains to "a rapt, religious consciousness." [17]

The next day Muir picked his route up a glacier flanking the side of Ritter until he had no other choice but to proceed straight up a sheer face just shy of 13,000 feet. At this point he faced a total failing in mind and spirit and a sense that he must fall. But something took over—something preternatural—enabling him to take control and scamper on up to the summit to view the entire Sierra Nevada Range all the way to Mount Whitney. At first the sight was too vast to behold, but after he studied each peak lovingly, he began to sense in Emersonian fashion a harmony, a harmony composed of "Nature's poems carved on tables of stone—simplest and most emphatic of her glacial compositions." [18] Picking a gentler route back to the valleys below, he rejoined the two artists so safe in their protected valley.

Before his marriage to Louie Wanda Strentzel, Muir made his first voyage to Alaska in 1879 to study the living glaciers of the fiords. He and his newly found companion, the Reverend Samuel H. Young, had the opportunity to explore the backcountry and discover new glaciers during missionary trips from one Tlinget settlement to another. Muir became a "transparent eyeball," to use an Emersonian image, to the wonders of nature; his mind and spirit deciphered glacial hieroglyphics and such gleanings became the basis of his ice sermons preached to the Indians, offsetting the Christian sermons preached by Reverend Young. More importantly, Muir's decipherings on this trip and

John Muir's Transcendental Imagery

two others (1880 and 1890) became the basis of *Travels in Alaska*, published posthumously in 1915.

Alaska, like the Sierra Nevada, was for Muir a place of light as well as ice. Such displays of light as sunrises, sunsets, luminous clouds, and aurora borealises were divine manifestations of "pure spiritual essence." In fact these phenomena made the very landscapes of mountains and fiords divine and as such became "pages from Nature's Bible." In such a land glaciers were described as ghostly, pale, and spiritlike. Calving or berging glaciers at the head of fiords made "the mysterious more mysterious." Muir's adjectives for the landscape, used over and over again, include: "ethereal," "celestial," "heavenly," "bodiless," "beatific," "luminous," "transfigured," "blazoned," and "radiating." Such adjectives evoke, certainly, a sense of the transcendental, the metaphysical. And they aid Muir in accounting for what he sensed to be divine harmony in Nature, a harmony so forcefully manifested in Alaska that his mind created a language effused with fire and burning ice.

John Muir's use of verbs also served his purpose well in *Travels in Alaska*. On his way to Alaska off the British Columbia coast, Muir writes, "when we contemplate the whole globe as one great dewdrop, striped and dotted with continents and islands, *flying* through space with other stars all singing and shining together as one, the whole universe appears as an infinite storm of beauty" (Emphasis is mine.)[19] The verbs "flying," "singing," and "shining" clearly convey a transcendental sense of the globe as a dewdrop in space. Not only is it a dewdrop, but it is a dewdrop that acts in harmony with the other stars. Our Earth's celestial relationship is indeed of transcendental significance.

In Alaska on the Muir Glacier in 1890, the California naturalist reflected upon the sounds of the glacier as he jotted down notes in his evening bed:

Solemnly growling and grinding moulins contrast with the sweet low-voiced whispering and warbling of a net work of rills singing

Richard F. Fleck

John Muir contemplating a glacier.
Pencil sketch by Jean Fader.

like water-ouzels glinting, gliding with indescribable softness and sweetness of voice. They are all around one another a few feet of my hard sled bed.[20]

The verbals "whispering," "warbling," "glinting," and "gliding" give an added dimension to the sweetness of the glacier's voice. Not only is the glacier leaving hieroglyphic messages on rocky walls at its side, it is also singing with a clearly discernible voice like Muir's favorite bird, the water-ouzel. Nature's own voice, then, stimulates the human mind to transcendental planes of thought beyond mere ice.

146

John Muir's Transcendental Imagery

Perhaps the chapter entitled "The Discovery of Glacier Bay" in *Travels in Alaska* (based on his 1879 trip) is the most transcendentally telling in that John Muir discovers far more than ice fields and glaciers.

Ralph Waldo Emerson asks in "Nature" (1836):

> Have mountains, and waves, and skies, no significance but what we consciously give them when we employ them as emblems of our thoughts? The world is emblematic. Parts of speech are metaphors, because the whole of nature is a metaphor of the human mind."[21]

Muir's description below of an aurora borealis in the Fairweather Mountains fully partakes of emblematic imagery:

> we were startled by the sudden appearance of a red light burning with a strange unearthly splendor on the topmost peak of the Fairweather Mountains. Instead of vanishing as suddenly as it had appeared, it spread and spread until the whole range down to the level of the glaciers was filled with the celestial fire. In color it was at first a vivid crimson, with a thick, furred appearance, as fine as the alpenglow, yet indescribably rich and deep—not in the least like a garment or mere external flush or bloom through which one might expect to see the rocks or snow, but every mountain apparently was glowing from the heart like molten metal fresh from a furnace. Beneath the frosty shadows of the fiord we stood hushed and awe-stricken, gazing at the holy vision; and had we seen the heavens opened and God made manifest, our attention could not have been more tremendously strained."[22]

Clearly Muir deduced that Nature at its height is a direct manifestation of the divine Creator and, all of Muir's emblems of thought point like iron filings to their magnetic source—God. Here John Muir came close to the native Alaskan in his spiritual beliefs.

Although John Muir did have some difficulty writing long books (as opposed to shorter magazine articles), one of his supreme achievements is a richly sensate metaphysical imagery that links finite aspects of the forested, glacial Sierra (and points north) with the cosmos. The strongest element of his literary

147

style, namely his imagery, skillfully conveys his transcendental philosophy.[23] Muir creates a vital link between Earth and the spirit world through his imagery, and his descriptions of the natural world are replete with the metaphysical, transcendental imagery.

Michael Cohen in *The Pathless Way* and Frederick Turner in *Rediscovering America* both discuss Muir's literary style. Cohen writes, "He was trying to find a strategy which would allow him to write essays that would not be artificial, but would capture the essential flow of nature."[24] The author concludes that he accomplished this strategy by recommending his transcendental experience as validated by the mountains.[25] And Turner notes that, despite Muir's great difficulties with literary composition, the philosopher-naturalist was continually sparked by the notion that Christianity and mountains are "streams from the same fountain."[26] Muir enhances his description of a nighttime Sierra forest with stars sparkling as blossoms on the upper branches.[27] The Milky Way becomes for Muir through his pen a "moraine of stars,"[28] and clouds in a Sierra sky become "glaciers in the canyon."[29] Waterfalls in Yosemite appear as "irised sunfire"[30] or the woven stuff spirits might wear.[31] Snowbanners (formed by blowing snow crystals mixing with air and sun on the lea side of a windy summit) become visible motion of sunglow[32] or "starry snow."[33]

His striking poetic language, typified by star blossoms on branches, easily fulfills the concept of beauty that Rosemond Tuve presents in her study, *Elizabethan and Metaphysical Imagery:* "Elements of formal beauty in images are not to be thought of as added on but as intrinsic."[34] Tuve further states, "an image is more than a plenum of qualities; it is an operative unit in an artistic structure."[35] Metaphysical conceit (imagistic construction) is an operative unit within artistic structure that is

> framed with especial subtlety. Indeed the formal defining element in any conceit, Elizabethan or medieval or Metaphysical, in any

John Muir's Transcendental Imagery

poem or in any language, seems to me to be this use of *multiple logical bases,* upon all of which the comparison obtains.[36]

John Muir's transcendental imagery strengthens his descriptive prose through multiple logical bases that imply a multiplicity of comparisons between nature and the spiritual cosmos. Let us take for example Muir's poetic image of the Milky Way being a "moraine of stars." What are the multiple logical bases in this one image beyond sensuous description? The multiple implications are: first, that God's creation is tellingly uniform in that glaciers on earth are similar to glaciers of stars in the sky; second, that the universe itself, though seemingly static, is constantly evolving and changing in form like glaciers gouging out mountains into moraines; third, that one learns from analogizing, an important Emersonian concept expressed in his essays "Nature" and "The Transcendentalist." In another example, Muir's image of a Yosemite waterfall as "irised sunfire," we can see again that there are multiple logical bases within the poetic prose description: First, God's creation is tellingly uniform in that mist and spray from a waterfall are similar to the fiery rays of the sun. Second, as the sun (one of Thoreau's favorite metaphysical images in *Walden*) gives off light, so too does a waterfall give off iridescence.

Muir's transcendental imagery truly enhanced what otherwise might be flat descriptive prose. The best of Muir compares favorably with Emerson and Thoreau because, as Tuve contends, elements of beauty are intrinsic. More importantly, his imagery of Nature concisely represented his own transcendental philosophy. The Creator speaks to our spirits through the analogy of His creation, and it remains the writer's task to transmit this spiritual essence through well-chosen and thoughtfully imagistic language. Muir's transcendental images are a cipher of Nature's hieroglyphics.

Richard F. Fleck

NOTES

1. John Muir, *John of the Mountains: The Unpublished Journals of John Muir*, ed. Linnie Marsh Wolfe (Madison: University of Wisconsin Press, 1979), p. 78.

2. *John Muir Papers*, John Muir Center for Regional Studies, University of the Pacific, Stockton, California.

3. Ibid.

4. Ibid.

5. Ibid.

6. Ralph Waldo Emerson, "Nature," in *The Complete Essays of Ralph Waldo Emerson* (New York: The Modern Library, 1950), p. 15

7. John Muir, *My First Summer in the Sierra* (Boston: Houghton Mifflin, 1911), pp. 14–15.

8. Ibid., p. 21.

9. Ibid., p. 102.

10. Ibid., pp. 108–109.

11. Ibid., p. 106.

12. Ibid., p. 109.

13. Ibid., p. 132.

14. Ibid., p. 229.

15. John Muir, *Steep Trails* (Boston: Houghton Mifflin, 1918), pp. 20–21.

16. John Muir, *The Mountains of California* (Boston: Houghton Mifflin, 1916), p. 57.

17. Ibid., p. 66.

18. Ibid., p. 79–80.

19. John Muir, *Travels in Alaska* (Boston: Houghton Mifflin, 1915), p. 5.

20. Ibid., p. 303.

21. Emerson, "Nature," p. 18.

22. Muir, *Travels*, pp. 152–153.

23. See Arlen J. Hansen, "Right Men in the Right Places: The Meeting of Ralph Waldo Emerson and John Muir," *Western Humanities Review* 39 (Summer 1985): 165–72, and Richard F. Fleck, "John Muir's Homage to Henry Thoreau," *The Pacific Historian* 29 (Summer/Fall 1985), pp. 54–64.

24. Michael Cohen, *The Pathless Way: John Muir and American Wilderness* (Madison: University of Wisconsin Press, 1984), pp. 130–131.

25. Ibid., p. 128.

26. Frederick Turner, *Rediscovering America: John Muir in His Time and Ours* (New York: Viking, 1985), p. 222.

27. John Muir, *Our National Parks* (Madison: University of Wisconsin Press, 1981), p. 301.

28. Muir, *John of the Mountains*, p. 236.

29. Ibid., p. 132.

30. Muir, *John of the Mountains*, II, p. 169.

31. Ibid., p. 169.

32. Ibid., p. 47.

33. Ibid., p. 51.

34. Rosemond Tuve, *Elizabethan and Metaphysical Imagery* (Chicago: University of Chicago Press, 1965), p. 29.

35. Ibid., p. 260.

36. Ibid., p. 264.

8.
On the Tops of Mountains

John Muir and Henry Thoreau

THE TOPS OF MOUNTAINS ARE AMONG THE UNFINISHED
PARTS OF THE GLOBE, WHITHER IT IS A SLIGHT INSULT TO
THE GODS TO CLIMB AND PRY INTO THEIR SECRETS, AND
TRY THEIR EFFECTS UPON OUR HUMANITY.

—*H.D. THOREAU*
"KTAADN"[1]

Edgar M. Castellini

John Muir entitled the fourth chapter of his major work, *The Mountains of California*, "A Near View of the High Sierra." This chapter, which Michael Cohen calls the "central chapter," is however every bit as much a *near view* of Muir himself, his imagination and his intimate and living understanding of nature, as it is a view of the high Sierra. It is Muir's great mountain-top chapter, his dramatic account of his climb of the highest and most central peak of the middle portion of the Sierra, Mt. Ritter. Cohen concluded that it was a "symbolic structure [where] every incident resonates with meaning."[2] *The Mountains of California* offers the nearest possible view of Muir, then, as he climbs and stands on the tops of Ritter and other great California mountains.

Muir began this fourth chapter describing the mid-portion of the high Sierra, above Yosemite, in terms of painting. Certain sections of the high Sierra, he realized, make dramatic *landscapes*, and as Muir sauntered down the valley of the Tuolumne River, he found that he "turned again and again to gaze on the glorious picture" of the Sierra Crown, often "throwing up my arms," he recounts, "to inclose it as in a frame."[3] In particular, a section of the highest peaks of the Sierra crown, seen from Tuolumne Meadows, "seemed now to be ready and waiting for the elected artist, like yellow wheat for the reaper." This last sentence now appears prescient; each passing year makes it clearer that John Muir himself has become the "elected artist" of the Sierra he spoke of, tacitly elected by generations of grateful readers. To understand how Muir in Chapter IV, maturely self-conscious and in command of the symbolic resources of language, is also describing his own artistic development requires the comparative study of his writing with that of another

153

Edgar M. Castellini

great artist of nature, Henry David Thoreau. Muir, as scholars increasingly realize, found "a spiritual and literary mentor" in Thoreau;[4] the kinship of Thoreau's account of his 1847 ascent of Maine's Mt. Ktaadn (now spelled Katahdin) to Muir's account of his ascent of Mt. Ritter is especially significant. With the aid of selections from the writings of Thoreau, this author demonstrates how Muir gleans from his mountain-top adventures not only a deeper perception of nature's mystical life but deeper truth about himself. These experiences entitle him to write *The Mountains of California* as the Sierra's own elected artist.

Muir's account of his climb of Mt. Ritter is carefully set within the context of his book, with each chapter, as their author claimed, "leaned . . . carefully against each other."[5] Thus, "A Near View of the High Sierra" leans upon Chapter III, "Snow," and Chapter II, "Glaciers," just as the highest mountains of the Sierra lean upon the snow-driven glaciers, their chief shapers. Snow and the glacial rivers of ice thus build to the highest peaks, the so-called Sierra Crown, as this fourth chapter itself crowns Muir's vision of a dynamic nature in "eternal flux," sculpting the rock of the Sierra. Nature itself is the greatest of artists.

Appropriately, Muir calls Ritter "king of the mountains of the middle portion of the high Sierra." If Ritter be a king, however, Muir describes its royal vestments rather curiously; he repeatedly calls this king *savage*, its face toward the summit "savagely hacked and torn." There was geological reason for this, of course; the mountain's top was never fully under the mantle of glacial ice. The heights of Ritter are therefore unfinished, an "undone extremity of the globe," as Thoreau says.[6] Ritter is "undone" or savage because its contours have been left unrefined by the ameliorating agency of glaciation. Muir thought of this mountain, then, as Thoreau thought of Mr. Ktaadn in Maine: "The tops of mountains are among the unfinished parts of the globe. . ."

Muir frames the story of his climb with the tale of his encounter with two painters whom he meets in Yosemite Valley

On the Tops of Mountains

North face of Mount Ritter. Photograph by Sean O'Grady.

upon his return in mid-October, his summer and autumn of research among the high peaks concluded. This meeting must have seemed all the more significant to Muir in that one of these painters, William Keith, subsequently became his life-long friend; this climb of Ritter was interwoven in Muir's life with his near view of the laws of artistic perspective. Destiny had seemingly framed this meeting. So to these artists' query whether the high Sierra had any truly picturesque mountains, Muir could give an enthusiastic Yes!, and agree to return immediately, while the fall weather held, to Tuolumne Meadows as guide for these artists.

As the painters studied the glowing beauty of the Sierra on their hike upward to the Meadows, Muir studied the painters: "the way that the fresh beauty was reflected in their faces made for me a novel and interesting study." The sense of beauty was contagious, and the like held good for these artists' enthusiasm: "Their enthusiasms was excited beyond bounds, and the more

155

impulsive of the two, a young Scotchman, dashed ahead, shouting and gesticulating and tossing his arms in the air like a madman." Muir intends their contagious sense of nature's beauty and this enthusiasm to operate reflexively in his own narrative; that is, the author strives in this chapter to fashion an art of words, a kind of verbal painting. The atmosphere of art in which he now moves makes his writing a kind of "poetry," as Cohen remarks.[7] Thus the chapter contains such adventurous word painting as this description of his near approach to Mt Ritter: "Just before the alpenglow began to fade, two crimson clouds came streaming across the summit like wings of flame." His verbal brush can also touch the little details of his diction. "God's glacial-mills grind slowly," he writes, each g, s, and l little brush strokes imitative of the "stormy sea" of glacial action. Again, he encloses books, bread, and cabin warmly encircled by the safe boundary of b: "warmly snow-bound in my Yosemite cabin with plenty of bread and books." His prose in many places strains toward the verbal intensities of poetry. Muir thus suggests in this chapter that he has found his words among the mountains on this journey, as the painters have found their long-sought landscapes and colors.

Muir, having arrived at the Tuolumne Meadows, determined to climb Ritter while the artists remained there to sketch. "The artists went heartily to their work and I to mine," Muir recalled, but his was now artistically conceived work. Mt. Ritter was a full day's walk south, a hike of "pure pleasure" and "mountaineering indulgence." Nearing, he observed that "Somber peaks, hacked and shattered, circled half-way around the horizon, wearing a savage aspect in the gloaming." The next day, approaching the mountain's base, he found himself "spellbound" in front of its "majestic mass"; seen from below, the heights of Ritter appeared "hacked at the top," with "huge, crumbling buttresses." Moreover, he stood on the north-facing side of this great peak, so that "the whole front was rendered still more forbidding by the chill shadow and the gloomy blackness of the rocks." The

On the Tops of Mountains

mountain is in fact appalling in its massive and lifeless desolation, "veiled with one blue shadow—rock, ice, and water close together without a single leaf or sign of life."

Ritter and its entire neighborhood is indeed unfinished in the most savage manner, somewhat unsettle Muir, and it is illuminating to compare with Muir's narrative Henry Thoreau's haunting description of Ktaadn's top:

> It was vast, Titanic, and such as man never inhabits. Some part of the beholder, even some vital part, seems to escape through the loose grating of his ribs as he ascends. He is more lone than you can imagine. There is less of substantial thought and fair understanding in him than in the plains where men inhabit. His reason is dispersed and shadowy, more thin and subtle, like the air. Vast, Titanic, inhuman Nature has got him at disadvantage, caught him alone, and pilfers him of some of his divine faculty.[8]

A few sentences further, Thoreau continues, "The tops of mountains are among the unfinished parts of the globe, whither it is a slight insult to the gods to climb and pry into their secrets, and try their effect on our humanity." Since the unfinished tops of mountains were home not to mortals, but to gods or Titans, they were accordingly *savage*, a word Thoreau emphasized throughout his Ktaadn account: "It was a savage and dreary scenery"; "Nature was here something savage and awful." Muir echoes this conception of the savagery of such mountain-tops. More pertinently, Muir's account of his ascent makes a deliberate record of Ritter's *effect on his humanity*, of this mountain's trial of his soul.

So Ritter was indeed vast, inhuman Nature, especially the forbidding north face that Muir confronted. What Thoreau discovered on Ktaadn, Muir also found at Ritter:

> I looked with awe at the ground I trod on, to see what the Powers had made there, the form and fashion and material of their work. This was that Earth of which we have heard, made out of Chaos and Old Night.[9]

As Thoreau had foretold, in effect, Ritter begins to "pilfer" Muir's fortitude and understanding as soon as he commences

157

the ascent. The difficulty of the north-face route causes Muir to begin "contending with" himself as to the feasibility of this climb. Making his way up an avalanche channel, he threads his way perilously "into a wilderness of crumbling spires and battlements." The more formidable obstacle, however, lurked within; Muir records that "my instincts, usually so positive and true, seemed vitiated in some way, and were leading me astray." Prior to his ascent, Muir had asserted "going to the mountains is like going home," and he had raptly spoken of the sun's "vital heat—rock crystals and snow-crystals thrilling alike." This same vitality filled and inspired him: "I strode on exhilarated, as if never more to feel fatigue, limbs moving of themselves, every sense unfolding like the thawing flowers . . ." Now, however, this mountain seems to "pilfer" his faculties, to "vitiate" his "instincts," as if, as Thoreau said, some "vital" part were escaping "through the loose grating of his ribs." Ritter assaults Muir in his life force as his word "vitiated" implies.

Muir's almost miraculous salvation, when his ordinary self proves inadequate to the task of scaling a particularly difficult part of Ritter, is well known. Midway up a sheer cliff, he is stopped spread-eagled upon the face of the rock and is saved from death by recourse to inner light only. Now, given a "strange influx of strength," he makes his way unerringly to the summit, even though above the scene of his greatest trial "the face of the mountain [was] still more savagely hacked and torn . . . a maze of yawning chasms and gullies, in the angles of which rise beetling crags and piles of detached boulders." Muir's special note of the loose and unsettled boulders recalls the significance Thoreau attaches to the "loosely poised" boulders atop Ktaadn: "The mountain seemed a vast aggregation of loose rocks, as if some time it had rained rocks. . ." [10] When Muir attains the summit, his instinctive response is notable: "first hour of freedom from that terrible shadow, the sunlight in which I was laving seemed all in all." This "terrible shadow" had been for Muir also the shadow cast by "Chaos and Old Night," assaulting his vitality,

On the Tops of Mountains

rendering his frail human reason "dispersed and shadowy," as Thoreau had said. Muir had realized, by the time he came to write *The Mountains of California* many years after this eventful climb, that his daring ascent had perhaps been "a slight insult to the gods," a challenge for the forces of nature to "try their effects upon (his) humanity."

His path upward had been a dark journey, through dark rock, ice, and air. But at the top of the mountain Muir laves, as he says, in the light; symbolically, this is also the light of science and far-seeing intelligence. He now proceeds to describe the mountains as if he were a guide to an inexperienced bystander, aware that "the inexperienced observer is oppressed by the incomprehensible grandeur, variety, and abundance of the mountains rising shoulder to shoulder beyond the reach of vision." Muir painstakingly points out the features to Ritter's south, west, north, and east, making the most complex characteristics of the Sierra's geology intelligible: "the most complicated clusters of peaks stand revealed harmoniously correlated and fashioned like works of art—eloquent monuments of the ancient ice-rivers that brought them into relief from the general mass of the range." As if to emphasize that glacial ice has been the great artist shaping these mountains, and to contrast the "works of art" wrought by glaciers with the "undone extremity" savage chaos of Ritter's uppermost portion, Muir finds his descent of the mountain by a different route quite easy, primarily because he finds a glacier and follows its path downward . The next day, he "sauntered home" to the artists who, after three days of sketching, had already begun to fret over their isolation.

Muir atop Ritter is thus providing his readers with a vision of the "comprehensive intelligence" that shapes the mountains and the planet, as Thoreau writes in "A Walk to Wachusett." [11] Thoreau atop Wachusett and Muir atop Ritter both sing the praises of far-seeing intelligence and its symbol of light. Indeed, this side of Muir is much more familiar to readers, the cheerful saunterer who proclaims "Climb the mountains and get

159

their good tidings," or "Of all the upness accessible to mortals, there is no upness comparable to the mountains." [12] In such passages, Muir is reading the lighted face of the mountains, yet he is neither naive nor unqualifiedly enthusiastic about the High Sierra, as Chapter IV shows. He had discovered that light necessarily purchases its opposite, its "terrible shadow." The mountains did not only proclaim to him their "good tidings." Rather, they taught Muir about their paradoxical nature: on the one hand they give birth to comprehensive intelligence, on the other to trial and terror. Muir's climb of Ritter has shown him that this mountain top was both a sublime and a terrible place—"vast, Titanic, and such as man never inhabits." Part of the election process for the artist in the Sierra is to have tried the effect of these peaks on his own humanity.

Mt. Shasta is to the northern Sierra what Ritter is to the middle of the range. John Muir's account of his climb to the top of Mt. Shasta on April 30, 1875, whereupon he and his partner become trapped by a fierce storm and must spend the entire night on the mountain top, makes a similar statement to his Ritter chapter. Both mountains try his humanity, both test his "election" through a severe probation.

Muir had been making barometric observations atop Mt. Shasta, and in the intervals, raptly following the boiling cloud masses of an approaching storm. This storm so suddenly struck the top of Shasta, however, that it became very dangerous for Muir and his partner to descend. An experienced reader of Muir, knowing his passionate love of storms, realizes that he almost certainly hoped to sample the force of this storm and to revel for a time in its effects. Nevertheless, this apparently proved to be the most severe short-term storm Muir had ever known, and the results were unexpected:

> the storm became inconceivably violent. The thermometer fell 22° in a few minutes, and soon dropped below zero. The hail gave place to snow, and darkness came on like night. The wind, rising to the highest pitch of violence, boomed and surged amid the desolate

On the Tops of Mountains

Mt. Shasta in winter. Photograph by C. Miller, ca. 1909. Holt Atherton
Library photo collections.

crags; lightning-flashes in quick succession cut the gloomy darkness; and the thunders, the most tremendously loud and appalling
I ever heard, made an almost continuous roar, stroke following
stroke in quick, passionate succession, as though the mountain
were being rent to its foundations and the fires of the old volcano
were breaking forth again.[13]

The storm was "appalling," the thunderclaps "passionate," the
mountain "rent"—by means of this storm, the slumbering Titan
of the old volcano stirs in its bed, its "fires" "breaking forth."
Muir experienced this storm as a visitation of Shasta's "passionate" nature. The wind, driving hail and snow, the intense cold,
the lightning, and thunder all were "appalling," equally as vast
and inhuman yet not inanimate, as were the elements of rock
and ice on the top of Ritter.

The strategy he and his partner, Jerome Fay, adopted of
spending the night and the hours of the storm lying on their backs
atop the fumaroles at Shasta's summit had not been Muir's plan.
He had prudently calculated the landmarks of a return course

in case of darkness or storm. He consented to this desperate tactic only out of obligation to Fay, who had become unnerved by the darkness and appalling contest of the elements and had bolted panic-stricken for the fumaroles. This was a mountain-top peril Thoreau had anticipated when be observed that the "gods" might indeed "pilfer" human reason on these heights. The night they spent there, their backs scorched and their upper sides frozen, proved yet another severe trial of Muir's humanity. Their sufferings were so severe that life itself came to seem an "easily quenched" flame: "Frozen, blistered, famished, be-numbed, our bodies seemed lost to us at times—all dead but the eyes." Shasta's trial of Muir's vital energies was vitiation indeed. Once again, as on Ritter, comprehensive intelligence is joined to intense suffering; Muir sees the stars as he had never beheld them before, "blessed immortals of light, shin-ing with marvelous brightness with long lance-rays, near-looking and new-looking." Self-knowledge and cosmic vision on the top of this mountain are conjoined to the intensity of his trial.

The light Muir won from his Shasta experience with the chaotic agencies of nature proved just as significant as his Ritter encounter, although on Shasta it took other forms. Fay and Muir lay atop this mountain, "icy and covered over with snow" like rocks on the ground, waiting for the light of day to release them from nature's savage grip. Every dark, chill, burning hour of the night seemed "like a year." With the utmost intensity, Muir "eagerly watched the pale light" of the dawn, light that now meant life and vitality. The scene inevitably recalls Dante's *In-ferno*, its rivers of lava in which scorched souls must swim, its vast deserts of ice. Likewise, Muir's and Fay's benumbed rising from the ground in the light and warmth of the new day was a resurrection; Muir, commenting on his safe return to the sunny valley below Shasta, says, "we seemed to have risen from the dead." He had returned "this memorable first of May" to his "old friends" among the plants and animals of earth's lower re-gions, as if "we had been away in some far, strange country."

On the Tops of Mountains

The tops of mountains were indeed a realm mankind cannot inhabit.

Shasta's trial of Muir's humanity differs from Ritter's only in that it was a lesson in the savagery of the elements of air and fire, whereas his Ritter experience was primarily a lesson about the primal chaos of rock and ice. The two experiences complement each other, therefore, especially if their contending elements are conceived in Aristotelian terms: earth, water, air, fire. Whereas Ritter had taught Muir that *earth* and *water* atop the highest peaks are "Powers . . . made out of Chaos and Old Night," Shasta instructed him that atop these peaks air and fire were likewise "vast, Titanic, and inhuman."

Let us now return to Muir's Ritter chapter, to the tale of the Sierra's elected artist. Muir concludes that chapter by recounting his confident "saunter"—Thoreau's playful word for the *art* of walking [14]—back through the high country toward the artists encamped in Tuolumne Meadows. In his three-day absence, the once-enthusiastic painters had become so uneasy that they had been deliberating ways to flee "back to the lowlands." [15] Note the connotations of the two adjectives Muir chooses to describe their state of mind: "Now their *curious* troubles were over. They packed their *precious* sketches. . ." Their anxieties were curious indeed, an aberration, compared to the life-and-death "troubles" Muir had endured on Ritter. Whose sketches, then, Muir's word painting or these painters' canvases, could conceivably be the more "precious"? The painters carry back from the mountains paper sketches. Muir carries back vital and transformative experience, the kind that breeds powerful and beautiful language.

Thoreau's diction, as has been suggested, has deeply tinged Muir's outlook. Thoreau's concepts of *savagery* and *vitality* helped structure Muir's narrative, these coming to him from his careful study of Thoreau's narrative of his ascent of Mt. Ktaadn. "Saunter," on the other hand, recalls Thoreau's "Walking," where he asserts that only those walkers who travel to "the Holy Land . . . are saunterers in the good sense, such as I mean." [16] "Holy Land:" all land (*-ter* or *-terre* in saun*ter*), all the surface of Earth, is holy. So Muir "sauntered home,—that is, back to the Tuolumne camp," stepping across the holy land of the high Sierra, a *ter*rain whose essential holiness became newly consecrated for him during his Ritter ordeal. [17]

Historian Michael Cohen says "Muir's experience on Ritter is the wilderness experience par excellence. Although it has aesthetic and scientific aspects, it is primarily a religious conversion, followed by a religious vision of a sacred cosmos." [18] The same might be said of Muir's experience atop Shasta. In each case Muir undergoes severe trial and comes close to death. In each he triumphs through his courage and insight, and from both he wins new awareness of the awful extent of nature's powers. He descends each mountain a wiser, more comprehensive human being.

Furthermore, it is now possible to understand more clearly the kind of religious experience Muir attained on these heights and the kind of sacred cosmos the mountains revealed. It was not of light alone, but of light and darkness—not of good and harmony only, but also of savagery and elemental fury; savage "gods" also dwelt there. The tops of mountains revealed a cosmos not solely of light and comprehensive intelligence, but rather of light subject to overwhelming by sudden darkness, of frail humanity easily eclipsed by chaotic natural forces.

Cohen observes Muir's telling use of the passive voice at critical junctures in his narrative, implying "a kind of dual consciousness. The climb happened to him." [19] A reader should recall the passive participles Muir uses to describe his climb: "hacked," "shattered," "torn." The subject or agent, Muir has left unnamed. Who or what has shattered these peaks, who has hacked and torn their rocks? This suggests the lesson Ritter had seared into Muir as Thoreau said, "Nature is mythical and magical always and works with the license and extravagance of genius." [20] Dynamic agencies were alive and at work on the

On the Tops of Mountains

mountains; earth, water, air, fire were some of the mythical and magical forces there, dwarfing in their action the human body and mind. These natural powers try Muir's humanity, they also transform him. And this train of thought also permits us to recognize the most important literary influence Thoreau exercised on Muir. He taught Muir how to organize his narrative around the symbolic events and features immanent in nature—to discern myth on the mountain tops.

Muir's use of the passive participle "elected" also has important connotations. Who might elect the Sierra's "elected artist"? Again the subject is left unnamed, but this is Muir's way of treating his "religious conversion" and vision in a suitably reverent manner. The import of "elected" is clear: creative nature, the earth's shaping intelligence, requires its elected interpreters to undergo severe trial before nature's laws can be truly seen, its words of power and beauty understood.

Readers of Muir's *Mountains of California* do not gain "A Near View of the High Sierra," or a full view of Muir, until his experiences atop the savage extremities of the Sierra are themselves more nearly seen. Atop Ritter and Shasta he has won new understanding of the vast extent of nature's powers, and he comes down these mountains to proclaim their "evangel," as he says. Muir's words, both in Chapter IV and elsewhere, have been wrested from the tops of mountains, those unfinished realms of "Chaos and Old Night"—words hard-won, words for which he climbed.

NOTES

1. Henry Thoreau, "Ktaadn," in *Maine Woods* (Boston: Ticknor and Fields, 1868), p. 65. This volume, along with other works of Henry Thoreau that were in John Muir's personal library, is now in the collection at the John Muir archives at the John Muir Center for Regional Studies, University of the Pacific, Stockton, California. The selections from Thoreau's "Ktaadn" are from this volume, which the Center kindly permitted me to peruse and copy in part. Many of these

Edgar M. Castellini

passages were marked in the margin by Muir himself. "Ktaadn" is now spelled "Katahdin."

2. Michael Cohen, *The Pathless Way: John Muir and American Wilderness* (Madison: University of Wisconsin Press, 1985), p. 67.

3. John Muir, *The Mountains of California* (Berkeley: Ten Speed Press, n.d., 1894 reprint edition), p. 50. All subsequent quotations from Muir dealing with his Mt. Ritter experiences are taken from Chapter IV of this work, pp. 48–73.

4. Richard Fleck, *Henry Thoreau and John Muir among the Indians* (Hamden, Conn.: Archon, 1985), p. 22.

5. Cohen, *The Pathless Way*, p. 285.

6. Thoreau, *Maine Woods*, p. 63.

7. Cohen, *The Pathless Way*, p. 285.

8. Thoreau, "Ktaadn," p. 65.

9. Ibid., p. 70

10. Ibid., p. 63.

11. Henry Thoreau, "A Walk to Wachusett," in *Excursions* (Boston: Houghton and Mifflin, 1906, reprinted 1968), p. 148. Muir's passage on the surrounding Sierra as seen from Ritter's summit seems strikingly anticipated by Thoreau's account atop Wachusett: "We could at length realize the place mountains occupy on the land, and how they come into the general scheme of the universe. When first we climb their summits and observe their lesser irregularities, we do not give credit to the comprehensive intelligence which shaped them; but when afterward we behold their outlines in the horizon, we confess that the hand which molded their opposite slopes, making one balance the other, worked round a deep centre, and was privy to the plan of the universe" (p. 148).

12. John Muir, *The Wilderness World of John Muir*, ed. Edwin Way Teale (Boston: Houghton Mifflin, 1954), pp. 311, 314.

13. Muir, *Wilderness World*, p. 260. This and subsequent citations referring to Muir's Shasta experiences are taken from the passage "A Perilous Night on Mount Shasta," pp. 251–265.

14. Thoreau, "Walking," in *Excursions*, p. 205.

15. Muir, *Mountains of California*, p. 73. Subsequent quotations also come from this chapter.

16. Thoreau, "Walking," p. 205.

17. I have in several places spoken of Muir's deep interest in Thoreau's outlook. To judge from the extent and frequency of Muir's margin notation and notes kept on the back pages of his copy of *Maine Woods*, the whole passage dealing with the ascent of Ktaadn engaged his special interest. Muir shares not only Thoreau's outlook, but his view of the earth as holy.

18. Cohen, *The Pathless Way*, p. 75.

19. Ibid., 68.

20. Thoreau, "Natural History of Massachusetts," in *Excursions*, p. 125.

PART
V
MUIR
AND THE
PHYSICAL
SCIENCES

9.
Muir and Geology

Dennis R. Dean

Those who know John Muir best describe him as primarily a naturalist and conservationist, not to mention an author, yet Muir himself insisted that he was also a geologist, interested particularly in glaciers but alert to other relevant phenomena. That Muir sometimes identified himself as a geologist is worth noting, because he rarely claimed to be a scientist of any other specific kind or, for that matter, a scientist at all.[1]

Since Muir held no degrees in geology (or, of course, earned ones in any other subject), never worked with or under geologists in any professional capacity, never joined any of their professional organizations, and never subscribed to the usual professional journals, some would argue that he has no place within the history of that science. Indeed, comprehensive studies of the development of American geology, or of geology in general, seldom mention his name. On the other hand, a well-known bibliography of American geology lists fourteen of his publications, which appeared between 1872 and 1917; clearly, it is upon the worth of such contributions that any evaluation of Muir as a geologist must rest.[2]

The fourteen geological publications with which Muir is credited divide rather easily into those that are primarily descriptive and those that are primarily analytical. Bifurcation is equally apparent in their subject matter, as they deal either with the Yosemite region or with Alaska. Keeping artificiality to a minimum, I shall review each of the fourteen publications (and certain others) pretty much in chronological order, adding only a few remarks intended to enhance our understanding of their implications—that is, to explain why Muir as geologist received the inordinate attention that he did.

Dennis R. Dean

John Muir evinced no pretensions to scientific status as a geologist until the fall of 1871, shortly before his discovery of living glaciers in Yosemite. His public career as a nature writer began then, with geology and glaciology as his subjects. Owing in part to Horace Greeley's interest in the topic, Muir's article "Yosemite Glaciers: The Ice Streams of the Great Valley," appeared in the *New York Tribune* of 5 December, 1871.[3] Anonymous and unusually placed, the article was overlooked in the bibliography of American geology mentioned above. Yet of all Muir's geological publications, this one may have been the most important; soon recognized as his, it represents the beginning of that long-involved public debate with J. D. Whitney and others regarding the origin of Yosemite Valley.

A statement of beliefs rather than an argument, "Yosemite Glaciers" has two parts, the first of which is dated 28 September [1871] from the Valley. In it, Muir eloquently compares the surviving glacial geology of Yosemite to a damaged but still readable book detailing the glorious actions of departed ice. "The Great Valley itself, together with all its domes and walls," he asserts, "was brought forth and fashioned by a grand combination of glaciers, acting in certain directions against granite of peculiar physical structure." His further claims are even more comprehensive. "All of the rocks and mountains and lakes and meadows of the whole upper Merced basin," he insists, "received their specific forms and carvings almost entirely from this same agency of ice." The remainder of part one, and nearly all of the other (dated 30 September) is then narrative self-portraiture, Muir depicting himself as a searcher among rocks and moraines for "readable glacier manuscript." He later referred to these explorations as nothing more than "preliminary rambles." And such they were, but his report of them, with its straightforward glaciological assertions, directly contradicted already published opinions of the testy state geologist, Josiah Dwight Whitney, who soon found in Muir an upstart amateur impossible to ignore.[4]

During a visit to Yosemite and Muir in 1871, John Daniel

Muir and Geology

Runkle, a major representative of the Eastern academic establishment, soon came to appreciate Muir's unique knowledge and well-thought out interpretations of natural phenomena. As Muir wrote proudly to Mrs. Carr on 8 September:

> Professor Runkle, President of the Massachusetts Institute of Technology, was here last week, and I preached my glacial theory to him for five days, taking him into the canyons of the Valley and up among the grand glacier wombs and pathways of the summit. He was fully convinced of the truth of my readings, and urged me to write out the glacial system of Yosemite and its tributaries for the Boston Academy of Science. I told him I meant to write my thoughts for my own use and that I would send him the manuscript and if he and his wise scientific brothers thought it of sufficient interest they might publish it.[5]

Having thus encouraged Muir to write him at length, Runkle subsequently shared extracts from the resulting letters with members of the Boston Society of Natural History.

The first such presentation, "On the Glaciers of the Yosemite Valley," read by the Society's secretary, Dr. Samuel Kneeland on 21 February, 1872, utilized Muir's *New York Tribune* article as well as his letters to Runkle but nonetheless endorsed Whitney's theory of the origin of the Valley rather than Muir's. A second paper, a description of the previous winter experienced by Muir in Yosemite and similarly presented by Kneeland on 6 March, stressed meteorology. Though his facts had potential relevance to past climates and the Ice Age, Muir proposed no such applications. All of the writing appears to be his own.

Finally, a third paper, read by Kneeland on 15 May, 1872, described the effects of the Owens Valley earthquakes of 26 March as they had manifested themselves in Yosemite. It has not previously been pointed out that much more than simple description was involved. For Muir (who inventively turned a pail of water into a seismoscope) demonstrated his familiarity with a number of up-to-date scientific concerns. These included the wave-like nature of earthquakes, the direction of the waves, the persistence of aftershocks, the likelihood of subterranean sounds, and the effects of earthquakes on animal behavior. Following current procedures, he noted both the time of day and the prevailing weather accompanying the shocks. His was the proper way, in contemporary practice, to describe an earthquake. Except for the Eagle Rock avalanche, however, Muir emphasized that even this major example had left few marks of its passage through the valley. Again, the writing was entirely his.[6]

Having discovered that his shrewd but sometimes form-less observations on natural phenomena were of interest to the more learned, Muir now searched for a more suitable outlet. Through the solicitous intervention of Jeanne Carr, he soon found it in a San Francisco-based periodical called the *Overland Monthly*, whose editor relished Western topics in natural history and quickly came to regard Muir as a major contribu-tor. His first appearance in its pages, a description of "Yosemite Valley in Flood," had originated in Muir's letter to Mrs. Carr of 1 January, 1872; sent on to the *Overland Monthly* by her, it was published three months later.[7] As opposed to the letters he sent Runkle, this one was written in his private, more lyrical, (and ultimately stronger) mode. Besides celebrating a marvelous display of adventitious waterfalls, however, Muir also recorded temperatures from his thermometer and later surveyed the val-ley floor to research the enhanced carrying power of its streams. Being a student of Lyellian uniformitarianism—and therefore convinced that the geological forces observable today are those that have always been at work—he was surely aware that simi-lar episodes of flooding must have occurred many times in the recent past.

A second *Overland Monthly* contribution, "Twenty Hill Hol-low," was geological only in part.[8] Less than a mile in length, the Hollow (a "Yosemite of the plain") lay between the Merced and Tuolumne rivers, surrounded by its eponymous twenty hemi-spherical hills, which alternated layers of slate with volcanic deposits. As Muir coyly wrote:

Muir and Geology

> Whatever may be the true theory of the formation of mountain Yosemites, Twenty Hill Hollow is a clear case of erosion. . . . The hollow canyons, cut in soft lavas, are not so deep as to require a single earthquake at the hands of science, much less a baker's dozen of those convenient tools demanded for the making of Yosemite, and our proper arithmetical standards are not outraged by a single magnitude of this moderate, comprehensible hollow.

Besides attesting to former Sierran volcanoes, then, Twenty Hill Hollow became for Muir a fine example of fluvial erosion—and an object lesson for all would-be geological theorizers.

Of still greater significance was his third contribution, a short narrative essay on the "Living Glaciers of California."[9] In it, Muir recalled that autumnal day in October 1871 when he had come upon a small mountain stream carrying glacial sediments easily traceable to a moraine of some sixty or seventy feet in height. After climbing to the top of the moraine, Muir discovered not a snowbank but an actual glacier, the movements of which were clearly evident. His subsequent examinations of Mounts Lyell and Maclure—both of them named for geologists—convinced him that their "snowbanks" were glaciers also. Since knowledgeable friends of his were inclined to dispute these claims, Muir returned to Mt. Maclure on 21 August, 1872, to plant a series of carefully positioned stakes across the glacier's surface, a technique borrowed from his predecessors. When he revisited the site on 6 October, all of the stakes had moved proportional distances toward the foot. "Thus," he was now able to confirm, "these ice-masses are seen to possess the true glacial motion." The existence of present-day Sierran glaciers had never before been demonstrated. That Muir's discovery was of professional interest is attested by the reprinting of this essay in the widely circulated *American Journal of Science*, which was edited by the geologist J. D. Dana at Yale.

In 1874, after patiently accumulating data for years, Muir unabashedly presented his geological analysis of Yosemite to the

173

public in a series of seven loosely coordinated essays collec-
tively entitled *Studies in the Sierra*. [10] (He was by now ambitious
to publish a book on California glaciers, past and present, but
the project never came to fulfillment.) Like some of the papers
already discussed, the *Studies* essays allude to Muir's contemporary science and its disputes more often than casual twentieth-
century readers might recognize. A few generalizations, therefore, may be of some use.

By 1874, both the science of geology as a whole and American
geology in particular had achieved considerable sophistication.
Among the scientifically informed, at least, scriptural literalism
regarding the creation and early history of the earth could no
longer be taken seriously. Contrarily, the vastness of geological time and the uniqueness of prehistoric life achieved general
acceptance. Though the tradition scarcely survived, it was still
possible to maintain some kind of "natural theology," a technical term meaning the discovery of divine attributes in the world
of nature. Geological discussions in both Europe and America,
however, stressed science rather than theology. Nevertheless,
disagreements continued on such surprisingly basic matters as
the nature and history of geological causality; the relative efficacy, past and present, of various geological forces; the origins of granite and other specific rocks; the histories of mountains, valleys, and other landforms; the mechanics of volcanoes
and earthquakes; the reality, causes, extent, and duration of
the Ice Age; the nature of glacial motion; and the respective
powers, constructive and destructive, of water, wind, and ice.
As these overlapping categories indicate, many geological issues
now more or less resolved were then still very much in dispute.
But it would be improper history merely to reward Muir for
points since accepted as our own. There have been innumerable
competing theorists of the Sierra. Among those of his own day,
however, Muir was the most influential of the nonprofessionals,
and we think today that he was partly right, whereas some of
those who bullied him with their more impressive professional
credentials were wholly wrong.

Muir and Geology

That *Studies in the Sierra* achieved immediate stature as a serious contribution to the science of geology is fairly remarkable. First, Muir's vehicle for publication, to begin with, was again *Overland Monthly*, a West coast periodical of more general purposes not widely read among the scientific establishment of the East. Second, Muir made almost no attempt to observe the normal conventions of scientific writing. Clearly preferring nature to books, he knew the truth because he had seen it. Thus, he used virtually no documentation, and so neither substantiated his points on the basis of agreement with others (excepting a general acknowledgement at one point of Louis Agassiz, John Tyndall, and James Forbes as glaciologists) nor established a theoretical context for his own observations, most of which either included unspoken assumptions or led on to dogmatic assertions, the latter self-consciously italicized. Third, despite a few technical terms (like "moraine"), Muir's language is not the language of science. In some cases, to be sure, standardized scientific terminology did not yet exist. But Muir stands well apart from the professionals in his unique diction, through which he relentlessly insists upon maintaining a stalwart individuality. As a result, somewhat unlike that of more orthodox scientific writers, Muir's style is inseparable from its author's perceptions and opinions. Necessarily, then, he offers us his conclusions in an arbitrary fashion. Given these characteristics of his work (which, I hope, have been described fairly), it is hardly surprising that cranky, professional geologists obsessed with their own importance found him not only irritating but intolerable. What does surprise is that such inauspiciously presented observations and opinions as Muir's had such an impact.

Part One, "Mountain Sculpture," is throughout an increasingly dramatic paean to the geological efficacy of snow.[11] Of all seven parts, this one also contains Muir's boldest and most far-reaching concepts. Prior to the glacial epoch, he asserts, the whole of the Sierra Nevada massif was relatively featureless, "one vast undulated wave, in which a thousand separate mountains, with their domes and spires, their innumerable canyons

Dennis R. Dean

A sketch by John Muir, ca. 1874, showing the direction of glacial flow on Half Dome, Yosemite National Park. John Muir Papers, Holt Atherton Library. Copyright 1984 by Muir-Hanna Trust.

and lake basins, lay concealed." Rejecting the theories of W. P. Blake and J. D. Whitney, among others, Muir dismisses such alternative geological agencies as earthquake, lightning, flood, and rain. For him, glacial ice alone carved out all of the features that make the Sierra both scenic and unique: its rugged mountains, rounded domes, pointed spires, steep-sided canyons, U-shaped valleys, and concave lakes.

When first glaciated, he continues, the Sierra lay entirely beneath a single, all-encompassing ice sheet, much like Greenland and Antarctica today. At some later time, the shrinking ice sheet separated into distinct glaciers, which then flowed down their separate valleys and canyons—much as one sees in the Himalayas, Alps, and Norwegian mountains today. In the Sierra, however, these glaciers have likewise vanished, but only recently; we can still trace their paths back to the summits from which they came, and on which smaller, residual glaciers still exist. From beneath this gradual withdrawal, the Sierra as we know it emerged.

Muir and Geology

The whole granitic mass of the Sierra, Muir has observed, consists of brick-like blocks that have separated from one another along well-defined "planes of cleavage" that are both vertical and horizontal. When these blocks are subjected to the "strain" of glaciers, he proposes, "they are torn apart in an irregular and indeterminate manner, giving rise to [an] endless variety of rock forms." These cleavage planes, moreover, run the length and breadth of the entire chain, with many of them traceable for miles. When vertical cleavages are more vulnerable than horizontal ones, the result is "majestic mural precipices" like El Capitan. Fully developed diagonal cleavage, on the other hand, produces sharp-pointed peaks and huge gables, like the numerous examples in Yosemite Valley and Tuolumne Canyon.

Besides rectilinear and diagonal examples, however, Muir has also found curved, or dome, cleavage. The resulting granitic domes are, for him, remarkably strong, being uncommonly able to resist both atmospheric and mechanical forces, including direct glacial pressure. Thus, they stand above the weaker rocks underlying them. That line of domes, which in Yosemite extends across the head of the valley from Mount Starr King to North Dome, was, it is true, breached by the combined forces of the Hoffmann and Tenaya glaciers, but the powerful South Lyell glacier, acting by itself, had been unable to force its way through. Rudimentary domes exist everywhere in the Sierra, he adds, but are nowhere more perfected than in Yosemite.

As Muir has now seemingly established, "the present sculptured condition of the Sierra is due to the action of ice and the variously developed cleavage planes and concentric seams which its rocks contain." Part One, then, asserts that of all possible erosive agencies, only glacial ice has been of any real significance in the shaping of Yosemite, through processes both gradual and recent. In reconstructing the region's geological history, however, Muir limits himself to only the very latest episodes. He takes the elevation of the Sierra Nevada massif for granted, without attempting to explain either its granite or the residual overlying layers of slate. Presumably, the planes of cleavage important to his remarks were created by the uplifting of the whole granitic mass, but Muir is concerned only with their subsequent dismemberment by glaciers, which "*do not so much mold and shape, as disinter forms already conceived and ripe.*" This was one of his more important observations.

Part Two of *Studies in the Sierra,* also called "Mountain Sculpture" but with specific reference to the "Origin of Yosemite Valleys," begins by classifying all the valleys and canyons of the western flank of the Sierra as valleys of erosion (another rebuke to Whitney).[12] They consist either of slate or of granite, are either V-shaped or not, and have still further characteristics. With four prevalent types thereby defined, Muir moves immediately to the last and proceeds to eulogize its type locality of Yosemite as "the noblest of Sierra temples, everywhere expressing the working of Divine harmonious law, yet so little understood that it has been regarded as 'an exceptional creation' or rather *exceptional destruction* accomplished by violent and mysterious forces." For Muir, any such assumption was entirely unacceptable.

Those who support the theory of exceptional creation, he tells us, have argued as follows: Yosemite is

> too wide for a water-eroded valley, too irregular for a fissure valley, and too angular and local for a primary valley originating in a fold of the mountain surface during the process of upheaval; therefore, a portion of the mountain bottom must have suddenly fallen out, letting the superincumbent domes and peaks fall rumbling into the abyss, like coal into the bunker of a ship.

This violent, chaotic hypothesis—an unmistakable parody of Whitney's—seemingly accorded with the remarkable sheerness and angularity of the valley's walls while conveniently invoking an uninvestigable source, its floor. Because that floor is blanketed with lakes, meadows, and gravel, field workers have been unable to ascertain whether or not the underlying bedrock displays the necessary fracturing. But it is central to Muir's argument that Yosemite represents a *type* of valley, not a unique example. As he expresses it a little later on:

Muir and Geology

Nature is not so poor as to possess only one of anything, nor throughout her varied realms has she ever been known to offer an exceptional creation, whether of mountain or valley. When, therefore, we explore the adjacent Sierra, we are not astonished to find that there are many Yosemite valleys identical in general characters, each presenting on a varying scale the same species of mural precipices, level meadows, and lofty water-falls.

Emphasizing a theme destined to recur throughout his works, Muir proclaims that the laws that control the distribution of Yosemites and their most salient characteristics are "as constant and apparent as those governing the distribution of forest trees."

It was his fervent belief in the existence of such laws that permitted Muir to contribute meaningfully to the science of geology. He is therefore able to cite as examples *other* Yosemites in which the bedrock floors of the valley lie more obviously exposed. Furthermore, exposed bedrock exists even in Yosemite itself—at its head and foot, though not its middle. If that middle portion had actually collapsed at some time (as the subsidence theory required), there would have to be clear indications of that foundering along the valley walls, but none appear. Finally, the conspicuous lack of talus within the valley had required proponents of the subsidence theory to argue that such debris must have been removed over a long period of time by natural agents, perhaps into some unique abyss underlying the valley. Muir, on the contrary, replies that the valley's formations are extremely recent, and that no vast quantity of debris has ever existed. Some rock masses, to be sure, *have* fallen but only because of earthquakes; where there is no talus, the valley wall shows glacial striations and polishing—and thus is very young. The idea of a unique abyss, he assumes, is logically absurd. All in all, Muir's demolition of Whitney's theory is an example of his geological reasoning at its best.

Other theorists stressed the role of water in the formation of Yosemite. At present, five important watercourses flow into the valley (often as spectacular falls plunging down its sides).

Dennis R. Dean

For Muir, these rivers and streams are not further excavating the valley floor but rather filling it up. "The granites of Yosemite," he knows, are "but slightly susceptible of water denudation." According to his calculations, "Throughout the greater portion of the main upper Merced Valley the river has not eroded its channel to a depth exceeding three feet since it first began to flow at the close of the glacial epoch." Even so, he admits that all these sources would have been far greater in the past, as melt water from the receding glaciers augmented their volume.

Before the watercourses, five immense glaciers from five to fifteen hundred feet in depth had flowed separately into Yosemite, then united to move throughout the valley with crushing force. Those who admitted to glacial agency sometimes explained their efficacy by postulating the existence of supplementary fissures in the granite, caused either by earthquakes or by the cooling or upheaval of the earth's crust. Because Muir had already pointed out the ubiquitous cleavage planes, however, he required no such hypothesis.

Having refuted three alternative explanations, Muir now presents his own. "*All Yosemites,*" he argues, "*occur at the junction of two or more glacial canyons,*" and are directly related to them. The cross-section of a Yosemite, moreover, is about equal to the sum of the glacial valleys that enter it, and its trend is always "*a direct resultant of the sizes, directions, and declivities of [its] confluent canyons,* modified by peculiarities of structure in their rocks." He would later recall this important rule in Part Three. Despite Yosemite Valley's unusual depth (more than 3,000 feet) juxtaposed cross-sections prove that all of the Yosemite-type valleys are fundamentally alike. Muir also compares their sculptured landforms more specifically, emphasizing Half Dome and El Capitan lookalikes. For him, the morphological similarity so evident in all of these geological examples necessarily implies a common origin.

Part Two, then, expresses a decided preference for gradualistic, uniformitarian geological theories ("Divine, harmonious law") rather than violent, catastrophic ones. Because the tectonic theory of Yosemite Valley's origin (as advocated by Whitney) is of the catastrophic sort—though it would not necessarily have to be—Muir finds Whitney easy to dismiss. He takes it for granted—perhaps wrongly—that the sudden collapse of Yosemite into valley form is regarded by its advocates as a unique (or, perhaps, miraculous) event. The argument that there are other Yosemites is important to Muir because it strongly supports his more general proposition that like causes will create like effects. In his view, Yosemites arise inevitably and even predictably as part of the normal workings of nature.

Part Three, "Ancient Glaciers and Their Pathways," begins with a memorable synopsis:

> Though the ancient glaciers of the Sierra are dead, their history is indelibly recorded in characters of rock, mountain, canyon, and forest; and, although other hieroglyphics are being incessantly engraved over these, "line upon line," the glacial characters are so enormously emphasized that they rise free and unconfused in sublime relief, through every after inscription, whether of the torrent, the avalanche, or the restless heaving atmosphere.[13]

Yosemite, he tells us, was shaped in large part by the confluence of five originally separate glaciers—the Yosemite Creek, Hoffmann, Tenaya, South Lyell, and Illilouette—that together almost completely covered the valley, although at a later stage they were so reduced in volume as to leave its walls mostly bare. "All the ancient glaciers of the Sierra," Muir reminds us, "fluctuated in depth and width, and in degree of individuality, down to the latest glacial days." His descriptions of the five, which follow, are intended to represent them in their senescence, when the sculpting of Yosemite had been nearly accomplished.

The Yosemite Creek glacier, in Muir's reconstruction, was about 14 miles long, 4 miles wide, and often no less than 1,000 feet in depth. He traces its magnificently curved progression from "lofty amphitheatres" in northern portions of the Hoffmann range down to Yosemite Valley and notes changes in both the glacier and its path through time. The main trunk, he believes, disappeared before its tributaries did, leaving the valley floor open for habitation by plants and animals. Retreats of the tributary glaciers, subsequently vanished as well, can be traced in a series of moraines, lake basins, meadows, and streams, all of which are now lush with vegetation.

As for the others, the Hoffmann glacier, a wedge of solid ice 6 miles in length by 4 in width, was primarily responsible for the shaping of Half Dome and adjacent rocks. Tenaya Glacier, about 12 miles long, 2½ miles wide, and more than 1,000 feet deep, gouged a trough 2,000 to 3,000 feet deep while sweeping over ridges as much as 1,200 feet high. The South Lyell glacier, fed by three important tributaries, was about 15 miles long, up to 1½ mile wide, and as much as 1,400 feet deep, but oscillated a good deal. Finally, there was the Illilouette glacier, 10 miles long, almost 5 wide, and only 700 feet or less in depth. The record that it left behind is still exceptionally clear.

Muir then follows these fine glaciers as they combine into a single large one that moves southward through the valley, up, and out. We are again reminded of what he has consistently assumed—"that all the valleys of the region are valleys of erosion, and that glaciers [not running water] were the principal eroding agents." The last few paragraphs of Part Three are appropriately devoted to the relative claims of water and ice. "With glaciers as a key," he assures us, "the secrets of every valley are unlocked. Streams of ice explain all the phenomena; streams of water do not explain any; neither do subsidences, fissures, or pressure plications." This, of course, is what the entire section is about. "Both in shape and sculpture," he concludes even more broadly, *"every Yosemite rock is a glacial monument."*

Part Four, "Glacial Denudation," begins with a general discussion of the water cycle (evaporation-precipitation-transportation) in which the origin of glaciers is explained and their behavior reduced to laws of nature.[14] The three chief categories of glacial phenomena observable in the Sierra, for Muir, are

Muir and Geology

polished or abraded surfaces, moraines, and sculpting of various kinds. Though he describes all three types enthusiastically, Muir emphasizes the scale and permanence of sculpting. For general guidance regarding glacial phenomena, he recommends supposedly "elementary" works by Agassiz, Tyndall, and Forbes but in all cases argues from what he has personally discovered around Yosemite. Such evidence plainly indicates to Muir that "the Sierra, from summit to base, was covered by a sheet of crawling ice, as it is now covered by the atmosphere." The "crushing currents" of that sheet, moreover, "slid over the highest domes, as well as along the deepest canyons, wearing, breaking, and degrading every portion of the surface, however resisting." When one seeks some kind of quantitative understanding as to the work of the ice sheet, however, several problems arise, in part because estimates regarding the length of the Ice Age vary from thousands to millions of years. Muir's best guess, the conclusion to Part Four, is that more than a mile of overburden was removed. The latter half of this chapter must have been extremely controversial.

Part Five, "Post-Glacial Denudation," imagines the differential emergence of a transformed landscape as it is revealed by slowly retreating ice.[15] (The ice sheet withdrew from the base of the range "tens of thousands of years ere it melted from the upper regions," Muir supposes.) Another effective geological force, he reasons, would have been avalanches, some of which were brought on by earthquakes. Astonishingly, he postulates a single post-glacial earthquake that by itself was responsible for no less than nine-tenths of all the cliff taluses now to be seen in Yosemite. In addition to avalanches, there would also be landslips. Muir then comes at last to consider running water, "usually regarded as the most influential of all denuding agents." As the ice sheet melted, streams would be formed at its foot, gradually moving upward with the receding glacier. "The transporting power of steeply inclined torrents," he declares surprisingly, "is far greater than is commonly supposed." They are capable of carrying heavy boulders, and these in turn powerfully grate along the channels in which they are carried. Within their channels, moreover, rivers can (like ice) remove boulders that have been separated from larger masses by cleavage planes. Impressive as the transporting power of streams may be in these rare instances, however, their more usual load consists almost entirely of mud, sand, silt, and gravel.

Atmospheric weathering, because of its universality, has often acted to obscure telltale signs of glaciation by eroding them into unintelligibility. But such erosion works with extreme slowness on hard rocks like granites (of which Yosemite is primarily composed) and so requires more time for its operations than has elapsed since the glacial era. In Muir's estimation, then, postglacial denudation in the Yosemite region probably amounts to no more than about three inches of loss. "From its warm base to its cold summit," he insists colorfully, "the physiognomy of the Sierra is still strictly glacial. Rivers have only traced shallow wrinkles, avalanches have made scars, and winds and rains have blurred it, but the change, as a whole, is not greater than that effected on a human countenance by a few years' exposure to common Alpine storms." Many of his contemporary geologists would have disagreed.

In Part Six, "Formation of Soils," Muir attributes the creation of soil deposits, more than a mile deep on the western slope of the Sierra, to glacial action (rather than rain, avalanches, floods, or earthquakes).[16] As the glaciers retreated, they dropped their loads, creating soil-rich moraines. But other glaciers, together with wind, rain, and the passage of time, carried much of that soil away. He again imagines various kinds of avalanches, together with a first post-glacial earthquake—perhaps only three centuries ago—that by itself "suddenly and simultaneously" deposited thousands of acres of fresh soil. Unlike rivers, which for Muir deposit soils only under special circumstances, glaciers enrich low and high places alike. "Notwithstanding the many august implements employed as modifiers and re-formers of

Muir and Geology

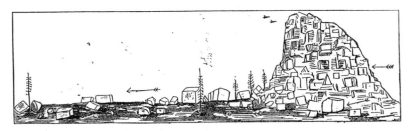

soil," he maintains, "the glacier is the only great producer." Despite the characteristically unsorted nature of moraine deposits, Muir insists that they are manifestations of natural order. "Every soil-atom," he observes, "seems to yield enthusiastic obedience to law—boulders and mud-grains moving to music as harmoniously as the far-whirling planets." Besides such enriching glacial moraines, Muir also recognizes other kinds of soil—derived, for example, from the decomposition of granite or the deposition of volcanic ash from the nearby volcanoes of Mono Lake.

Part Seven, the final one, concerns itself with the much-disputed topic of "Mountain Building." [17] Unlike his contemporaries, however, Muir himself thinks the problem "easily solved by the patient student." Discussing pinnacles, peaklets, and major mountain peaks in turn, he soon establishes that all of them—differing only in scale—were created "not by cataclysmic fissures, but by the gradual development of orderly joints and cleavage planes." It is obvious, therefore, that all were once part of an originally solid mass. In his view, the now missing portions had been carried away by glaciers, not running water. Thus, it is notable that very little debris has been wrested from glacially sculptured rocks during the post-glacial era.

Muir's conclusion to Part Seven sums up his entire series. "No matter how the preglacial mass of the range came into existence," he supposes all of its constituent landforms "owe their

Dennis R. Dean

development to the ice-sheet of the great winter and the separate glaciers into which it afterward separated." "In all this sublime fulfillment," moreover, "there was no upbuilding, but a universal razing and dismantling, and of this every mountain and valley is the record and monument." As throughout the series, Muir will countenance no tectonic arguments of any kind. The Sierra, he is convinced, remains wholly a product of erosion, virtually all of it glacial.

Despite the unconventionality of its presentation, *Studies in the Sierra* is clearly serious geology. As a prospective scientist, what Muir lacked then was the proper audience. That he found the next year when his "Studies in the Formation of Mountains" was published by the prestigious and widely influential American Association for the Advancement of Science (AAAS).[18] Unfortunately, we do not know for sure just what Muir submitted to it, but that considerable editorial revision took place is likely. Three facts seem particularly germane. First, the AAAS "Studies" is an augmented version of the *Overland Monthly*, Part Seven, essay "Mountain-Building." The augmenting includes passages derived from other parts of the series, particularly Four and Five. Second, even the reprinted passages have often been rearranged and are at times significantly abridged or even rewritten. Muir, for example, describes what we now call cirques as "glacial wombs"; "Studies" calls them "glacial amphitheatres." Greater formality and a closer approximation to scientific regularity have been imposed throughout. Third, all of Muir's numerous illustrations, which the *Overland* published, have been deleted here, together with portions of the text that discussed them. The resulting essay is a faithful precis of Muir's ideas that utilizes his own words to the maximum extent possible. It was obviously created from Muir but not altogether by him. Two years later, the same journal published a second paper of his "On the Post-Glacial History of *Sequoia Gigantea*" that includes geological remarks.

The two papers that Muir published with the American Asso-

Muir and Geology

ciation represent—so far as geology is concerned—his closest approach to orthodox professionalism in print. Until the later years of his life, moreover, they were also the last of his publications to deal significantly with the geology of the Sierra. Beginning in 1879, his new "library" of geological phenomena would be the recently acquired American possession of Alaska, which he visited seven times.[19] Two book-length narratives eventually resulted in *The Cruise of the "Corwin"* (1917) and *Travels in Alaska* (1915), as did two specifically geological papers.

The first and more important of these, "On the Glaciation of the Arctic," based upon the *Corwin* reconnaissance of 1881, was published by the United States government in 1884.[20] It then reappeared, slightly revised by Muir before his death, as an appendix to *The Cruise of the "Corwin."* In general, Muir found the glacial abrasions and moraines of Alaska and the Bering Sea region (including a brief visit to Siberia) "much broken and obscured" because strong forces were actively at work upon weak rocks. He found no granites like those of Yosemite. Even so, the shaping power of glaciers upon landscape being so distinctive, it was still possible to trace their paths. In his paper, Muir also surveyed Pacific Coast glaciers in general, beginning with those of the Sierra, then moving northward through the Cascades to British Columbia and southeastern Alaska. The region between Mount Fairweather and Mount St. Elias, he declared, contains more glaciers than any other, perhaps in excess of 5,000. Farther north than that, however, their numbers progressively diminish.

At Glacier Bay, first explored by Muir in 1879, one sees not only the colossal Muir Glacier but part of a more general ice sheet from 1,000 to 3,000 feet thick. "This ice-sheet," he thought, "together with the multitude of distinct glaciers that load the lofty mountains of the coast, evidently once formed part of one grand continuous ice-sheet that flowed over all the region hereabouts, extending southward as far as the Straits of Juan de Fuca;" the islands and coastline in between attest to "a vast press of over-sweeping ice" and "the grinding action of a continuous ice-sheet." In his view, that same offshore labyrinth of channels, straits, and passages had been part of "the general pre-Glacial margin of the continent, more deeply eroded [than the islands], and, therefore, covered with the ocean waters which flowed into them as the ice was melted out of them." In consequence, Muir showed particular interest in fiords, a highly relevant land-form not available to him in California. He was again convinced that "these valleys, fiords, forges, and gaps, great and small, like those of the Sierra, are not a result of local subsidences and upheavals, but of the removal of the material that once filled them." Like the Sierra, Alaska everywhere manifested the shaping power of glaciers whereas the effects of running water seemed negligible. Throughout the *Corwin* voyage, Muir con-sistently read northern landscapes with Sierran eyes, the major thrust of his analyses being to establish that points he had made about glacial phenomena in California genuinely rested upon laws of nature and were therefore equally valid in Alaska or anywhere else. Dealing briefly with other landscapes (mostly offshore islands) that no longer supported glaciers, he thought many of them once had. The Bering Sea, he believed, had for-merly been covered by an ice sheet not less than 2,500 feet thick. Its gradual withdrawal, at the very end of the glacial period, led to the separation of Asia and America. On both continents, Muir also explored sections of tundra, regarding such layers of marshy soil as an originally glacial deposit (from a shrinking ice sheet) subsequently reformed by the running water.

Muir's final geological paper, somewhat derivative from the preceding one, was "Notes on the Pacific Coast Glaciers" (1901), written as his contribution to the remarkable Harriman expe-dition of 1899, on which he accompanied a number of other distinguished American scientists and naturalists.[21] Eschewing any claim to scientific status, Muir modestly identified himself as only a "Student of Glaciers" but was considered their foremost investigator of them anyway—or at least the most vociferous. As John Burroughs joked in his official narrative of the trek,

Muir and Geology

"In John Muir we had an authority on glaciers, and a thorough one—so thorough that he would not allow the rest of the party to have an opinion on the subject." The Indians, Burroughs added, used to call Muir "the Great Ice Chief"; if so, it was a shrewd appellation.

For all the latitude accorded him, however, Muir generally restricted his "Notes" to well written description. Those parts of it dealing with the glaciers and volcanoes of California, Oregon, and Washington were borrowed from his earlier "Glaciation of the Arctic," and his remarks on the distribution of glaciers throughout Alaska likewise reemerged essentially unchanged. At Glacier Bay, the expedition tarried nearly a week, which gave him ample time to discover how much Muir Glacier and the others had diminished since his first visit. As he reported, "the Hugh Miller and Muir [glaciers] have receded about two miles in the last twenty years, the Grand Pacific about four, and the Geikie, Rendu and Carrol perhaps from seven to ten miles." Thus, inlets were longer now and new islands had appeared in the fiords. On the other hand, some buried forests were evidence of recent glacial advances. Muir then repeated almost verbatim the great ice-sheet theory he had originally published in 1884.

For Muir, a highlight of this trip was the expedition's reconnaissance of Prince William Sound, where he had never been. Bold navigating led to the discovery of Harriman Fiord, with which Muir was thoroughly delighted, but for aesthetic rather than scientific reasons. "It is full of glaciers of every description," he rhapsodized, "waterfalls, gardens and grand old forests—nature's best and choicest alpine treasures purely wild—a place after my own heart." By all indications, he thought, Prince William Sound had once been filled by a large glacier, 1,000 years ago or more. Other destinations included Cook Inlet, Kodiak Island, Unalaska, and the Bering Sea; he called the Aleutians a "wonderful chain of volcanoes." On the whole, Alaska, in all seven of Muir's explorations, allowed him the joy of seeing large-scale living glaciers at work, an experience that strongly confirmed many of the observations he had previously made about those once in the Sierra.

Though Muir in his later years visited classic geological sites worldwide, only those involving glaciers left much of an impression upon him. He fully realized that such narrowness of perspective was of limited value in theorizing. But Muir remained his father's child in that respect, as stubborn regarding glaciers as his parent had been about religion. Even when back in the United States, he failed to confront theoretically certain evidence of which he had been thoroughly aware—about the Grand Canyon, for example.[22] And he seems never to have been seriously interested in stratigraphy or fossils, or the early history of man, though such topics were current and had close associations with glaciology. That Muir, despite his lack of formal education, might have been a great geologist seems to me beyond dispute. Why he failed to become one takes us beyond the realm of mere historicizing, but it is not difficult to see that the two chief dogmas of Muirian geology—the ubiquity of natural law and the significance of glaciers—were both somehow reflections of deep-seated psychological needs, the eventual satisfaction of which then required no further explorations.

NOTES

1. Muir's introduction to science took place during his student years at the University of Wisconsin. Prior to 1871, he sometimes identified with botany; geology prevailed thereafter. In 1889 (to Robert Underwood Johnson, 13 September) he described himself as a "poetico-trampo-geologist-bot, ornith-natural, etc." but often preferred "naturalist." Though the word "ecologist" existed during his latter years, he seems never to have used it.

2. John M. Nickles, *Geologic Literature on North America, 1785–1918*, 2 vols. (Washington, D.C.: United States Geological Survey, 1923), I, 768–769. George P. Merrill, *The First Hundred Years of American Geology* (New Haven: Yale University Press, 1924; reprinted New York and London: Hafner, 1969) criticizes Whitney on Yosemite and other issues without ever mentioning Muir.

3. Greeley had himself visited Yosemite in 1859. Anon. [but Muir], "Yosemite Glaciers. The Ice Streams of the Great Valley. Their Progress and Present Con-

Muir and Geology

dition—Scenes among the Glacier Beds," *New York Tribune,* 5 December 1871, p. 8; reprinted in John Muir, *To Yosemite and Beyond: Writings from the Years 1863 to 1875,* edited by Robert Engberg and Donald Wesling (Madison: University of Wisconsin Press, 1980), pp. 76–87. From the latter, I quote p. 80 three times. "Preliminary rambles" is from John Muir to Mrs. Carr, 13 February, 1872 p. 110.

4. Josiah Dwight Whitney et al., *California Geological Survey; Geology, Volume I, Report of Progress and Synopsis of the Field Work from 1860 to 1864* (Philadelphia: Caxton, 1865), pp. 421–423. Also, California Division of Mines and Geology, *The Yosemite Book: A Description of the Yosemite Valley and the Adjacent Regions of the Sierra Nevada, and of the Big Trees of California* (New York: Bien, 1868), p. 73; second through fifth editions, as *The Yosemite Guide-Book* (Cambridge: Welch, Bigelow and Co., 1869, 1870, 1871, and, somewhat revised, though not in its geological portions, 1874). Muir owned a copy of the 1874 edition and had presumably seen earlier ones.

5. John Muir, *Letters to a Friend: Written to Mrs. Ezra S. Carr, 1866–1879* (1915; reprinted, Dunwoody: 1973), p. 107.

6. Samuel Kneeland, "On the Glaciers of the Yosemite Valley," *Proceedings of the Boston Society of Natural History* 15 (1873): 36–47; "Winter Phenomena of the Yosemite Valley," ibid. 15 (1873): 148–151 (also Muir, *To Yosemite,* pp. 113–117); "On the Effects of the Earthquake of March 26, 1872, in the Yosemite Valley," ibid. 15 (1873): 185–186 (also Muir, *To Yosemite,* pp. 119–121). All three of Muir's contributions were excerpted by Kneeland in his *The Wonders of the Yosemite Valley, and of California,* 3rd ed. (Boston: Houghton, Mifflin, 1872), pp. 84–91; the earthquake paper had also appeared in his second edition (1872), p. 78. More polished versions of the latter by Muir can be found in *Our National Parks* (1901) and *The Yosemite* (1912). Muir's earthquake techniques, where not traditional or his own, were those of Robert Mallet.

7. John Muir, "Yosemite Valley in Flood," *Overland Monthly* 8 (April 1872): 347–350 (also Muir, *To Yosemite,* pp. 122–128 [see too pp. 99–100, 111], but the citation is flawed).

8. John Muir, "Twenty Hill Hollow," *Overland Monthly* 9 (July 1872): 80–86, 82; (also John Muir, *A Thousand-Mile Walk to the Gulf,* ed. William Frederic Badè [Boston: Houghton, Mifflin, 1916), pp. 192–212, revised.

9. John Muir, "Living Glaciers of California," *Overland Monthly* 9 (December 1872): 547–549, 548. *American Journal of Science* (series 3) 5 (January 1873): 69–71.

10. John Muir, "Studies in the Sierra," *Overland Monthly* (May 1874–January 1875). The seven parts, cited individually below, were reprinted in the *Sierra Club Bulletin,* 1915–1921. Publication in book form was not achieved until 1950 with *John Muir's "Studies in the Sierra,"* edited by William E. Colby (San Francisco; Sierra Club, 1960, revised edition, 1960, 1968). Both reprintings include minor textual differences. Drafts and other manuscripts (including sketches) pertinent to the entire series and to Yosemite more generally are preserved at the John Muir Center, University of the Pacific, Stockton, California.

11. John Muir, "Mountain Sculpture," *Overland Monthly* 12 (April 1874): 393,

394, 403, 403. Reproduced in part as E. S. Carr (sic), "On Mountain Sculpture in the Sierra Nevada, and the Method of Glacial Erosion," *American Journal of Science* (series 3) 7 (May 1874): 515–516. Authorship corrected, ibid., 8 (1874): 80. William Phipps Blake, "Sur l'action des anciens glaciers dans le Sierra Nevada de Californie et sur l'origine de la vallée de Yo-Semite," *Comptes rendus, Académie des Sciences*, Paris 65 (1867): 179–181 (Blake attended the Paris Universal Exposition of 1867 as California commissioner).

12. John Muir, "Mountain Sculpture.—Origin of Yosemite Valleys," *Overland Monthly* 12 (June 1874): 489–500, 490, 490, 496, 496, 493, 496. It is promised in a footnote (p. 496, but omitted in certain reprints) that "We shall hereafter endeavor to show how glaciers have formed their own channels." That Yosemite Valley is indeed U-shaped was established in John P. Buwalda, "Form and Depth of the Bedrock Trough of Yosemite Valley," *Yosemite Nature Notes* 20 (1941): 89–93; cited in Muir, *John Muir's Studies*, p. 103n.

13. John Muir, "Ancient Glaciers and Their Pathways," *Overland Monthly* 13 (July 1874): 67–79, 67, 67, 74, 78, 79.

14. John Muir, "Glacial Denudation," *Overland Monthly* 13 (August 1874): 174–184, 182. Louis Agassiz, John Tyndall, and James Forbes wrote several books each dealing with glaciers. Works by the first two, annotated and indexed by Muir, are preserved at the John Muir Center.

15. John Muir, "Post-Glacial Denudation," *Overland Monthly* 13 (November 1874): 393–402, 394, 398, 399, 402. He had mentioned "the storms of ten thousands of years" in part four (p. 176). Recollections of the 1872 earthquake appeared in parts two (p. 493) and four (p. 178), but the avalanche of 12 March, 1873, reported here (p. 394) was, for him, caused by erosional weakening and gravity, with no seismic implications.

16. John Muir, "Formation of Soils," *Overland Monthly* 13 (December 1874): 530–540, 536, 539, 540. I follow Colby in emending "farewhirling." In a minor paper of 1866, Whitney had written: "While we have abundant evidence of the former existence of extensive glaciers in the Sierra Nevada, there is no reason to suppose that this ice was to any extent an effective agent in the transportation of the superficial detritus now resting on the flanks of the mountains. The glaciers were confined to the most elevated portions of the ranges, and although the moraines which they have left as evidences of their former extension are often large and conspicuous, they are insignificant in comparison with the detrital masses formed by aqueous erosion," ("On the Absence of the Northern Drift Formation from the Western Coast of North America," *Proceedings of the California Academy of Sciences* 3 (1866): 271–272, 271).

17. John Muir, "Mountain Building," *Overland Monthly* 14 (January 1875): 64–73, 65, 65, 73. Orogeny had long been one of the most controversial topics in nineteenth-century geology. See Mott T. Greene, *Geology in the Nineteenth Century: Changing Views of a Changing World* (Ithaca and London: Cornell University Press, 1982), chapter four, "The Origin of Mountain Ranges: European Debate, 1830–1874," and chapter five, "The Debate in North America, 1840–1873"; Muir, however, is nowhere mentioned.

Muir and Geology

18. John Muir, "Studies in the Formation of Mountains in the Sierra Nevada, California," *Proceedings of the American Association for the Advancement of Science*, 23, part 2 (1875, for December 1874): 49–64. "This paper [published as an "abstract"] was accompanied by a large number of illustrations, and it is greatly to be regretted that the funds of the Association would not permit of their being reproduced as cuts. This has necessitated the abbreviation of portions of the communication, and in justice to the author I must state that he has not read proofs owing to his absence from Oakland, where they were sent.—Editor" (p. 49n); "On the Post-Glacial History of *Sequoia Gigantea*," ibid., 25 (1877): 242–253.

19. The seven visits took place in 1879, 1880, 1881, 1890, 1896, 1897, and 1899 (but none of the full-length biographies lists them all). See Frank Buske, "John Muir's Alaska Experience," *Pacific Historian* 29 (1985): 113–123. The entire double issue is devoted to "John Muir: Life and Legacy," with several essays of geological interest.

20. John Muir, "On the Glaciation of the Arctic and Subarctic Regions Visited by the United States Steamer *Corwin* in the Year 1881," in Calvin L. Hooper, ed., *Report of the Cruise of the U. S. Revenue Steamer* Thomas Corwin *in the Arctic Ocean, 1881* (Washington, D.C.: G.P.O., 1884), pp. 135–147; John Muir, *The Cruise of the Corwin* (Boston and New York: Houghton, Mifflin, 1917), pp. 255–280. My quotations are from the former (pp. 136, 138). At this time, Muir even opposed interpretation of the Aleutian chain as a series of individually uprisen volcanoes; for him, it was simply "a degraded portion of the North Pacific pre-Glacial coast mountains" (p. 137) and therefore the product of glacial erosion.

21. John Muir, "Notes on the Pacific Coast Glaciers," in C. Hart Merriam, ed., *Harriman Alaska Expedition*, 13 vols. (New York, 1901–1914), I, pp. 119–135 (quoting pp. 18, 128, 132, 133); John Burroughs, "Narrative of the Expedition," ibid., pp. 1–118. See also III (1904): G. K. Gilbert, "Glaciers and Glaciation of Alaska," pp. 1–231.

22. Muir's essay, "The Grand Canyon of the Colorado," written in 1902 and published that year in *Century* Magazine (then again in the posthumous *Steep Trails* of 1918) is a fine example of scenic and geological appreciation but does not generalize beyond the canyon itself.

10.
Botanical Exploration of California

from Menzies to Muir (1786–1900) with Special Emphasis on the Sierra Nevada

Nancy G. Slack

Introduction

This article chronicles the botanical exploration of California from the end of the
eighteenth century, when the first botanists
of many nationalities arrived by ship to the end
of the nineteenth century. During this period
a surprising number of people explored California's
seacoasts, valleys, and mountains for plants, recording
their observations and collecting specimens for herbaria
around the world. Some were shipboard surgeon-naturalists,
some were San Francisco physicians for whom botany was a serious avocation. Others were members of government surveys,
horticulturists, and university professors. A surprising number
of them were women. One of these explorers was John Muir.

Early exploration was carried out largely near ports where
shipboard naturalists could spend the time in port exploring for
new plant species. New horticultural species, including California's many endemic tree species found nowhere else in the
world, were the focus of some of the first inland explorers. In
the second half of the nineteenth century, the Sierra was thoroughly explored, first by William Brewer, the official botanist of
the California State Survey and, not long after, by John Muir,
by Berkeley and Stanford botanists, and by famous botanists
visiting California from the east and from England.

The institutions that supported these botanical explorers,
often by providing colleagues rather than funding, are also important. The California Academy of Sciences included a nucleus
of men, and later also women, particularly interested in plants.
By degrees it evolved into a major institution providing the bota-

nist with a library, herbarium and curator, its own journals, as well as a meeting place and often instruction from other members. The California State Legislature played an important part in the funding of a state survey for the exploration of the whole state, primarily for new mineral resources, but for plants and animals as well. The University of California at Berkeley and later Stanford University provided additional resources, including professional employment for botanists. Finally, at the end of the century, the Sierra Club was founded, destined to play a role in the preservation of the discoveries of botanists and other explorers.

This chapter examines the plant explorers and also presents a picture of the exploration itself and of how the explorers camped and traveled in California's varied climate and topography. Important changes occurred during this period, with travel by shipboard, by mule, by railroad, and eventually by automobile. Changes also took place in physiology and laboratory studies in the science of botany toward the end of the nineteenth century, but plant exploration and plant taxonomy, dependent on that exploration, continued to be the most important activity of botanists. Preservation of California's natural heritage, including its plants, became an important movement by the end of the century, a movement in which John Muir had a primary role.

John Muir as Botanical Explorer

The year in which John Muir arrived in California, 1868, was the year of the completion of the transcontinental railroad and of the first University of California classes. Muir, like Brewer before him, made the trip to California by sea, except for the crossing of the Isthmus of Panama. Both were immensely impressed by the tropical forests they saw in Panama. Muir wrote:

> Never shall I forget the glorious flora, especially the first fifteen or twenty miles along the Chagres River. The riotous exuberance of

great forest trees, glowing in purple, red, and yellow flowers, far
surpassed anything I had ever seen of flowering trees.[1]

When Muir got off the boat in San Francisco in 1868 and,
when asked where he wished to go, answered, so it is said, "Anywhere that's wild." He was directed to travel inland via the Oakland Ferry. There he met a young Englishman, a Mr. Chilwell,
who set off with him to Yosemite by a roundabout route. In
Muir's very first writings about California, more botany reflections are found than in most of Brewer's journals and all of King's.
For example:

> in this rich garden pass we gathered many fine grasses and carices,
> and brilliant penstemons, azure and scarlet, and mints and lilies,
> and scores of others, strangers to us

And later:

> At the top of the [Pacheco] Pass I obtained my first view of San
> Joaquin plain and the glorious Sierra Nevada. Looking down from
> a height of fifteen hundred feet, there, extending north and south
> as far as I could see lay a vast flower garden . . . like a lake of
> gold. From the eastern margin of the golden plain arose the white
> Sierra. At the base ran a belt of gently sloping purplish foothills
> lightly dotted with oaks, above that a broad dark zone of conif-
> erous forest, and above this frost zone the lofty mountain peaks,
> clad in snow.

Muir seemed often to take an ecological rather than purely
taxonomic view of the vegetation.

Even more than the uncomplaining Brewer, Muir exalted in
the simple camp life:

> Our bill of fare in camps was simple—tea and cakes, the latter
> made from flour without leaven and toasted on the coals. Chilwell,
> being an Englishman, loudly lamented being compelled to live
> on . . . flour and water, as he expressed it and hungered for flesh;
> therefore he made desperate efforts to shoot something to eat, par-
> ticularly quails and grouse but he was invariably unsuccessful.

Nancy G. Slack

When Muir wrote of the flora, he was very specific, often using Latin names in the absence of common ones. His viewpoint is again ecological:

> Many of the herbaceous plants of the flowing foothills were the same as those of the plain and had already gone to seed. But at a height of one thousand feet or so we found many of the lily family blooming in all their glory, the Calochortus especially . . . and many species of two new shrubs, Ceanothus and Adenostoma. The oaks, beautiful trees with blue foliage and white bark, forming open groves gave a fine park effect. Higher, we met the first of the pines with long gray foliage, large stout cones and widespreading heads like palms. Then yellow pines, growing gradually more abundant as we ascended. At Bower Cave on the north fork of the Merced the streams were fringed with willows and azalea, ferns and flowering dogwood.

Later he and Chilwell followed the Mariposa trail through deep snow and reached Wawona, where their flour sack was refilled and someone gave them a piece of bear meat. Muir wrote:

> We then pushed eagerly on up the Wawona ridge through a magnificent sugar pine forest and into the far-famed Mariposa Sequoia Grove. . . . We soon had a good fire and at supper that night we tasted bear meat for the first time. My flesh-hungry companion ate it eagerly. . . . After supper we . . . gazed enchanted at the vividly illuminated brown boles of the giants towering about us, while the stars sparkled in wonderful beauty above their huge domed heads. We camped here long uncounted days, wandering about from tree to tree, taking no note of time. The longer we gazed the more we admired not only their colossal size, but their majestic beauty and dignity. Greatest of trees, greatest of living things, their noble domes poised in unchanging repose seemed to belong to the sky, while the great firs and pines . . . looked like mere latter-day saplings.

Here is another botanical description, this one from Dry Creek where he was following the sheep in December. The winter rains had just begun.

> Being out every day I had the advantage of watching the coming of every species of plant. Mosses and liverworts, no trace of which

could be seen when dry and crumpled, now suddenly covered the entire plain with a soft velvet robe of living green. Then, at first one by one, the different species of flowering plants appeared, pushing up with marvelous rapidity and bursting into bloom, until all the ground was covered with golden compositae, interrupted and enriched here and there with charming beds of violets, mints, clover, mariposa tulips.[2]

There are many botanical descriptions in Muir's *First Summer in the Sierra*. Often he described plants or at least genera that he had seen before coming to California, but there are also descriptions of plants entirely new to him, many of them California endemics. For example, he wrote early in that summer (June 6, 1869):

I have been examining the curious and influential shrub, *Adenostoma fasciculata* [chamise or greasewood], first noticed about Horseshoe Bend. It is very abundant on the lower slopes . . . forming a dense almost impenetrable growth that looks dark in the distance. It belongs to the rose family, is about six or eight feet high, has small white flowers, round needle-like leaves, and reddish bark that becomes shreddy when old. It grows on sun-beaten slopes, and like grass is often swept away by running fires, but is quickly renewed from the roots. Any trees that may have established themselves in its midst are at length killed by these fires, and this no doubt is the secret of the unbroken character of its broad belts. A few manzanitas, which also rise again from the root after consuming fires, make out to dwell with it, also a few bush compositae—baccharis and linosyris, and some liliaceous plants, mostly calochortus and brodiaea, with deepset bulbs safe from fire. . . . A most admirable plant!

This was a most admirable description of both the plant itself and its fire ecology and community structure; all before ecology was a scientific discipline. He even has some good words for and interesting observations on poison oak (June 7):

Poison oak or poison ivy (*Rhus diversiloba*) both as a bush and a scrambler up trees and rocks, is common throughout the foothill region up to a height of at least three thousand feet above the sea. It is somewhat troublesome to most travelers, inflaming the skin

Nancy G. Slack

and eyes, but blends harmoniously with its companion plants. . . . I
have oftentimes found the curious twining lily (*Stropharium Cali-
fornicum*) climbing its branches. . . . Sheep eat it without ill effects.

He continued, already expounding one of his most persistent
themes: "Like most other things not apparently useful to man,
it has few friends, and the blind question 'Why was it made?'
goes on and on with never a guess that, first of all, it might have
been made for itself."

Later in that first summer, on August 21 he made a "wild
excursion" over Bloody Canyon Pass and observed both plants
and signs of glaciation:

> Early in the morning I tied my notebook and some bread to my
> belt, and stole away full of eager hope, feeling that I was going
> to have a glorious revery. The glacier meadows that lay along my
> way served to soothe my morning speed, for the sod was full of
> blue gentians and daisies, kalmia and dwarf vaccinium, calling for
> recognition as old friends [from Wisconsin and the East], and I
> had to stop many times to examine the shining rocks over which
> the ancient glacier had passed with tremendous pressure, polish-
> ing them so well that they reflected the sunlight like glass in some
> places, while fine striae, seen clearly through a lens, indicated the
> direction in which the ice had flowed.[3]

John Muir did not name the new California plants he collected. Many had already been named by earlier botanical explorers. He sent pieces of some of them to his friend Jeanne
Carr. He sent others to specialists for identification. There were
no Sierra floras in his day. Yet it is clear from these writings that
he knew the plants, at least the genera, well, even in his first year
in the Sierras, and could describe them so that another botanist
including this author, a plant ecologist, can recognize them.

Before examining John Muir's role further as botanical explorer, pioneer ecosystem ecologist, or preservationist of the
Sierra flora, it is necessary to examine the earlier California botanists, some of whom had arrived on these shores by boat and
by land long before Muir was born, some long before California

200

Botanical Exploration of California

was a state. Several of these crossed the Sierra, the territory that Muir was to claim for his own, in search of plants new to science.

Early Botanical Exploration

California became a new center of botanical exploration even before it came under American control. San Francisco had been visited by botanist-naturalists as early as 1786.[4] French naturalists sailing with Jean-François La Pérouse were the first to collect plants there. Archibald Menzies, Scottish surgeon-naturalist with the Vancouver expedition visited both San Francisco and Monterey in 1792. The plants he collected, together with a specimen of the California condor, were sent back to England. Russian ships arrived as early as 1806, and ten years later another Russian ship arrived carrying two naturalists, Johann Friedrich Eschscholtz and Albert von Chamisso. They visited San Francisco in 1816 and again for two months in 1824. Plant collections were made on both voyages and taken back to St. Petersburg. Menzies, Eschscholtz, and Chamisso all found plants new to science on these early trips and gave them names. One of these, the California poppy, was named *Eschscholtzia* by Chamisso. Two beautiful redwood forest shrubs, *Menziesia* or mock azalea, and madrone (*Arbutus menziesii*) were both named for Menzies. Botanical exploration was very exciting in California at that time because so many of the plants found were unknown to science, such as the California poppy which would become the state flower.

These men botanized while their sailing ships were on shore, while others followed, who explored overland, including David Douglas from Scotland, and Thomas Coulter from Ireland. Thomas Nuttall and John Townsend crossed the continent from Missouri in 1834. Both collected in California. Their specimens were sent east to Philadelphia, though some of Nuttall's many important plant collections also ended up in England.

Thomas Nuttall was actually the first trained scientist to

Nancy G. Slack

cross the present United States in 1834. He collected both plants and molluscs on all his American travels, including Hawaii (then the Sandwich Islands) in 1835 and 1836. In the spring of 1836 he arrived in Monterey, then went to San Diego and Santa Barbara. David Douglas, for whom the Douglas fir is named, had collected on the California coast before Nuttall. He had arrived there in 1831 at the age of 32, on his travels for the Horticultural Society of London. Douglas collected many new species in California, some of horticultural value. He was killed three years later while collecting in Hawaii, trampled by a wild bull.

Nuttall was well enough known to be described by R. H. Dana and caricatured by Washington Irving. He also found many new plants, including new genera, on the California coast. Douglas's California journal of his year and a half in California has not been found, but Nuttall's journal is extensive, and his comments on travels, observations, and collections were much quoted by his biographer, Jeanette E. Graustein. Nuttall found many new plant species along the California coast, which he visited by ship like his predecessors. In the vicinity of Santa Barbara, then a village of 700, he even found three new plant genera. Nuttall also observed birds and collected molluscs, including 54 new species of the latter on the California coast. Of Santa Barbara his journal reads:

> The forest trees were new to my view. A magpie chattered from the branches of an Oak with leaves like those of the Holly. A thorny gooseberry, forming a small tree appeared clad with pendulous flowers as brilliant as those of a Fuschia. A new [species of] Plane tree spread its wide arms over the dried up rivulets. . . . The scenery was mountainous and varied, one vast wilderness . . . and the prowling wolves [coyotes], were as tame as dogs, and every night yelled familiarly through the village.[5]

Before 1847 most botanical collectors in California took themselves and their collections back to the east, but the discovery of gold by James Wilson Marshall on the American River that year set off a phenomenal migration to California. Along

Botanical Exploration of California

with the gold seekers came a number of naturalists, some of whom stayed. In 1849, arrivals included John Graham Bell, Dr. John B. Trask, and Dr. Jacob Stillman. The latter collected California plants and sent them to John Torrey as did another 1840s collector, Reverend Augustus Finch.

The Horticultural Collectors

The best-known forty-niner botanist is probably William Lobb, an English horticultural collector for the firm of James Veitch. During the winter of 1852–1853 he scooped the American botanists by hearing about the "Big Tree" from a hunter and finding the trees in the Calaveras Grove. He collected what parts he could, seeds, bark, and cones, and took them back to England. A tree section 115 feet high was put together for the Crystal Palace exposition in London in 1857 where it was called the "Mammoth Tree."

Horticulture continued to be an important motivation for botanical exploration. John Jeffrey collected seeds and plant specimens for his sponsors in Edinburgh. He was in San Francisco in 1853 but disappeared on an expedition after sending back a box of tree seeds in 1854. William Murray, another Britisher, continued his work; conifer seeds in particular were much in demand by British gardeners. Murray, together with a local botanical collector, A. F. Beardsley, traveled through the Sierra Nevada in the 1850s collecting conifer seeds.

Yet another Britisher, Thomas Bridges, came to California in 1856 and collected in the Sierra Nevada. He collected the bulbs of the Washington lily, which blooms in July and August at 4,000–7,000 feet in the Sierra. It was named *Lilium washingtonianum*, by Albert Kellogg, who probably found it first. Bridges's lily specimens never reached England but were lost at sea.[6]

Nancy G. Slack

The Early Government Surveys

Even before the 1850s, paid positions for botanists existed in the west. The great exploring expeditions and surveys made the federal government itself the "foremost information collecting instrument."[7] This information included plants as well as other resources. Along with the Army Topographical engineers, largely employed to make surveys and maps, were surgeon-naturalists and other civilians to collect plants and animals. Spencer Baird of the Smithsonian Institute equipped naturalists for these expeditions and even paid some of them. Others worked with the collections after they returned, separating these botanists from the "collectors" in the field who often worked in rough and even dangerous territory. "Experts" at the Smithsonian, Harvard, and elsewhere examined the collections and reported on them. Sometimes the expedition officers themselves did the collecting. Most of these collections came back to Cambridge, and sets were sent to many herbaria in the east and in Europe; there were none in California or elsewhere in the west as yet.

Historian Anderson Hunter Dupree referred to these surveys as graduate schools for an entire generation of naturalists, but these "graduate students" were paid; salaries of $60 to $130 per month were quoted for one such survey, respectable salaries for 1858. Botanical collectors C. C. Parry, Charles Wright and John Bigelow all took part in the Mexican Boundary Survey.[8]

These men were neither uneducated nor inexperienced at plant collection. Some had excellent credentials. Wright, for example, had graduated from Yale and had already been on two expeditions in Texas, one during the Mexican War and another accompanying United States troops to Western Texas. He had brought back new plants described in Smithsonian publications. On the early surveys he was not paid although the army carried his collecting equipment. On the Boundary Survey he was paid as a botanist and surveyor, one of the first botanical collectors to be paid specifically to do botany. Wright went on to collect in Hong Kong, Japan, and Cuba as well as in California.

204

Charles Wright, Professional Plant Collector. Archives,
Gray Herbarium, Harvard University,
Cambridge, Mass., U.S.A.

Botanists also took part in the great railway surveys of the 1850s. Six potential cross-continental routes from the Mississippi to the Pacific were surveyed by army-civilian teams. Jefferson Davis, then secretary of War, secured a $150,000 appropriation for this work. Surveys included all kinds of resources of the country traversed including zoology , botany, and Indian tribes.[9] The railway provided a wealth of scientific data for the whole west, and the results were published promptly, within seven years, providing more work for civilian specialists, botanists among them. They were also printed in large quantities and well circulated, later proving useful to indigenous western botanists, including the Californians. Later in the nineteenth century much botanical exploration was also done along these routes by California botanists with free railroad passes.

Naval expeditions also included civilian botanists; Charles Wright went to Japan with one, bringing back plants that would enable Asa Gray to provide his own data for Darwin's theories. The Coast Survey under Alexander Bache was probably the most important continuing federal government scientific undertaking. The exploring expeditions were temporary by contrast, but they also funded civilian scientists. The Coast Survey, originally funded for chart making on the East and Gulf coasts, expanded to include many branches of science. It also expanded from the Atlantic coast and the Gulf of Mexico to the Pacific when Oregon became a territory and California was acquired. Botanists, including Albert Kellogg, a founder of the California Academy of Sciences, were included on these western coast surveys. Collections from that survey at least did not all go to the east; some stayed in California.

The California Academy of Sciences

Thus, the first half of the nineteenth century included much activity by botanists and other naturalists. Still, in 1850, naturalist John LeConte, brother of Joseph LeConte, who was later to be Berkeley's first botany professor, could write about California to a friend in the east: "the climate is heavenly . . . San Francisco is damnable . . . a scientific man is completely lost and useless in this country." [10]

In 1853, the California Academy of Sciences, the most important scientific, and particularly botanical institution of this period in the West, was founded in San Francisco. It was founded by five physicians, a realtor, and a colonel. The latter, Thomas Nevins, had earlier convinced the San Francisco Common Council to establish a free public school system. For twenty years the Academy meetings were held in his office.

Many plant specimens came to the Academy in the 1850s and 1860s, largely through the efforts of Dr. Kellogg, an eastern physician who came to California in 1849. He had a pharmacy business and secondarily a medical practice. He was an important founding member and supporter of the Academy. Support for the institution and for its publications at that time came entirely from the professional earnings of the members.

By 1860 serious botanical exploration and collection had begun in California. Kellogg took part in the 1867 United States Coast Survey to Alaska. This time, while one set of specimens went to the National Herbarium in Washington and another to Philadelphia, a third set remained in the West, going to the California Academy. In the 1860s Kellogg and another Academy member, William Harford, collected plants in California and Oregon and sent sets to Torrey and Gray and to European herbaria, as well as adding to the collections of the Academy, which also had a good botanical library, including the first California flora by Dr. Hans Behr.

Some of the new California botanists were not forty-niners but forty-eighters who came as political refugees to this country after the failure of the 1848 revolutions in Europe. One of these was Behr, a physician trained in Berlin who had emigrated to California. He taught at the new California College of Pharmacy, collected plants, and wrote a *Flora of San Francisco* for his students. He joined the California Academy in 1854 and was associated with it for most of his remaining fifty years.[11]

Behr served as mentor to a number of botanists including Kate Curran, better known as Kate (Curran) Brandegee, a physician who became the Academy's first professional curator.[12] She was the first woman curator in a paid position in the United States. The California Academy had voted at one of its early meetings in 1853 to "approve the aid of females in every department of natural history" and "invite their cooperation." It was not until 1878, however, that the first seven women became members.[13]

William Brewer and the California State Survey

1860 was another landmark year in the professionalization of science in California. In that year the State Legislature authorized a geological survey of the state, and appointed a state geologist, Josiah Whitney. The 1860 act appointing the state geologist directed him to appoint assistants and, in addition to the geological survey of the whole state, to provide a scientific description of "botanical and zoological productions, together with specimens of the same."[14] Whitney wrote to his father that he had "found the state of California a prodigiously large place," and that with twice the staff he might complete the task in about 450 years![15]

William Brewer was appointed his principal assistant in charge of the botanical department. Brewer had good scientific credentials for 1860. He had been a graduate of the first class of the Sheffield Scientific School in 1852 and had studied chemistry in Europe with Justus von Liebig and Robert Wilhelm Bunsen. He was 32 when he was hired for the California State Survey.

Brewer traveled 3,600 miles as he and Whitney visited forty counties of the state. He has left us excellent accounts of his explorations. His field notebooks are at the Bancroft Library at

Botanical Exploration of California

William Brewer, California State Botanist, in the field about 1864.
Reprinted from Farquhar, *Up and Down California in 1860–1864*.
© 1949 The Regents of the University of California.

Nancy G. Slack

Berkeley. Hundreds of his letters are in the Yale Archives and Francis P. Farquhar collected many of his letters, written in the field, often by firelight or candlelight, into a narrative called *Up and Down California*. [16] The letters tell a great deal about how the expedition was run and of the organization of field parties which he led, but less than one would like to know about the plant life he studied. Nevertheless, the methods of exploration are of great interest.

Farquhar characterizes Brewer as "first and last a farmer," one who was able to keep going through all kinds of adversities of weather and who enjoyed hard labor. He, indeed, grew up on a farm near Ithaca, New York, and went to Yale originally to study agricultural chemistry for one year. He stayed longer, taught in several schools, receiving his bachelor's degree in 1852. He was a college professor in Pennsylvania when he was appointed to the California survey. [17]

Brewer's letters are generally not very literary. He was not John Muir or even Clarence King, who wrote about his adventures with Brewer and the Survey for the *Atlantic Monthly*. Brewer's were "an unabridged, undecorated record of the times, replete with significant facts."

Brewer's letters do, however, contain some wonderful descriptions, as with his first sight of the Sierra in 1861 from above the San Joaquin Valley not many years before John Muir saw them, Brewer wrote:

> In places we could see the Snows of the Sierra Nevada glittering in the sun through the veil of dust that hung between us. They looked grand and sublime in the faint outlines we could see and appeared ten or twelve thousand feet high.

and shortly thereafter, on a day of botanical collecting:

> Last night I returned on foot to a cragged ridge 1500 or 2000 feet above camp for specimens. . . . The sun set while I was there coloring with orange light the barren mountains north and east and even showing plainly the snowy Sierra in the distance. The view was glorious but desolate as a desert. [18]

Botanical Exploration of California

The next time we hear about the Sierra he has been invited to lecture in Stockton, where "I was well received, hospitably entertained and had a good time generally—got tall puffs in the three daily papers for my lecture." He also visited the State Lunatic Society there and noted that California had a far higher percentage of insane people than any other state, which he attributed to the effect of gold rush fever on miners and their families. He reported a "good house for so small a place" for his lecture, but had to refuse all pay except for traveling expenses, an oyster and champagne supper at the mayor's house, and "fifteen dollars toward the botanical wants of the Survey" [19]

One gets a good picture of Brewer in the field, walking up 4,000–foot peaks carrying a barometer, clearing trails, recommending the "luxury of camp life" including sleeping on gravel stones and eating bacon and beans. He was sleeping near an easy tree to climb after seeing an "exceeding abundance" of grizzly tracks. He had bet a co-worker a keg of beer "to be drunk at the first place where it could be got that we would neither hear nor see a bear that night." He won the beer; a bear passed within 100 feet during the night but no one woke.[20]

In May of 1863 the Survey members planned a trip across the mountains to Aurora via Yosemite. Brewer rode to the Big Trees, the celebrated Calaveras Grove referred to earlier. Here he does describe the botany, as always primarily interested in trees.

The way is mostly through an open forest and there is nothing to indicate the near presence of any such vegetable wonders . . . until crossing a little hill, one enters the valley and the grove [and sees] two faithful sentinels . . . and huge ones they are.

There are about ninety trees of this species in this grove which is in a valley sheltered from the winds. The prevailing trees are sugar pine, pitch pine, false cedar (called here *arbor vitae*), Douglas spruce and silver fir—all of which grow to a large size, often over two hundred feet high and ten feet in diameter, so the "big trees" always disappoint the visitor. . . . On acquaintance they grow on the mind so that in a day or two they can be appreciated in all of their gigantic proportions. . . . I measured over a dozen.

The largest one he measured was 82 feet in circumference. Many of them were three hundred feet high; a fallen one was 116 feet around and over 400 feet high. A tree had been felled a few years before, which took four men twenty-seven days to get down. Rings were counted on this tree. It proved to be 1,225 years old. Brewer commented: "It is remarkable that the wood should be sound that was already over eight hundred years old when Columbus set out on his voyage of discovery. Brewer reported that large numbers of seeds had been sent to Europe and that one English nursery had over 200,000 young trees.[21]

Brewer, Whitney, and Charles Hoffman, the long-time expedition topographer, planned to cross the Sierra via Yosemite Valley by the Coulterville Trail and return by the Sonora. Two pack-mules carried provisions and blankets. They had tin cups, a coffee pot, a tin pail to cook beans in, dishpan, and a frying pan to fry meat and bake bread. They did not carry a tent but did have two barometers and other instruments. The days were hot, but Brewer wrote that "ice froze on their blankets" when they camped out at night. After camping at 6,000 feet at Crane Flat, they found another grove of big trees but not so large—only twenty feet in diameter. Then they crossed the river and camped directly in front of the great Yosemite Falls. He wrote: "the first thing we see in the gray dawn of morning, the last thing at night,"

> Yosemite Valley is not only the greatest natural curiosity in this state but one of the most remarkable in the world. . . . The stream is so large that it cannot be forded here. I tried it two days ago but . . . my horse was carried off his feet. We had to swim and got a good wetting. . . . The Bridal Veil Fall is in front. It is a stream larger than Fall Creek in Ithaca, and falls clear in one leap over eight hundred feet!

He then discussed Cathedral Rock, nearly 4,000 feet high and Tutucanula, a 3,600–foot bluff of granite, which he measured. He described it as nine cliffs the height of Taughannock Falls in Ithaca piled on top of each other.

Botanical Exploration of California

Brewer went on to describe Sentinel Rock, Half Dome, and Vernal Fall. He climbed Nevada Fall and measured it to see if the heights previously given were correct. "Few visitors ever attempt it," he wrote. He reported also measuring the 2,600–foot Yosemite Fall after a terribly hard climb, exciting from its danger. They got back after "fourteen and a half hours of severe fatigue."

Shortly thereafter at Soda Springs he wrote on a restful Sunday: "I have attended to my botanical specimens, baked two loaves of bread, washed my clothes, and am at last ready for writing." At one of their campsites they got news of the progress of the Civil War from another party. They froze in late June at a campsite three miles from the summit of Mono Pass at almost 10,000 feet. From there they started over rocks, ice, and snow for an unexplored peak that turned out to be over thirteen thousand feet high, and saw fifty more unknown peaks over twelve thousand feet. To the east lay Mono Lake, an inland sea surrounded by high deserts. They found the first traces of ancient glaciers on the Pacific slope.

At this point he made what he called a "digression" and discussed the vegetation:

> As we leave the plain where there are but few trees, the grass is already dry and withered. In the foothills to the height of four thousand feet, there are scattered oaks and pines. Above this come the fine forests of gigantic trees, all evergreen. Oaks have disappeared, and in their places are pitch pine, sugar pine, false cedar and some Douglas spruce. Above this at six thousand to seven thousand feet are the noble fir and silver fir; . . . at nine thousand feet a scrubby pine (*Pinus contorta*) is almost the only tree. Above nine thousand feet a low scrubby pine, *Pinus flexilis,* comes in and extends up to eleven thousand feet or more but is a mere shrub. It will grow where fifty feet of snow falls on it every winter and lies on it for seven months of the year. . . .
>
> Above this peculiar alpine plants come in, all very small, which extend to the summits of the highest peaks here, a little over thirteen thousand feet. . . . Snow is abundant above 10,000 feet. I have collected over a hundred species of mountain plants.

213

Brewer stated at the end of this Sierra trip that though he found glacial striae, there is "now no glacier in this state—the climatic conditions do not exist."[22] He and Whitney were wrong; John Muir discovered active glaciers in the Sierra in 1870, and many have been found since in California.

Brewer met several other botanists on his survey travels. One of them was Dr. William Hillebrand, born in Westphalia, who had visited Australia, the Philippines, and then California. He had gone to Hawaii in 1844 and stayed more than twenty years, serving as physician to King Kamehameha V. He made important studies of Hawaiian plants, and in 1888 wrote a flora of the Hawaiian Islands still in use.[23] Hillebrand was visiting California and came along on one of Brewer's trips to the Big Trees and the Sierra foothills in July of 1863, carrying his package of collecting papers. He collected plants included in the state survey as did others such as William Holden, also mentioned by Brewer.

Brewer noted in one of his letters from the expedition that he had met A. F. Beardsley, mentioned above, in a tavern in the Napa Valley in the course of his botanical travels. He was invited home for a glass of real cider and was quite surprised to find that this "hired man" on a ranch had rare and expensive botanical works. Beardsley was one of a number of California residents who did not have professional botanical positions but made some money collecting seeds of California plants, particularly conifers, for English and Scottish gardens. Beardsley, who made wine and cider and sold fruit for a living at this time, was apparently quite a knowledgeable and sophisticated botanist.[24]

Brewer also met the English botanist, horticulturist and ornithologist, Thomas Bridges, cited above. Bridges had come to California in 1856 and collected specimens for nine years, on the coast and in the Sierra Nevada. Brewer ran into Bridges in 1863 in an aspiring mining town near Ebbetts Pass in the Sierra in 1863. He wrote:

> It was a relief to meet Mr. Bridges, an old rambler and botanical collector well known to all botanists. A relief . . . to talk botany;

Botanical Exploration of California

yet even he is affected—he has dropped botany and is here specu-
lating in mines. "Mining fever" is a terrible epidemic. . . . Yet a *few*
[italics his] become immensely rich.[25]

Not Bridges. He went back to botany but his luck was not good
there either; two years later he died at sea on a collecting trip to
Nicaragua.[26] After his death his wife gave many of his California specimens to the National Herbarium in Washington, where
they eventually became part of the second volume of the Botany
of the California Geological Survey. A beautiful Yosemite pen-
stemon as well as a lupine were named for him.

Brewer himself, meanwhile, was collecting everywhere. By
the end of the first year of the Survey he had traveled 2,600 miles
on horse and muleback, 1,000 more on foot. He and Whitney
had visited forty of the forty-six counties of the State. In August
of 1863 he wrote, "Professor Whitney and I climbed the Silver
Mountain, . . . a very rugged climb. It is . . . the highest in the
region. . . . I collected some fine alpine plants and, curious [sic]
enough, . . . myriads of red bugs—beetles—red and brilliant—
a pint could easily be collected." [27]

Brewer kept meticulous field notes during the entire expedition in a series of very small notebooks. In these he wrote
specimen numbers and careful botanical descriptions of each of
the plants he collected, many of which were unknown to him. In
some cases he did not even know the plant family. These notes
indicate, that Brewer, although a good botanical explorer and
meticulous collector, was not an accomplished botanist. John
Muir, who arrived before the end of the decade, knew California
plants much better.

Clarence King, a youthful member of the California Survey and later director of the U. S. Geological Survey, wrote
articles about his mountain adventures (as cited above) for *Atlantic Monthly* and also the *Overland Monthly* starting in 1871, later
published in book form. His literal, colorful descriptions introduced many Easterners to the Sierra Nevada. A follower of John
Ruskin, King seemed to view nature, including the vegetation,

as a work of art. He painted the landscape in many-colored prose that seem more like semi-abstract watercolors than the more specific if romanticized oils of Bierstadt.

Describing the conifer forests from south to north he wrote, "At one extremity are magnificent purple shafts ornamented with an exquisitely delicate drapery of pale golden and dark blue green; at the other the slender spars stand crowded together like the fringe of masts girdling a prosperous port." He described an oasis in the desert approaching the Sierra from the east: "with its . . . bright parterre in which were minute flowers of turquoise blue, pale gold, mauve and rose, and its two graceful palms, this oasis evoked a strange sentiment." Near Kings River canyons he described

> forests, dense and unbroken, green to the base of our cliff. The southern sunlight reflected from its polished foliage gave to this whole sea of spiry tops a peculiar golden green, through which we looked down among giant red and purple trunks upon beds of bright mountain flowers. . . . The granite flushed with rosy brightness between the fields of glittering golden snow.

The mill people and Indians near Thomas's Mill told him about a group of giant sequoias, and especially one tree, which King later measured as forty feet in diameter and two hundred and seventy-four feet high. He later measured it and wrote:

> The bark, thick but not rough . . . is of brightest cinnamon color mottled in purple and yellow. That which impresses one most after its vast bulk and grand pillar-like stateliness, is the thin and inconspicuous foliage, which feathers out delicately on the boughs like a mere mist of pale apple-green.

When he went on to describe its companion trees, color became all-important:

> a sugar pine (*Pinus lambertiana*) of about eight feet in diameter and hardly less than three hundred feet high . . . delicate purplish-blue in hue . . . [the branches] well covered with dark yellow-green needles. The two remaining were firs (*Picea grandis*) . . . whose load of polished blue-green foliage, for the most part, hid

Botanical Exploration of California

the dark wood-brown trunk . . . the foliage and trunk of each separate tree contrasts finely—cinnamon and golden apple-green of
the Sequoia, dark-purple and yellowish green for the pine, deep
wood-color and blueish green of the fir.

King, a geologist rather than a botanist, painted observant word
pictures of trees but largely ignored other plants, apart from the
mountain gooseberry (possibly *Ribes roezellii*) that he claimed
saved his life on his difficult ascent of Mount Tyndall:

My shoulder struck against the rock and threw me out of balance;
for an instant I reeled over upon the verge and seized a small
alpine gooseberry-bush, the first piece of vegetation we had seen.
Its roots were so firmly fixed in the crevice that it held my weight
and saved me.

Contrary to both John Muir and Alice Eastwood (see below)
who waxed both lyrical and scientific about the flora of Mt.
Shasta, King mentioned only one unidentified yellow flower:

A few scanty bunches of alpine plants began to deck the grey earth
and gradually to gather themselves in bits of open sward, here
and there decorated with delicate flowers. Near one little spring
meadow we came upon gardens of a pale yellow flower with an
agreeable aromatic perfume.

King was, however, more scientific about his geology and
gave memorable descriptions of the people he met, both white
and Native American. He was celebrated for the fossil he found
"in the bottom of Hell's Hollow, a canyon whose profound
uninterestedness is quite beyond portrayal." He was perhaps
goaded to continue his exploration of this dull place by the senior
paleontologist of the survey who said of him, "I believe that
fellow had rather sit on a peak all day and stare at those snow
mountains, than find a fossil in the metamorphic Sierra." Find a
fossil he did:

Jagged outcrops of slate cut through vulgar gold-dirt at my feet.
Picking up my hammer to turn homeward, I noticed in the rock
an object about the size and shape of a small cigar. It was the fos-

Nancy G. Slack

sil, the object for which science had searched and yearned and despaired! . . . a plump pampered cephalopoda . . . whom the terrible ordeal of metamorphism had spared. The age of the gold-belt was discovered!

Many years later King was introduced to an old German paleontologist who said: "Ach! . . . I have pleasure you to meet, when it is you which the cephalopoda discovered has."

King also provided one of the first reports on the ancient flora of California from plant fossils:

During the Cretaceous and Tertiary periods, the entire basin from the Rocky mountains to the Blue Mountains of Oregon, was a fresh-water lake. . . . Enough relics of the land vegetation remain to indicate a flora of subtropical climate. Living among these subtropical plants were animals now associated with Africa, including elephants and camels.[28]

Botanical and geological exploration in the high Sierra was not exactly comfortable. Occasionally hotels of sorts were found but the collectors do not seem to have ever carried tents. Brewer wrote from 10,000 feet in the Sierra:

You cannot imagine how uncomfortable it is without any shelter. I stayed in camp alone, while Dick and King went out to shoot a bear, [for food] if they could. At about noon it began to snow violently and it continued all the afternoon. The boys came back wet and numb with the cold, but I had made a big kettle of soup, which was pronounced an eminent success. We made our preparations for an uncomfortable night.[29]

Brewer noted that it was hard to write because his fingers were so cold. It had been reported, moreover, that hostile Indians who had been driven out of Owens Valley were somewhere near.

Brewer rarely complained in his letters. One can almost feel his exhilaration just to be there. He made the first ascent of what was to be Mount Brewer, found trees at elevations as high as 11,500 feet and wrote, "Such a landscape! A hundred peaks in sight over thirteen thousand feet, cliffs in every directions almost rivaling Yosemite, sharp ridges almost inaccessible to man, on which [a] human foot has never trod." In addition to his beloved peaks, he never lost his enthusiasm for California trees. Of the redwood forest near Crescent City he wrote at the end of 1863:

> the redwood is a sort of gigantic cedar. . . . The forest is narrow, and mostly made up of gigantic trees—large groups of trees, each ten to fifteen feet in diameter, and over two hundred feet in height, the straight trunks rising a hundred feet without a limb. The bark is very thick and lies in great ridges, so that the trunks seem like gigantic fluted columns supporting the dense canopy of foliage overhead. . . . They grow so dense that the sun cannot penetrate through the dense and deep mass of foliage above. A damp shady atmosphere pervades the forests. . . . The wood is so durable that a century may elapse before the fallen giant decays and mingles with its mother earth. . . . Mosses accumulate in the hollows and nooks, bushes, and ferns take root and grow . . . among the trees to a great height, trailing lichens festoon from the branches.[30]

A year earlier, however, Brewer had objected to the use of the redwood as a Christmas tree: "yet to me, as a botanist, it looks exotic." He was homesick for the snowy Christmas of his childhood. In addition, Brewer atypically complained in a letter home in August 1863 of "the same old trouble about getting money."

If Whitney had been as good a politician as was geologist James Hall in New York, the California state legislature might have more amply funded the Survey and for a longer period. Hall convinced the State of New York that even paleontology and other noncommercial aspects of geology were worthy of state funding. The California legislature, however, had funded its state survey in order to find lucrative mining sites rather than the fossils and new plants and animals that were discovered. When no such lucrative sites were found, funds for the California Survey were not easily forthcoming. Brewer wrote home that the state owed Professor Whitney about $25,000, including all the unpaid salaries, and that Whitney "has borrowed until he cannot raise any more. . . . I have to borrow for my personal expenses. I am tired of it. . . . It is infamous," Brewer wrote, "political hacks get their money more regularly. . . . We must wait, as our bills have less 'political significance' as the comptroller calls it."

Meanwhile, as a result of the Morrill Act, Yale received funds for a new professorship. "If the place is offered me I shall surely accept it, gladly," Brewer wrote, "and next year will turn my back to the Pacific, and my face eastward and homeward once more." It was offered and by November 1864, he was headed home on the steamer, *America*. [31]

Brewer spent the rest of his professional life at Yale, although he did return to California much later to serve with John Muir on a forestry commission. He identified and wrote up, together with Sereno Watson, some of his California botanical finds while visiting the Gray Herbarium at Harvard but without any funding from the California legislature.

The legislature funded only three reports; others had to be privately funded, including Brewer's botanical volume. That natural history had its private patrons in California as elsewhere in the United States [32] is shown by the names of those involved in funding these publications: Judge S. C. Hastings, Leland Stanford, and Alexander Agassiz.

After the departure of Brewer for Yale, Henry Bolander became California's state botanist. Bolander was born in Germany and came to Columbus, Ohio, at the age of fifteen. Two very important botanists were already there, William Sullivant and his protegé, Leo Lesquereux. Bolander became Lesquereux's protegé, and in 1861 arrived in San Francisco where he served as state botanist from 1864 to 1873. He botanized all over the state including the Sierra, paid attention to lesser known groups, especially grasses and mosses, and made California plants known in European herbaria. Over 1,000 species that he had personally collected can be found in the Geneva herbarium alone.

"J. G. Lemmon and Wife" and California's Women Botanists

John Lemmon, a prisoner of the Confederacy during the Civil War, went to California in 1866, explored the Sierra for plants, married Sara Plummer, and started the "Lemmon Herbarium" at their house in Oakland. The two of them were a botanical couple, collecting in the Mount Shasta region and the San Bernadino Mountains, making up sets of specimens. He published a guide to the conifers of California. The labels on their specimens often said "J. G. Lemmon and wife."

Other women also took part in the early botanical exploration of California. Rebecca Merritt Austin came to California to the gold mines in Plumas County in 1865. Lemmon saw her plant specimens there, displayed in a soap box herbarium case. Later her family moved to Butterfly Valley where she studied the pitcher plant, *Darlingtonia*. She did experiments feeding the pitchers pieces of meat, about which she corresponded with eastern and European botanists, and she eventually published some results. New California species were named both for her and for her daughter, a botanist known only as Mrs. C. C. Bruce. According to Willis Jepson, who included Rebecca Austin in his early series of "The Botanical Explorers of California," she collected a number of species in Butte, Plumas, Lassen, and Modoc Counties that even more than sixty years later were not found again in that region or even in all of California.[33]

A later and more famous California botanical couple were Kate Curran Brandegee and Townshend S. Brandegee Kate Curran, an early California medical graduate, studied botany at the California Academy and, as mentioned above, became its curator in 1883. She was the editor of a botanical journal, *Zoe*, in which she published her own botanical discoveries and those of others and also wrote many reviews.

Townshend Brandegee had come to California originally to collect tree trunks for the American Museum of Natural History.

Nancy G. Slack

In 1889 he married Kate Curran; they are said to have walked and collected plants on a honeymoon that started in San Diego and ended in San Francisco. Each collected plants widely, but mostly separately, for many years. Kate Brandegee made extensive journeys into the Sierra by stage and on foot and also used the free railroad passes available to botanists after the completion of the transcontinental railroad in 1869. She wrote to Townshend from a solo trip she made, stating: "Tomorrow I leave on the stage for the Giant Forest where I will be for nearly a week. Then I try to get higher—with a packer guide and finally fetch up across country to Mineral King. It may be 3 or 4 weeks before I reach there." The next letter was on the way to Alta Meadows which she described as "a great deal higher." [34]

The Brandegees made a trip to lower California (Baja California) together with Academy expedition leader Gustavus Eisen, which was reported on in the *San Francisco Chronicle*, with the title "Off on an Odd Expedition" subtitled "Two Men and a Woman Chasing after Snakes and Bugs." It reads:

> After a week's stay at the village on the Cape a mule train was organized and with a couple of guides and . . . some boys to help chase butterflies and bugs, the scientists started for the mountains where Mr. and Mrs. Brandegee were to begin their real botanical work. Mrs. Brandegee on this trip rode astride of her mule, man fashion in the pantalooned suit that she took with her for the purpose. Her strong leather leggings were found to be a wise precaution for in passing through the thorny cactus regions, the narrow defiles of the mountains or the washed out canyon trails the mules cannot be induced to estimate on more that the exact width of their own bodies.[35]

The best-known woman botanist in California in the late nineteenth and early twentieth century was Alice Eastwood, famous for rescuing botanical specimens in the 1906 earthquake and fire. She had taken Alfred Russell Wallace up Pike's Peak in Colorado in 1887, a trip he described in *My Life*. She first came to California in 1890, became Kate Brandegee's protegé and successor as curator, explored the coast ranges, and climbed Mt. Whitney at the turn of the century. She published an early handbook of California trees and rebuilt the Academy herbarium after the disastrous fire. She was also a friend and correspondent of John Muir, as will be discussed.

The University of California

In 1868 another institution important to botany was established, the University of California, whose early botanical history has been written by Lincoln Constance. It was first housed in Oakland and the first person to teach botany there was Joseph LeConte, a physician with a Harvard degree in geology under Louis Agassiz. LeConte was a professor in South Carolina but after the Civil War he made California his adopted state. In 1870 he made his first trip to Yosemite and across the High Sierra to lakes Mono and Tahoe, a six-week trip with eight students. In Yosemite LeConte met John Muir whom he called "a gentleman of rare intelligence" and considered the greatest authority on the geology and botany of the Sierra. Muir led the group to Mono Lake and Tenaya Lake; the two shared geological interests as well and discussed the effects both believed glaciers had produced on the landscape. LeConte and Muir continued to meet over the years, Muir providing LeConte with both geological and "detailed botanical information on the flora of the region." [36]

In 1873 the University moved from Oakland to the new campus at Berkeley that had two buildings only. The total Berkeley enrollment was 228 in 1875. In that year, the College of Agriculture and the Agricultural Experiment Station were established, and a German agronomist, Eugene Hilgard, taught botany from 1875 to 1882.

Many other botany courses were taught in spite of the small enrollment. Economic Botany was taught by Charles Bessey, visiting from the University of Iowa. Forestry was taught by Bolander, Field Botany by Gibbons and Kellogg, and lower plants by Harkness. The latter four were all Californians and members of the Academy of Science, Gibbons and Kellogg being charter members. Bessey wrote of Berkeley at this early period (1875):

> Arriving in Oakland we were advised that it would be best for us to find quarters in town rather than to attempt to do so in Berkeley then only a much scattered village of but a few people. A horse car ran toward Berkeley at long intervals. . . . A couple of miles out in the country it stopped . . . and the passengers were obligated to wait on an open platform for a smaller car drawn by a single mule at a very slow pace. . . . We crossed the brook on a plank and walked . . . to the two buildings which housed the University. . . . I think it took a full hour to make the trip from Oakland to Berkeley.[37]

The 1884 report of the president of the University of California recommended a botany department with a professor at $3,000 a year, an assistant at $600, and expenses of $200 a year. The latter were to be used for the "formation of a large herbarium." Edward Lee Greene was hired as "Instructor in Botany" in 1885.[38] He was probably the most avid California plant collector within the time period under consideration, and certainly the most controversial.

Edward Lee Greene and the Independence of California Botanists

Greene's life story is well known, most recently described by Robert P. McIntosh.[39] In short, he was born in 1843 in Rhode Island, read Almira Lincoln Phelps's botany text as a child, and moved to Wisconsin at seventeen. There he became the protégé of Thure Kumlien, an Uppsala graduate, who became his botanical mentor. Greene attended Albion Academy but did not graduate until after the Civil War in which he served two years as a private in the Union army. He seems to have managed much botanical activity while on his army travels, always carrying a

Botanical Exploration of California

botany text and writing to Kumlien about the plants he had found. In 1870, he went to Colorado to collect plants, corresponding from that time on with Asa Gray, the patriarch of the eastern botanical establishment at Harvard.

Greene remained in Colorado, entered an Episcopal seminary in Golden in that same year, and was ordained a priest in 1873. He had several mission churches in Colorado and later in California. He wrote on September 3, 1874, to Kumlien's son, "I have had a fine time, also have worked my way into the pulpit so as to have no trouble about the wherewithal to pay my expenses" [but "that with my pastoral work] my scientific studies were interfered with not a little."[40]

His moves brought him into many out of the way places, for example Silver City, New Mexico, and Yreka in northern California, in which little botanical exploration had yet been done. About Yreka he wrote to Gray on February 27, 1876:

> The place that I am going [to] . . . sounding like a cross between ancient Greek, and modern Digger Indian . . . is to be *Yreka, Siskiyou Co.;* away up between Mt. Shasta and Klamath River!! I can hardly sleep of nights since I have secured my appointment to that field of Missionary labor . . . . I have got a pretty ample supply of sermons on hand; don't mean to compose a single new one all next spring, summer and fall, just herborize to my heart's content.

The flora of California had not yet been carefully studied. Brewer's work with the California Survey took a long time to be published. Greene wrote to Asa Gray in 1876 about the botanical report of the California Survey, "How about the *Flora of California?* Is any part of it out yet?"[41] This was the period of the great naming game. Many California plants were western American endemics and, thus, many were new to organized science. Finding a new species and either naming it or having a new plant named for the discoverer provided instant immortality. Sending the plant elsewhere for identification could mean either losing the "new" species, if Gray or someone else decided it was not new, or losing the priority if someone else found and published it in the interim. Gray, of course, had often named plants for the collectors who sent them to him, including John Muir.

To name a new plant oneself only required enough knowledge of Latin to write a description, which Greene and many others had, even those only educated through secondary school. Greene had named a number of species himself in 1881, but he wrote to Gray that he had done so only because of the latter's absence in Europe. But he continued to publish his new species in the *Gazette* after Gray's return and eventually in his own journal, *Pittonia*.

George Engelmann, St. Louis physician and one of the most respected American botanists after Gray, understood the Californians' desire for independence. He commented to Gray that the Californians wanted their flora for themselves.[42] The question in Engelmann's mind (and presumably in Gray's) was whether they could do it well enough. Gray had early recognized the importance of visiting European herbaria to see the plants previously collected; Greene did not see the corresponding need to visit the Harvard herbarium to compare plant specimens, although other Californians did, for example Kate Brandegee.

Many other botanists corresponded with Gray during the 1870s and 1880s including several who then or later worked in California. They similarly went through a period of complete dependence on Gray (and sometimes on Gray's curator, Sereno Watson), but later became independent botanists who not only collected but published in California. California botany by the 1870s was being done by residents, all of whom were from the East Coast or midwest or of European origin, to be sure, but they were no longer transients. There were increased numbers of plant collectors, and they no longer had to be able to survive in wild and often dangerous places. The first transcontinental railroad had been completed in 1869 and railroads provided botanists with many opportunities in little explored areas. C. C. Parry, noted Colorado botanical explorer, collected in California in 1878 and in the early 1880s. In 1883 he had a Southern Pacific

Botanical Exploration of California

Railroad pass, and in 1886–1887 he was back in California. He wrote letters about his finds to many other botanists including Asa Gray. One letter to Samuel Parish reads:

> I made a short trip to Ione in Amador Co to look up an anomalous *Arctostaphylos* collected in leaf only by Mrs. Curran last year— I found it on her directions abundant and in full flower. . . . I conclude it is a good n[ew] sp[ecies]—I will probably offer it for publication in the Cal Acad Bull.[43]

The California botanists were by this time numerous and had in the Academy their own institution with its own herbarium, library, and journals. Solid evidence seems to suggest that they wished to be in charge of their own flora rather than dependent on Gray and the eastern establishment, just as Gray had sought independence from European botany at an earlier date.

Parry, on visiting the Academy herbarium in 1875, reported to Gray that the Academy botanists had not sent Gray a number of newly discovered plants that he ought to have for his *North American Flora*. It was apparently frowned on by Albert Kellogg and other members of the California Academy to send new plant specimens east for identification; they wanted to determine the plants themselves.[44] Two botanists with such views were Marcus Jones and Townshend S. Brandegee.

Marcus Jones, along with Christopher Parry, John Coulter, Cyrus Pringle, and John Lemmon, all corresponded with and sent specimens to Gray. Jones was an established botanist by the late 1870s when he was working on the Rocky Mountain flora. He worked later in California, publishing in *Zoe*, a California Academy of Sciences journal and in his own *Contributions to Western Botany* in which he gave candid biographical sketches of many California botanists.

In a letter of February 27, 1881, it is clear that Jones did not always agree with the identifications of eastern experts. He wrote to Gray, "I have several new species which I will endeavor to send you soon with the names which I have given them. . . .

Nancy G. Slack

The plant which you think looks like *Cymopteris amisotus* . . . is much different in habit and grows in the clefts of rocks in the arid region of St. George. *C. amisotus* . . . is a plant growing only on the mountain tops at an elevation of 10,000–11,000 feet.

Marcus Jones seems to have expressed the frustration of many western botanists. Writing in *Zoe* in 1894, he explained:

> For a long time it has been the custom of western botanists to provide themselves with the necessary literature and then study their home plants, naming such plants as accord with the descriptions given; the rest they send with such notes as they consider valuable to certain persons in the East who have been regarded as authorities. The authorities compare them with the types of species . . . and if the plants do not vary too much from the species are considered the same and so named; if they deviate too much, then they are erected into new species, usually on the strength of a single specimen. . . . The notes of the field botanist they usually have dismissed . . . with a remark like this: "flowers said to be white but they appear to be yellow." If the field botanist has been so bold as to write out a full description of the real characters, the closet botanist will cut out all except those which strike his fancy and are found in the specimen before him, and will add such as he thinks have been overlooked by the field botanist. At last when the description is published the weary field botanist goes out into the home of the plants, where perhaps there are acres of them, and he finds that his description does not describe. . . . Of late this kind of thing has become a nuisance, and field botanists have taken to describing their own species.
>
> The occasional republication of an old species by a western man is pointed to as "an exasperating blunder" . . . but, dear me, that does not begin to express our feelings when we see a new monograph from men who would not know their own new species if they saw them alive.

This is basically a declaration of independence for field botanists in the West to publish their own discoveries. Jones declared that the eastern botanists were "ignoring and underestimating the work of [western] field botanists . . . . One would think that the only persons who have any rights are the people who sit in their warm and cozy herbaria and manufacture species which other men have sent them at great expense of health, time and money."[45]

Meanwhile, Edward Lee Greene was out in the field in much of California finding and naming many new species of plants. Greene's philosophical views involved fixity of species; unlike many of his contemporary California botanists, he did not accept evolution. In his botanical studies Greene was certainly an ardent splitter; any character distinctive to him, even plant height, led him to consider a plant a new species. Michael Smith's comment that Greene's "habit of declaring his discovery of a new species at every turn exasperated his colleagues at the university and the Academy of Sciences" is undoubtedly an understatement. Dayton and Blake wrote that Greene would write on the folder of a specimen he could not identify on sight 'New to me, hence new to science' or drop the specimen in a waste basket and observe that 'if the Almighty wished to preserve this plant creation .... He could doubtless reproduce it again!' Many contemporary vitriolic comments on Greene's taxonomic methods appeared in print, particularly in *Zoe*. Rogers McVaugh pointed out, however, that about 70 percent of Greene's several thousand new species have stood up to time and botanical revisions.[46]

In the currently used California flora Greene's name is ubiquitous. One genus at random, *Cryptantha*, in the borage family consists of about sixty-five species, fifty-eight of which grow in California. Of these, thirty-one bear Greene's name either as the discoverer (or at least the person who named it) or as the individual who moved the plant into this genus![47] That is only one genus; examining the flora as a whole it is clear that Greene, splitter and anti-evolutionist though he probably was, was also a superb plant explorer. He explored and collected all over the state and trained many botanists of the next generation, including his successor at Berkeley, W. L. Jepson, before returning to the East in 1895.

Nancy G. Slack

Stanford University

Stanford University was established after the death of Leland and Jane Lathrop Stanford's only son in 1884. The Stanfords built the university on their Palo Alto estate and hired David Starr Jordan as president. When hired, Jordan, a Cornell graduate, was already a noted zoologist and president of Indiana University. Jordan's original interest had been in botany, and in his first position at Lombard College in Illinois he taught Botany, as well as five other sciences, Paley's "Evidences of Christianity," German, and Spanish. He became president and an important supporter of the California Academy of Sciences during his Stanford years.

It was Jordan who hired one of California's most ardent plant explorers and conservationists, William R. Dudley, his former roommate at Cornell. In the 1870s and early 1880s, Dudley collected all the plants he could find in the vicinity of Ithaca, New York, then studied in Europe in the late 1880s.

Dudley came to Stanford as its first botany professor in 1892. He brought many of his New York plant specimens with him and collected more all over California, for what was to be the Dudley Herbarium at Stanford. Originally, Dudley had few facilities. His specimens and laboratory were housed in the attic of a shop building. Better facilities were ten years in coming.

Dudley meanwhile explored the forests of the Sierra and Coast Ranges. He knew the trees and other flora of these forests extremely well. He objected to the lumbering of 2,500–year-old giant sequoias, writing, "I cannot help thinking we are here in the presence of one of the most remarkable products of the globe, not excepting those of human civilization."[48] Dudley, together with John Muir, was an important actor in the fight to preserve these remarkable forests.

John Muir's Role in
the Botany of California

Muir was cognizant of, but not very interested in the competitive "name game" then going on among rival California botanists. He was not a lumper, splitter, or classifier. Muir's name does not appear as an author of any species in Philip A. Munz's California flora. Some of his plant specimens are still extant, however, and at least three species were named after him.[49] His major botanical contribution was in his marvelous ability as both observer and writer to describe the beauty, diversity, and ecology of the plants for those who were not there in person and to recruit these readers for future preservation battles.

Muir made other important contributions to botany itself. He was a guide, associate, and botanical resource, especially in the Sierra, for the best-known botanists in the world, Asa Gray, John Torrey, and Joseph Hooker, all of whom came to California. His correspondence with Gray dates from at least 1871. His advice was sought by one of California's best-known botanists, Alice Eastwood. These activities are well documented in his letters as will be shown briefly here.

Muir had already served as guide to Joseph LeConte and his eight University of California students in the Sierra in 1870. LeConte was surprised at Muir's knowledge of the botany of the region. LeConte himself had studied with both Torrey at medical school in New York and with Gray at Harvard. Both LeConte and Muir described this excursion in letters and journal.

Muir wrote to Jeanne Carr on August 20, 1870, "I have just returned from a ten days' ramble with Professor Le Conte and his students in the beyond" and described all their campsites, including one on the "velvet gentian meadow of the South Tuolumne." He also offered in this letter to send her some choice mountain plants, which he often did, but few of these became herbarium specimens.

Jeanne Carr, the wife of his former geology professor at Wisconsin, Ezra Carr, sent Muir a string of famous visitors. In 1871 he took Ralph Waldo Emerson to the Mariposa Grove and tried to persuade him to camp among the Big Trees. He promised to "build a glorious camp-fire, and the great brown boles of the giant Sequoias will be most impressively lighted up." But the "house habit was not to be overcome, nor the strange dread of pure night air." The aging Emerson declined. Emerson did, however, stop in Oakland at the Carrs' on his return to thank Jeanne Carr for the letter introducing him to Muir. Moreover, the following year Emerson wrote to Muir, "I have everywhere testified to my friends . . . my happiness in finding you—the right man in the right place—in your mountain tabernackle."[50]

In 1872, the Harvard botanist Asa Gray was president of the American Association for the Advancement of Science (AAAS). As already suggested, the transcontinental railroad gave botanists easy access to previously quite inaccessible places where Gray had sent collectors like Charles Wright. The AAAS meeting was in Dubuque, Iowa, and Gray gave his presidential address on "Sequoia and its History"—but not before seeing both the trees and Muir in California. He came by rail, botanizing at every stop, although from his herbarium labels it appears that he did not always know exactly where he was.[51]

In July 1872, Gray was due to arrive in Yosemite to be guided by John Muir. Muir wrote to Jeanne Carr: "I have been longing for Gray, whom I feel to be a great, progressive unlimited man like Darwin and Huxley and Tyndall," and two days later he wrote to his sister, Sarah: "I have had a great day in meeting Dr. Asa Gray, the first botanist in the world."[52]

They were already well acquainted by mail. Asa Gray wrote to Muir early in 1872 that he had received a "glorious" package from him, had "taken out the plentiful *Torreya* [California nutmeg] seeds, poked thru a wilderness of superb *Pellea mucronata* [bird's foot fern] all in first-rate condition."[53]

They had a good excursion but Muir was disappointed that Gray and his wife had not climbed with him into the high peaks

Asa Gray, patriarch of American botany, 1873. Archives, Gray Herbarium, Harvard University, Cambridge, Mass., U.S.A.

north of Yosemite: "If you and Mrs. Gray had only exposed your-selves to the plants . . . of our High sierra, I would have been content to have you return home to your Cambridge classes and to all the just and proper ding dong of civilization." [54]

Gray was to return to California, but in the meantime Muir was kept busy sending him plant specimens. On September 21, 1872, Gray wrote, "If you get up to that *Primula suffrutescens* [Sierra primrose] on Crow's Nest or Mt. Jefferson, pray collect a quantity of it and dispatch it, packed in damp moss." In re-sponse, on December 18, 1872, Muir wrote to Gray: "I climbed there [South Dome] and ran up to Clouds' Rest for your Primu-las. And as I stuffed them in big sods into a sack, I said, Now I wonder what mouthfuls this size will accomplish for the Doctor's primrose hunger. Before filling your sack I witnessed one of the most glorious of our mountain sunsets."

In return, Gray sent Muir several of his books including *How Plants Behave*, his *Manual, School and Field Book*, and *Structural Botany*, so that Muir could "set to studying Botany again" as Gray wrote to Muir in September 1872. In February, 1873, in addition to sending plants to be named, Muir wrote Gray:

> I call your attention to the two large yellow and purple plants from the top of Mt. Lyell, above all of the pinched and blinking dwarfs that almost justify Darwin's mean ungodly word, "struggle." . . . . They are the noblest plant mountaineers I ever saw climbing above the glaciers into the frosty azure and flowering in purple and gold, rich and abundant as ever responded to the thick creamy sungold of the tropics.

One of the plants Muir sent was new to science, and Gray named it after him and encouraged Muir to go on collecting:

> If you will keep botanizing in the high Sierra you will find curi-ous and new things, no doubt. One such, at least, is in our present collection . . . the wee mouse-tail *Ivesia*. And the rare species of *Lewisia* is as good as new, and is so wholly to California. . . . *Ivesia Muirii* is the first fruit. . . . Get a new alpine genus, that I may make a *Muiria glacialis*. [55]

Botanical Exploration of California

Muir continued to collect plants and to send them to Asa Gray for many years, sometimes in regions far from California, for example in the polar regions of Wrangel Land and Herald Island.

Later that same summer, Gray's original botanical mentor, John Torrey came to Yosemite, and was guided by Muir. He wrote in September 1872, from the home of botanist George Engelmann in St. Louis that he had enjoyed the "pleasant and instructive hours he had spent with Muir in Yosemite." Muir sent him plants, too, one of which, a little *Botrychium* (fern) looked peculiar and Torrey promised to report on it when he got home. He never did, however. Torrey died in 1873 and the *Botrychium* (perhaps *B. lunularia* var. *minganense*) was not rediscovered in the High Sierra until the turn of the century.[56]

In 1877 Asa Gray, his wife, Jane, and Sir Joseph Hooker, president of the Royal Society of London and the most important English botanist of the era, undertook a western botanical expedition. It was paid for by F. V. Hayden, then head of the U.S. Geological and Geographical Survey of the Territories. In California they visited the Mount Shasta region and again Muir was the guide. One night around the campfire, Gray asked why *Linnaea borealis* (twinflower) had never been discovered in northern California. The next morning Hooker and Muir found it on "an excursion westward across one of the upper tributaries of the Sacramento."

Muir thought "Gray [who had stayed in camp] felt its presence the night before on the mountain ten miles away." It is, however, not rare; Munz records it in a large elevation range in at least six counties. Gray would have known its habitat in the eastern mountains. Dupree commented on Muir's transcendental view of such occurrences:

The gulf between the tradition of the nature lover which descended on Muir from Emerson and the tradition of the botanist represented by Gray was never more clearly demonstrated than at these campfires . . . in Northern California. . . . Muir would build up the

Nancy G. Slack

Joseph Hooker and Asa Gray (both seated at left) and party, 1877, Western Botanical Expedition.

fire to "display the beauties of the silver fir" . . . and shout "Look at the glory." The botanists, Gray and Hooker, remained silent.[57]

Nevertheless, Muir said they talked of trees and argued about species relationships, and decided with world traveler Hooker's concurrence that the Sierra conifer forests were unrivaled for diversity and beauty. Perhaps the gulf was not so wide. In a Thanksgiving letter to his sister, Sarah, that same year (1877) Muir wrote:

> The Professor Gray I was with on Shasta is . . . the most distinguished botanist in America and Sir Joseph Hooker is the leading botanist of England. We had a fine rare time together in the Shasta forests, discussing the botanical characters of the grandest coniferous trees in the world, camping out, and enjoying ourselves in pure freedom. Gray is an old friend of mine that I led around Yosemite years age [in 1872] and with whom I have corresponded a long time.[58]

Muir wrote after Parry's death in 1890, "It seems as though all the good flower people, at once great and good, have died now that Parry has gone—Torrey, Gray, Kellogg, and Parry.

Botanical Exploration of California

Plenty more botanists left, but none we have like these." He continued, "Oh dear, it makes me feel lonesome. Never shall I forget the charming evenings I spent with Torrey in Yosemite, and with Gray."[59]

Good California botanists there still were. Muir corresponded with Alice Eastwood near the end of the period under consideration. Eastwood, before coming to California in 1892 had made important contributions to the botany of Colorado, including a published flora. She had been Alfred Russel Wallace's guide up Gray's Peak in Colorado in 1888, as Wallace described in his autobiography. Eastwood after accepting the California Academy position in 1892, collected plants on pack trips in the Santa Lucia Mountains, Kings-Karn Divide, Yosemite, and elsewhere in California. In December of 1896, she wrote to Muir and asked him about the ripening of the cones of the giant sequoia. She had herself studied redwood, and wanted his knowledge about the Big Tree. In another letter she inquired about estimates of standing timber in California since "the U.S. Govt. seems at last to be making an effort to discover how many trees it owns or ought to own."

Muir was clearly the expert on forest trees. He and Alice Eastwood seem to have been kindred spirits in terms of mountains and mountain plants. In the same letter, she had asked him to come with her botanical group to the "beautiful spots on Mt. Tamalpais of which only the true lovers of the mountain know."[60]

In addition to Muir's botanical exploration of the Sierra, his able guiding of the most famous botanists to visit them, and his knowledge of many aspects of the biology of trees, how else did he contribute to California botany? He of course contributed greatly to its preservation in the formation of Yosemite National Park and in the founding and activities of the Sierra Club. The establishment of Yosemite as a park and as a botanical preserve had been initiated before Muir's arrival, in part because of Whitney's and Brewer's explorations of the Sierra described above.

Nancy G. Slack

President Lincoln signed a bill passed by Congress in 1864 assigning Yosemite Valley and the Mariposa Big Tree Grove to the state of California, but the Sierra Club was of prime importance to Yosemite as a National Forest. Muir was president of the Sierra Club from its inception in 1892 until his death in 1914. On May 18, 1892, John Muir met with three professors of the University of California: J. H. Senger, William D. Armes, and Willis L. Jepson in the office of lawyer Warner Olney of San Francisco to launch the Sierra Club. Many others in this narrative, Kellogg, Dudley, LeConte, and Jordan were officers of the Sierra Club and had an important part in its work. These events, including the preservationist battle lost at Hetch Hetchy are discussed elsewhere in this volume and by previous authors.[61]

John Muir contributed something else, a viewpoint on nature in general and plants in particular, quite new in his time. Now we would call it an ecosystem perspective. As his discussion of "what is the use" of poison oak during his first summer in the Sierra shows, he rejected the then prevalent anthropocentric view of nature. He was always describing the plants he saw in the Sierra not in terms of their uses to the human species but in relation to each other and to their physical environment, as in his description of chamise (*Adenostoma*) above, and in his discussion of alpine flora.

Muir had come to these views even before he came to California. He discussed them in his journal of 1867, satirizing the then-held views:

> whales are storehouses of oil for us, to help out the stars in lighting our dark ways until the discovery of the Pennsylvania oil wells. Among plants, hemp . . . is a case of evident destination for ships' rigging, wrapping packages, and hanging the wicked.

and asks whether the logical outcome of such thinking should not be that man is the "divinely intended prey of lions, tigers, alligators, and the myriads of noxious insects that plague and destroy him." He concludes that the idea that the world was

238

made especially for man is "a presumption not supported by all the facts."[62]

Wolfe wrote that while forming his glacial theory and collecting evidence on Mount Dana, Lyell, and Bloody Canyon, he "learned the supreme lesson that nature is one living, pulsing organism" and stated his certainty of this by writing 'when we try to pick out anything by itself, we find it hitched to everything else in the universe . . . the whole wilderness in unity and interrelation is alive and familiar.'[63] He made it very clear to Gifford Pinchot in person and to those who listened to him speak and to his many readers that the activities of man, and especially of their sheep and their forestry operations, were destroying the unity and interrelation of this wilderness.

Muir saw all organisms as interrelated, and related to their changing environments. Perhaps even more than botanical or geological explorer, Muir was California's first ecosystem ecologist.

Notes

1. William Frederic Badè, *The Life and Letters of John Muir*, 2 Vols. (Boston: Houghton Mifflin, 1924), I, p. 76.

2. Ibid., pp. 180–181, 183, 187, 193 (from unpublished memoirs).

3. John Muir, *My First Summer in the Sierra* (New York: Viking Penguin, 1911; Penguin Books edition, 1987), pp. 19, 26, 215.

4. For a compilation of those who worked in all fields of natural history in the San Francisco Bay area, see Joseph Ewan, "San Francisco as a Mecca for Nineteenth Century Naturalists," in California Academy of Sciences, *A Century of Progress in the Natural Sciences, 1853–1953* (San Francisco, CA: California Academy of Sciences, 1955), pp 1-56. A Spanish botanist, José Longinos Martínez, also arrived in California in 1792.

5. Jeanette E. Graustein, *Thomas Nuttall, Naturalist: Explorations in America, 1804–1841* (Cambridge, Mass.: Harvard University Press, 1967), pp. 313–316.

6. Ewan, "San Francisco as a Mecca," pp. 1–6, 14–15.

7. Anderson Hunter Dupree, *Science in the Federal Government* (Cambridge, Mass.: Harvard University Press, 1957), p. 91.

8. Ibid., pp. 91–95.

9. Ibid., p. 94.

Nancy G. Slack

10. Robert V. Bruce, *The Launching of Modern American Science, 1846–1876* (Ithaca, N.Y.: Cornell University Press, 1987), p. 56.

11. Ewan, "San Francisco as a Mecca," pp. 9–12.

12. Nancy G. Slack, "Nineteenth-Century American Women Botanists: Wives, Widows, and Work," in P. G. Abir-Am and D. Outram, eds., *Uneasy Careers and Intimate Lives; Women in Science 1789–1979*, ed. (New Brunswick, N.J.: Rutgers University Press, 1987), pp. 77–103.

13. Michael L. Smith, *Pacific Visions: California Scientists and the Environment, 1850–1915* (New Haven, Conn.: Yale University Press, 1987), p. 117.

14. William H. Brewer, *Up and down California in 1860–1864*, Francis P. Farquhar, ed. (Berkeley Calif.: University of California Press, 1966), p. x.

15. Quoted in Smith, *Pacific Visions*, p. 50.

16. Brewer, *Up and Down California.*

17. Farquhar, in ibid., pp. xi-xiii.

18. Brewer, in ibid., pp. 140–141.

19. Ibid., pp. 259–261.

20. Ibid., p. 282.

21. Ibid., pp. 398–400.

22. Ibid., pp. 401–412.

23. Farquhar, notes, in ibid., pp. 448–449.

24. Brewer, in ibid., pp. 218–219.

25. Ibid., pp. 432–433.

26. Ewan, "San Francisco as a Mecca," pp. 16–17.

27. Brewer, *Up and Down California*, p. 433.

28. Clarence King, *Mountaineering in the Sierra Nevada* (Lincoln: University of Nebraska Press, 1970; reproduced from the 1872 edition published by James R. Osgood and Co., Boston), pp. 10, 18, 31, 40–42, 67, 183–185. For Ruskin's influence on King's vegetation "paintings," see Smith, *Pacific Visions*, pp. 83–86.

29. Brewer, *Up and Down California*, pp. 519, 524–525.

30. Ibid., pp. 490–491.

31. Ibid., pp. 448, 548, 564.

32. In regard to professionalization of botany in New York, see Nancy G. Slack, "Charles Horton Peck, Bryologist and the Legitimation of Botany in New York State," *Memoirs of the New York Botanical Garden* 45 (1987): 28–45; and Douglas Sloan, "Science in New York in the Nineteenth Century," in A. Oleson and S. C. Brown, eds., *The Pursuit of Knowledge in the Early American Republic* (Baltimore, Md.: Johns Hopkins University Press, 1976), pp. 33–69.

33. Ewan, "San Francisco as a Mecca," pp. 19–20, 23–26; Willis Linn Jepson, "The Botanical Explorers of California XI," *Madroño* 2 (1934), pp. 156–157.

34. Letters in the Brandegee archives of the Jepson Herbarium, University of California, Berkeley.

35. Newspaper article in the Brandegee archives, California Academy of Sciences.

36. Lincoln Constance, *Botany at Berkeley: the First Hundred Years* (Berkeley,

Botanical Exploration of California

Calif.: University of California Press, 1978); Lester D. Stephens, *Joseph LeConte, Gentle Prophet of Evolution* (Baton Rouge: Louisiana State University Press, 1982), pp. 120–122, 128.

37. Letter written by Charles E. Bessey in 1911, quoted by Constance, *Botany at Berkeley*, p. 3.

38. Constance, *Botany at Berkeley*, p. 4.

39. Robert P. McIntosh, biographical sketch of Edward Lee Greene, in Edward Lee Greene, *Landmarks of Botanical History*, ed. Frank N. Egerton (Stanford, Calif.: Stanford University Press, 1983).

40. Letter from Edward Lee Greene to Kumlien, September 3, 1874 quoted by Robert P. McIntosh in Greene, *Landmarks*, pp. 25–26.

41. Letter from Edward Lee Greene to Asa Gray, February 27, 1876, in Gray Herbarium archives, Harvard University.

42. Anderson Hunter Dupree, *Asa Gray* (Cambridge, Mass.: Harvard University Press, 1959), p. 398. See also controversy, note 39.

43. Letter from Charles C. Parry to Samuel B. Parish quoted by Ewan, "San Francisco as a Mecca," p. 32.

44. Dupree, *Asa Gray*, p. 396. See Chapter 19, "The Patriarch of New Plant Sciences," pp. 384–402 for the background of this controversy between Gray and the California botanists, especially Edward Lee Greene.

45. Letter from Marcus Jones to Asa Gray, February 27, 1881, Gray Herbarium archives, Harvard University and Jones's comments in *Zoe* (California Academy of Sciences, 1894). Other correspondence of Jones with Gray and with Sereno Watson are in the Gray Herbarium archives.

46. Smith, *Pacific Visions*, p. 127; W. A. Dayton and S. F. Blake, "Ivar Tidestrom (1864–1926)," *Rhodora* 59 (1957): 161–168; Rogers McVaugh in Greene, *Landmarks*.

47. Philip A. Munz, *A California Flora* (Berkeley, Calif.: University of California Press, 1959); for the genus *Cryptantha*, see pp. 563–577.

48. William R. Dudley, "The Vitality of *Sequoia Gigantea*," *Dudley Memorial Volume* (Palo Alto, Calif.: Stanford University Press, 1913), pp. 40–41; Smith, *Pacific Visions*, p. 134–135.

49. Munz, *A California Flora*, a letter from Asa Gray to John Muir quoted by Badè, *Life and Letters*, p. 381, about the new species *Ivesia muirii* named for Muir; Andrew Denny Rodgers, III, *American Botany 1873–1892* (Princeton, N.J.: Princeton University Press, 1944), p. 156.

50. Badè, *Life and Letters*, I, pp. 231–232, 254–259.

51. Dupree, pp. 345–347.

52. Badè, *Life and Letters*, I, p. 335 (letter from John Muir to Mrs. Carr, July 14, 1872); p. 337 (letter from John Muir to Sarah Muir Galloway).

53. Letter from Asa Gray to John Muir, January 4, 1872 in the Microfilm Edition of the *John Muir Papers*, University of the Pacific, Stockton, California.

54. Badè, *Life and Letters*, I, p. 342.

55. Letter from Asa Gray to John Muir, September 21, 1872; letter from John

Nancy G. Slack

Muir to Asa Gray, December 18, 1872; letter from John Muir to Asa Gray, February 22, 1873, *John Muir Papers*.

56. Badè, *Life and Letters*, I, pp. 342–343.

57. Dupree, *Asa Gray*, p. 407.

58. Badè, *Life and Letters*, II, p. 83.

59. Ibid., II, pp. 242–243.

60. Letters from Alice Eastwood to John Muir, December 21, 1896, *John Muir Papers*. Eastwood went on living and working into her 90s, maintaining her curatorship at the California Academy for 57 years. In 1950 when over 90, she flew to Sweden for the International Botanical Congress of which she was honorary president, returning by freighter in a month-long trip through the Panama Canal (described in letter from Alice Eastwood to Miss Woodward, June 29, 1952). In Joseph Ewan archives, Missouri Botanical Garden.

61. See for example, Smith, *Pacific Visions*, Chapters 7 and 8, pp. 143–185; and Richard J. Orsi, " 'Wilderness Saint' and 'Robber Baron': The Anomalous Partnership of John Muir and the Southern Pacific Railroad for the Preservation of Yosemite National Park," *The Pacific Historian* 29 (Summer/Fall 1985): 136–156.

62. Quoted in Linnie Marsh Wolfe, *Son of the Wilderness: The Life of John Muir* (New York: Knopf, 1947), pp. 254, 360, n. 24.

63. Badè, *Life and Letters*, I, pp. 166–167.

PART
VI
MUIR'S
PLACES

11.
After Yosemite

John Muir and the Southern Sierra

Paul D. Sheats

For reasons that have as much to do with symbolism as history, the popular imagination often assigns its heroes a particular landscape, a place that bears witness to their power. No one, I think, would doubt that for John Muir this place is Yosemite. Although Muir's full-time residence in the famous valley lasted only for three years, from 1870 to 1873, the place is haunted by his legends, the nooks and bowers he loved, his hair-raising *scootchers*, or adventures, and the intensities of the relationships he forged and of the first mountain writings he composed there. In Yosemite, we assume, Muir was inspired by formative experiences of nature that ultimately shaped a national park system and a national conservation movement.

For all its intuitive truth, this Yosemite-centered version of Muir's legend requires qualification of several kinds. It was never promulgated by Muir himself, who sensed the ending of the "Merced and Tuolumne chapters" of his life with remarkable clarity in September 1874 and who regularly directed the attention of his growing audience of readers beyond the walls of the Yosemite Valley to the features of the entire range.[1] A good deal of symbolic value might be given, in fact, to the landscape he chose for the introduction to both his first substantial Yosemite article and his first book, the *Mountains of California*—a long view of the entire range as he first saw it in 1868 from across the Central Valley, "miles in height, reposing like a smooth cumulus cloud in the sunny sky."[2] On this occasion Muir avoided appearing partial to any particular region, and indeed in the first chapter of his book referred only to "valleys of the Yosemite kind" as a feature of the middle elevations of the range.[3] As Frederic Gunsky's valuable anthology demonstrated over two decades ago, Muir took a lifelong interest in the entire range, especially in the southern watersheds of the Kings and the Kaweah rivers, an area that inspired some of his finest descriptive writing.[4]

In the "old free Sierra times," Muir recalled in a letter of 1891, the Valley of the Kings was "a favorite haunt," and he visited it frequently.[5] During the 1870s, the most decisive and changeful decade of his life, he went south four times in five years: in the fall of 1873, the summer and fall of 1875, and the summer of 1877. Hopes for a new national park prompted a three-week trip to the Kings in 1891, and in 1902 and 1908 he joined outings held by the recently founded Sierra Club in the Kings and Kern Canyons. On the first of these, at the age of 64, Muir is reported to have inspired his companions to dance a Virginia reel on the summit of Mt. Whitney. In 1912, two years before his death, he drove to Giant Forest in an automobile. Although all of these southern trips produced accounts and anecdotes, two illustrate with special clarity the importance of this region in Muir's career. In 1873 and 1875, I would suggest, the southern Sierra provided the setting for a distinct, post-Yosemite phase in Muir's growth as writer and thinker, and, in 1875 especially, served as a catalyst for a reformulation of his vocation.

In September 1873, Muir and three companions set out from Clark's, at Wawona, and worked their way south along the tributary canyons of the San Joaquin to the south fork of the Kings, then across the range to Owens Valley, where Muir climbed Mt. Whitney. Mingled with delighted exploration of this new landscape was a serious scientific purpose: the confirmation of his controversial theory of the glacial origin of the Sierra landscape.

The geological purpose of this first trip south may be understood within a broader context still, that of the nineteenth-century debate between special and general creationists that lay behind Muir's well-known controversy with Josiah Whitney, the state geologist. In arguing that Yosemite had been formed by a sudden, catastrophic subsidence along fault lines, Whitney made the valley an impressive example of special creation, with all the theological assumptions implicit in that theory. As the product of an unknown and unpredictable cause, Whitney's Yosemite was something very like a miracle, the work of a Creator who chose to cloak His methods and purposes in a mystery impenetrable to human reason. Such a view suited the impressive features of Yosemite and was welcomed by those who for commercial or artistic motives sought to impress far-away urban audiences who had never seen the mountains and to bring them as tourists to the valley. As represented by landscape painters like Albert Bierstadt, whose sunset scenes of the valley were as famous as they were inaccurate, the right word for Yosemite was indeed "incomparable."[6]

For John Muir, on the other hand, close and thoughtful comparison was exactly what was needed to explode the theory of special creation. His first printed attack on that theory in 1874 mingled gentle mockery with theological debate:

> Such is Yosemite, the noblest of Sierra temples, everywhere expressing the working of Divine harmonious law, yet so little understood that it has been regarded as an "exceptional creation," or rather *exceptional destruction* accomplished by violent and mysterious forces.

The following explanation by Muir of Whitney's theory makes it laughable: the "mountain bottom" falls out, letting peaks and domes fall "like coal into the bunker of a ship," or into a kind of "Tophet" or Hell prepared for "the reception of bad mountains."[7] In a newspaper letter a year later Muir again stressed the perversity of the special creationists' assumption that Yosemite "stood unrelated and alone among all the known valleys of the world," like "a special church or temple in which all the landscape-loving world would do extraordinary worship," or a geological wonder that "like ancient miracles, lay at a hopeless distance beyond the boundaries of exact science."[8]

Such misreading of the landscape proceeded from what Muir by now recognized as a widespread methodological error, a habit of abstracting particular phenomena from their natural contexts. "The greatest obstacle" to understanding the valley's history, he wrote in 1874, results from just such a narrow view, produced by the sheer "magnitude" of its several features as seen from the valley floor. Examined from above, on the other hand, from some "commanding outlook," the valley exhibits

> a far more natural combination of features than is at all apparent in partial views obtained from the bottom. Its stupendous domes and battlements blend together and manifest delicate compliance to law, for the mind is then emancipated from the repressive and enslaving effects of their separate magnitudes.[9]

In a context that might seem to require a cool empiricism, Muir's language exerts passionate ideological and theological force. Through the sublimity of its parts, its individual domes and cliffs, Yosemite acts very much like a political tyrant: it "enslaves" and "represses" the mind observing it. To "emancipate" the mind from such tyranny of the sublime, Muir recommended delaying scientific judgement until Yosemite's particular features could be related to "an all-unifying, all-explaining law." He sought, in other words, to neutralize the valley's overwhelming power, and by extension to demystify the violent yet unknowable God implied by Whitney's catastrophism, a God Muir himself had known only too well in the Calvinist theology of his childhood. Properly seen, he argued, nature will not enslave the mind but set it free—"emancipate" it—from fearful awe. If the compliance to law that nature secures is ultimately irresistible, it is also, in Muir's word, "delicate."

If his reasons for leaving Yosemite in the fall of 1873 were in part personal, he thus had a clear scientific motive as well. By 1873 he had gathered solid local evidence that Yosemite was created by glacial ice. His two most important discoveries up to this time, of the Hetch Hetchy "Yosemite," and the survival of living glaciers in the Yosemite backcountry, both exemplified the efficacy of looking beyond the valley itself in order to understand it as an effect of more general causes. To press home the case against Whitney it thus became all the more necessary to extend the geological context down the length of the range, on a trip that would show the valley to be the effect of general, not special, causes, and by no means, "unrelated and alone." Put plainly, Muir's purpose in 1873 was to collect as many Yosemites as he could find.

He found them, and in abundance. "Groping through unexplored regions," he wrote Mrs. Jeanne Carr from the canyon of the San Joaquin in late September, he had discovered not only "15 glaciers" but "Yosemite Valleys 'many-O'" Muir's suffix, "O," echoes the refrain of such Scottish lyrics as "Green grow the rushes O!" and celebrates his geological discovery by turning it into a brief but joyful song.[10] Journal entries suggest that he was especially struck by the way the individual features of the various Yosemites repeated themselves. A dome in the canyon of the San Joaquin showed a "remarkable resemblance to the Yosemite Half Dome."[11] Nine years earlier William Brewer had noticed that the canyon of the South Fork of the Kings "much resembles Yosemite and almost rivals it."[12] But Muir went further, applying the Merced nomenclature itself to this "Kings yosemite," which he noted has not one but two "tissiacks," or Half-domes, and "two Washington Columns and nearly two North Domes."[13] When he first described Kings Canyon for the public, in a letter to the *San Francisco Bulletin* dated August 1875, he emphasized these homologies, citing them as evidence that "in the Sierra Nevada are many Yosemites."[14]

In the following year, 1874, Muir put his collection of Yosemites on public view. Working at an Oakland desk for much of the winter and spring, he shaped these observations into his "Studies in the Sierra," a series of articles on the glacial origins of the range that he long regarded as his most "ambitious" work.[15] A footnote to the second installment, "Mountain Sculpture," warned the reader that his language will be general as well as specific; he will use "the word Yosemite both as a specific

John Muir sketch, ca. 1874, illustrating several fractured granite domes in the Sierra, similar to Half Dome in Yosemite National Park. Courtesy Yosemite National Park Research Library.

and geographical term"—a usage he had already adopted in his journals and letters, as we have seen and that characterized his published work for the rest of his life.[16] An accompanying illustration eloquently corrected those who regarded Yosemite as an exceptional creation: a map of the Merced Yosemite is placed between maps of its sisters on the Tuolumne and the Kings rivers. All three Yosemites are clearly members of the same family, offspring of a single parent. Muir concluded by stressing such family relationships: "the abundance, therefore, of lofty angular rocks, instead of rendering Yosemite unique, is the characteristic which unites it most intimately with all the other similarly situated valleys in the range." [17] The journey of 1873 demonstrated the truth that Muir would insist on for the rest of his career, that no single element in nature can be understood in isolation, be it a single flower or a stupendous valley.

Such multiplication of Yosemites had a predictable side effect: it raised the possibility of competition between old and new, north and south. In his journal of 1864 Brewer had described Kings Canyon as a "rival" of Yosemite, a word Charles D. Robinson, the artist and illustrator, used again in his 1889 series on Kings Canyon for the *San Francisco Sunday Chronicle*. [18] It was Muir's editor, Robert Underwood Johnson, who entitled his 1891 article on the Kings "A Rival of the Yosemite." [19] Such comparisons of the "incomparable" valley could seem to dim the starring role the "old" Yosemite had so long enjoyed, and indeed Johnson recalled that Muir was accused in the press of being a "traitor to California" for daring to multiply Yosemites. [20] Robinson made the relative superiorities of the two Yosemites a principal theme of his *Chronicle* articles, expatiating freely on the kind of visitors each attracts. Kings Canyon, he wrote, will appeal to "the practiced and more eminent in all the liberal professions . . . the geologist, the writer, the artist, . . . the scholars of the world." The old Yosemite, on the other hand, is a good place for the "average tourist," and "the life-is-too-short 'rustler and summer butterfly' cast of humanity." [21]

A rather different sort of comparison lay at the heart of Muir's geological method, as we have seen, and he did not go on to deduce from his comparisons a hierarchy of preference. The many Yosemites of the Sierra differ, he wrote, "in no other way or degree than one man or mountain differs from another." [22] When a noble purpose justified it—to persuade readers to come to the mountains or to support the creation of a national park— Muir was not above praising the new at the expense of the old. "The new Yosemite of Kings Canyon," he wrote in the *Bulletin*, is "larger, and in some respects more interesting than the Yosemites of the Tuolumne and Merced." [23] In his journals, and occasionally in his published work, on the other hand, he acknowledged that in certain respects the "old" Yosemite remained without peer. The southern "El Capitan" lacks the stature of its northern brother, he pointed out, and no other valley matches the Merced's grand waterfalls.

Instead of exploiting such comparisons, however, Muir characteristically sought to soften and balance them, interpreting difference as a form of reconciling compensation, and avoiding or mocking the simple-minded superlatives favored by the press. On the trip of 1875 a small cascade on Dinkey Creek prompted a thought of "the booming cataract of Yosemite, half a mile high." That, he wrote, "is one thing; this little woodland fairy is another. Its plain spiritual beauty is most impressively brought forward." [24] Although most writers agreed that the cascades of the Kings were far inferior to the falls of the Merced, Muir defended them in his newspaper letter of 1875. They are, he wrote

> exceedingly beautiful, more beautiful than vertical falls, and belong to a higher type of water beauty. Nevertheless, it may be long ere waterfalls have their beauty measured in any other way than by plumb-lines and tapelines.[25]

If not ultimately irrelevant to Muir, sheer size was less important than "spiritual beauty." It is with waterfalls as it is with mountains: "as in all the mountains I have seen about the head of Merced and Tuolumne this region is a song of God." [26]

Two years later, in August 1875, Muir set out on what may have been his most memorable journey south, his purpose a close study of the Big Tree. "I want to go with the Sequoias a month or two," he wrote Mrs. Carr, "into all their homes from north to south, learning what I can of their conditions and prospects, their age, stature, the area they occupy, etc." [27] It was an arduous and eventful trip. Accompanied only by a tough, short-legged mule named Brownie, Muir followed earlier routes along the flank of the range to the Kings. He ran out of provisions, and was fed by a party of Indian sheepherders. He encountered and admired the beauty of a forest fire. Muir met a hermit, and fought a running battle with the weary and "jaded" Brownie, a battle he did not always win. He followed the sequoia to Giant Forest and beyond, across the Kaweah River to its southernmost groves along Deer Creek, and did not return to the northern Yosemite until November 1, two and one-half months after he started.

Two themes intertwine in the journal of this trip, and in the published writings that issued from it over the next fifteen years. Muir's principal purpose was to ascertain the health of the sequoia, in light of the then current Darwinian assumption that the species, hitherto known in small straggling northern groves, was a living relic verging on extinction. Although prepared to report that the sequoia was in a "period of decadence," a kind of "mastodon of the vegetable kingdom" that was doomed to extinction, Muir modified his opinions.[28] "The farther south I go," he reported to his *Bulletin* audience, "the thriftier and more numerous they become." [29] Repeatedly Muir described the sequoia as "thrifty," a word he gives its old sense of "thriving, prospering" and that in turn gives the tree the aspect of a plucky, hardworking husbandman, like the "thrifty fellows" Muir met down on the farms of the Tulare Flats.[30] In several letters and articles, accordingly, he presented a cogent demonstration of the species's vitality, based on his discovery of substantial new forests south of the Kings River, on observations of the tree's ecological success, and on evidence that its range had not diminished in thousands of years. One of these arguments brought his glacial theory into play, as he attributed the gaps in the sequoia's distribution not to any organic infirmity but to the absence of the glacial moraines on which it thrives. As he put it with admirable simplicity, "the wider the ancient glacier, the wider the corresponding gap in the sequoia belt." [31]

If the sequoia's abiding vitality was clear, that good news

was ironically overshadowed by the second lesson of the trip: the species was in mortal danger. Unlike the mountain sculpture he had celebrated up to now, these giant patriarchs were terribly vulnerable to man, to fire, and the ax. For Muir they fell into the category of natural objects that are "destructible"—a word that echoes through his writing at this time. "I wonder," he reflected in his journal, "what man will do with the mountains—that is, with their utilizable, destructible garments." [32] A sheepherder's sign in meadows along the Kings leads him to the gloomy prediction that "all the destructible beauty of this remote Yosemite is doomed to perish like that of its neighbors." [33] The same word dominates his letter, in February 1876, to the legislators of Sacramento: "The forests of coniferous trees growing on our mountain ranges are by far the most destructible of the natural resources of California." [34]

The consequences of this 1875 trip were thus quite different from those of 1873. Muir's exploration of mountain sculpture had prompted an elegant demonstration of the harmony of glacial action across the range, which if it drove home the argument against Whitney was nevertheless a celebration of the spirit he found in nature. The botanical work of 1875 inspired a similar celebration of the sequoia tree itself, but it also pointed beyond, to the necessity of human action. A new urgency entered Muir's writing at this time, as he sought to give the written word power to save the forests.

He now began to reach out to new audiences in new ways. His letters to the *Bulletin* grew more frequent in 1875, and in February of 1876 he wrote a trenchant letter to the *Sacramento Union* in an attempt to reach the state legislature. In August of 1876 his report to a distinguished national audience in the American Academy for the Advancement of Science called for the "most watchful attention of government." [35] An influential article on "The New Sequoia Forests of California" appeared in 1878 in *Harper's Magazine.* and three years later two articles on the remaining conifers of the range appeared in *Scribner's.*

After Yosemite

In 1875 Muir imagined the audience that was reading his words: "tame law-loving citizens," who "plant and water their garden daisies without concern, wholly unconscious of loss." [36] As his irony suggests, he was painfully aware that the fate of the sequoia lay with good-minded people who dutifully tend their own gardens and whose only fault is their ignorance, or as he would later call it, their "death-like apathy." [37] As he labored to give his language power to reach and move such people, his writing took on a new flexibility and power, from the often jocular informality of the *Bulletin* letters to the finely honed descriptive prose of the *Harper's* article. On occasion Muir admitted the intensities of his private correspondence into his public writing. At the conclusion of a letter to the *Bulletin*, for example, he wrote that, despite the difficulties of the terrain, he "will make a way, and love of King Sequoia will make all the labor light," offering himself as a role model for his city-dwelling readers. [38] He began to use concrete details to shape political attitudes. In the journals of 1873 he had passed the Kings River lumber mills without comment. In an entry of 1875, however, a mill on the Kaweah seems a sinister and predatory intruder: "booming and moaning like a bad ghost, [it] has destroyed many a fine tree from this wood— two million feet of lumber this year. And it has been running three years." [39] Sounds suggest the forest's vulnerability: "magnificent groves of King Sequoias . . . still flourish in cool glens and hollows from Kings river southward to the Kaweah, and yet beyond. Here we heard the sound of axes." [40] "When felled," he wrote, "the sequoia breaks like glass." [41] In 1875 he encountered a group of busy loggers preparing a section of sequoia trunk to be exhibited in Philadelphia at the 1876 Centennial Exhibition, and wryly noted that the imitation trunk they are constructing "will therefore appear as a huge tub cut from a hollow log," a "rustic tub." "Many a poor, defrauded town dweller will pay his dollar and peep, and gain some dead arithmetical notion of the bigness of our Big Trees, but a true and living knowledge of these tree gods is not to be had at so cheap a rate. As well try

Paul D. Sheats

to send a section of the storms on which they feed."[42] Humor provides one possible response to the pride and blindness of this human attempt to build a sequoia for exhibition in Washington by destroying the living tree in California. Another response, however, is dismay, and a sense of doom darkens many of the 1875 descriptions and makes Muir's earlier celebrations of mountain sculpture seem almost innocent by comparison. He now seems to take "The Doom of the Coniferae" as inevitable.[43]

Another of Muir's rhetorical strategies is descriptive. The task of defending the trees calls forth a richer, more focused descriptive style, which instead of preaching makes evident the value of what is being described. As we might expect from Muir's mistrust of comparative statistics, his descriptions of the giant Sequoia seldom dwell on superlatives—the sheer size of the tree or even its great age. In a first attempt to catch its spirit he noted in his journal that it is a "supremely noble kind of tree."[44] In the *Harper's* article, however, he analyzed the way we perceive its beauty before its size: its "real godlike grandeur in the meantime is invisible, but to the loving eye it will be manifested sooner or later, stealing slowly on the senses like the grandeur of Niagara or of some lofty Yosemite dome."[45] In a journal note he adopted a particularly novel point of view, sensing the tree's weight from the inside, as it were:

> The sequoias are the most venerable-looking of all the Sierra giants, standing erect and true, in poise so perfect they seem to make no effort—their strength so perfect it is invisible. Trees weighing one thousand tons are yet to all appearances imponderable as clouds, as the light which clothes them.[46]

What is remarkable, especially in the *Harper's* article, is Muir's penetration, beyond picturesque or sentimental responses, to an imaginative grasp, of the spirit of what he called "the great master-existence of these unrivalled woods."[47] Although not explicitly polemic, such descriptions attempt to make the reader feel as well as think that the tree is worth preserving, not for its size or rarity, but for its very existence.

256

After Yosemite

Even in the formal Academy report of 1876 the imagery of vitality dominates Muir's descriptive prose. The big trees grow "in brave and comfortable independence, over hill, and dale, and rocky ridgetop."[48] As he goes south they "become more and more irrepressibly exuberant, tossing their massive crowns from every ridgetop, and waving onward in graceful compliance to the complicated topography of the basins of the Kaweah and Tule."[49] For every "old storm-stricken tree there is one or more in all the glory of prime, and for each of these many young trees, and crowds of exuberant saplings."[50] Similar language appeared in the *Harper's* article: a grove is termed a "vigorous company of trees." He gladly recognizes the "well known crowns swelling grandly against the sky." The trees compete aggressively for sun and air, and even their limbs compensate for a lost crown "like a colony of bees that have lost their queen."[51] Descriptions and anecdotes incidental to the sequoia—a bear dell, a visit from a trusting deer, the encounter with the hermit, a relic of the "clang and excitement of the gold battles" who yet cares for the sequoia saplings—emphasize the harmony and delicacy of natural communities, and remind us obliquely that the only predator these woods need fear is ourselves.[52]

The effect of Muir's sequoia study and of this second trip south, was thus to change his conception of himself and his purpose. Bidding farewell to Yosemite a year earlier, he had described that purpose as one of celebrating the wilderness by describing it: "I care to live only to entice people to look at Nature's loveliness."[53] Now his task has become more complex: to assert not only the good news of the abiding vitality of the trees, but their ironic vulnerability to man, and to move his audience to save them. On the one hand he continued to resemble the biblical namesake to whom he compared himself for years, John the Baptist: he preaches the good tidings from the wilderness. But from now on he also recalls the angry prophet Jeremiah, who warned his people of the destruction that awaited them if they continued blindly in their evil ways. If this mixed role of preacher and prophet began to resemble the fire-and-brimstone fundamentalism of Muir's father, it also announced a new and mature voice of his own, and proclaimed a clear conception of his vocation.

What that vocation became may be seen in Muir's visit to Kings Canyon sixteen years later, in the early summer of 1891. This outing was made on assignment, as it were, for Robert Underwood Johnson, the associate editor of *Century Magazine*. A year earlier Muir had written two articles on Yosemite, which Johnson featured in his campaign for a National Park Bill, and as early as 1889 Johnson had suggested that he write on the Kings River country.[54] "I hope you will be able to go at the Kings River Cañon[*sic*]," he wrote Muir in August 1890 "for I want to have a bill introduced to reserve it."[55] Although Muir agreed that "it would be a fine thing to save the magnificent Kings River region," he did nothing for nearly a year, citing his ranch duties and his dislike of writing.[56] In the spring of 1891 Johnson's requests became urgent; his good friend, the Secretary of the Interior, seemed sympathetic to this new park, and he went so far as to compose a title for the unwritten article, which was to be called "A Rival of the Yosemite." As we have seen, he suggested that Muir mention that he had been labeled a "traitor to California" for daring to suggest that Yosemite had a competitor.[57] Muir never replied to this suggestion, and, distracted by the illness and death of his father-in-law, he did nothing until May, when he proposed a three-week trip to the canyon to take new measurements and to survey the state of the valley.

"I am bending and stretching at the oar on this Kings River article hard as I can," he wrote a few days after his return, and he finally sent it off, by registered mail, on August 15.[58] It appeared, lavishly illustrated by Charles Robinson in the November issue, a compendium of themes and images from 1875 and 1877; as in the books to come, Muir relied heavily on earlier journal writing and articles, especially the *Bulletin* letter of 1875. The article describes the various features of the Canyon and recommends side trips, minimizing the physical difficulty a visitor might en-

After Yosemite

"View from talis at foot of North Dome," Kings Canyon National Park. From a sketch by Charles Dorman Robinson, 1891. John Muir, "A Rival of the Yosemite," *Century Magazine*, 43 (November 1891), 89.

counter descending 3,000 feet of bear trail. A carriage road, it suggests, might be built to Cedar Grove and over the divide into Tehipite. Two maps describe the "proposed" park—proposed, Johnson noted with amusement in a letter, so far only by the two of them.[59] Muir dutifully elaborates on the "rivalry" of Johnson's title, adding new heights and depths to earlier comparisons between the "new" Yosemite and the old, and changing several of the names Robinson had given the features of the canyon in 1889. The spire Robinson had named "Mt. Hutchings" is not in fact a mountain at all, as he noted to Johnson, and he renamed it "The Sphinx."[60] To Robinson's gothic imagination a "monstrous" mass of white granite at the upper end of the valley seemed to resemble a corpse—"a dead woman of harsh features" laid out beneath a "white winding-sheet."[61] He called it the "White Woman," a name Muir questioned on grounds of both taste and accuracy. "Think of White Woman for a rock a mile high & two broad," he wrote to Johnson. "No whiter than any other mass of gray granite in the valley." And he proposed the less sentimental name we use today: "Glacier Monument." [62]

Johnson had urged Muir to avoid sentimentality and concentrate on description, and Muir himself found this article "guidebookish" and "dry." [63] There are, however, several interesting stylistic developments in the way he describes the valley. He had confessed to Johnson that his "stock of cliff and cascade adjectives are all used up, and I am too dull to invent new ones." [64] But his prose gathers energy when it arrives at the old waterfall comparisons. In Kings Canyon, he acknowledges, "we look in vain for a stream shaken loose and free in the air to complete the glory of this grandest of Yosemites." The description that then follows, of the comparatively unimpressive cascades of the Kings, deserves to be quoted in full:

> Nevertheless when we trace these cascading streams through their picturesque cañons, and behold the beauty they show forth as they go plunging in short round-browed falls from pool to pool, laving and plashing their sunbeaten foam-bells; gliding outspread in smooth shining plumes, or rich ruffled lace-work fold over fold; dashing down rough places in wild ragged aprons, dancing in up-bulging bosses of spray, the sweet brave ouzel helping them to sing, and ferns, lilies, and tough-rooted bushes shading and brightening their gray rocky banks,—when we thus draw near and learn to know these cascade falls, which thus keep in touch with the rocks, and plants, and birds, then we admire them even more than those which leave their channels and fly down through the air.[65]

As we move through this paragraph, Muir converts the very smallness of the Kings cascades into their chief virtue, a power to draw us into a close appreciation of ecological interconnection, the way the various elements of the landscape "keep in touch" with each other. The passage recalls other descriptions of Sierra waters, but in this context it becomes an exemplary act of compensation, in which Muir's language—a veritable cascade of enthusiastic verbs, not adjectives—takes on the task of righting the balance, and attests to the craftsmanship of this second Yosemite, this waterfall-poor sister of the south.

After Yosemite

A second, largely stylistic alteration takes place halfway through the essay. After citing the stupendous measurements that make the Kings Canyon a true "rival" of Yosemite Valley, Muir directs our attention again to the diminutive: a meadow on the canyon floor, and in that meadow, a tiger lily. The passage first appeared in the *Bulletin* article but now revises the earlier description, pruning it of enthusiastic adjectives:

> Near the Roaring Fall we came to a little circular meadow which was one of the most perfect gardens I ever saw. It was planted with lilies and orchids, larkspurs and columbines, daisies and asters. . . . One of the lilies was six feet high, and had eleven open flowers, five of them in their prime. . . . It was as if nature had fingered every leaf and petal that very day, readjusting every curving line and touching the colors of every corolla. Not a leaf, as far as I could see, was misbent, and every plant about it was so placed in reference to every other that the whole meadow-garden seemed to have been thoughtfully arranged like a tasteful bouquet.[66]

Emphasized by the precision of Muir's specification ("eleven" flowers), the movement from grand to exquisite takes place step by step, making the point once more that the sublime is not the only home of the spirit. In 1873 Muir had found the glacial patterns of the range "delicate" in their harmonies; in 1891 he finds the same harmony in a single flower.

Another survival from earlier days was indignation. As Muir decried the continuing inroads of sheepherders and lumbermen, he refined the work of 1875 in a style that prophesies his future jeremiads against the damming of Hetch Hetchy. "It seems incredible," he wrote, "that Government should have abandoned so much of the forest cover of the mountains to destruction. As well sell the rain-clouds, and the snow, and the rivers, to be cut up and carried away if that were possible."[67] No thanks, clearly, were due the Government for the Bill of 1890, which set aside only two small sequoia groves, Giant Forest, and the Grant Grove. The 1891 article ended with a brief assurance to the "law-givers"—mentioned here for the first time as his audience—that if they create "one grand national park" they will

Paul D. Sheats

be blessed—a prospective blessing Muir conferred, one senses, with less than complete confidence.[68]

That grand national park took a long time in the making. Although this 1891 article reached its intended congressional audience, no park bill was passed in 1891 or for the next 35 years, and Kings Canyon National Park did not attain its present borders until 1965. That it and Sequoia became parks at all, however, owes much to Muir's interest in the southern Sierra. What Muir himself owed to the southern trips he took in the 1870s is equally great. What he said of Sierra geology—that in order to understand Yosemite Valley one had to leave it—might be said of his own career as well. Contemporaries like Galen Clark, the valley's first guardian, and the landscape painter Thomas Hill, remained in the valley for many years and made a livelihood there. For Muir, however, it seems that further growth as a thinker and writer demanded that he put the intensities and potential fixations of his Yosemite years behind him. He began his wanderings anew, asking questions about the glacial past and the forest future, and he returned from the southern Sierra not only with answers geological and botanical but with a new literary and political purpose that continues to touch us all.

NOTES

1. William Frederic Badè, *The Life and Letters of John Muir* (Boston, Mass.: Houghton Mifflin, 1924), Vol. II, p. 26.

2. John Muir, *The Mountains of California* (Dunwoody, Ga.: Norman S. Berg, n.d.), p. 4.

3. Ibid., p. 6.

4. John Muir, *South of Yosemite: Selected Writings of John Muir*, ed. Frederic R. Gunsky, 1966 (Berkeley, Calif.: Wilderness Press, 1988). In the following discussion I am especially indebted to this fine anthology of writings, which has been recently reprinted in paperback, pertaining to the southern Sierra.

5. Muir to Janet Moores, July 2, 1891. *John Muir Papers*, University of the Pacific, Stockton, California.

6. See, for example, Bierstadt's "Yosemite Valley," painted in 1868 and now in the Oakland Museum.

After Yosemite

7. John Muir, "Studies in the Sierra, No. II," *Overland Monthly* 12 (June 1874): 490.

8. John Muir, *John Muir: Summering in the Sierra*, edited by Robert Engberg (Madison: University of Wisconsin Press, 1984), pp. 92–93.

9. Muir, "Studies in the Sierra," pp. 495–496.

10. To Jeanne Carr, late September 1873. I have silently corrected the spelling and punctuation of printed versions of this sentence. Like several other famous songs that use this refrain, "Green grow the rashes, O!" is by Muir's beloved Robert Burns.

11. Muir, "Studies in the Sierra," p. 498.

12. William H. Brewer, *Up and Down California in 1860–64: The Journal of William H. Brewer*, ed. Francis P. Farquhar, 3d ed. (Berkeley, Calif.: University of California Press, 1966), p. 530.

13. John Muir, *John of the Mountains: The Unpublished Journals of John Muir*, ed. Linnie Marsh Wolfe (Madison: University of Wisconsin Press, 1938), p. 184.

14. Muir, *Summering in the Sierra*, p. 92.

15. Muir to unidentified recipient, October 20, 1891, *John Muir Papers*.

16. Muir, "Studies in the Sierra," p. 490.

17. Ibid., p. 500.

18. Brewer, *Up and Down California*, p. 590; Charles D. Robinson, "Yosemite's Rival," *The Sunday Chronicle*, November 10, 1889: 8.

19. Johnson to Muir, May 1, 1891, *John Muir Papers*.

20. Ibid.

21. Charles D. Robinson, "Far Up King's River," *Sunday Chronicle*, November 3, 1889, p. 8.

22. Muir, *Summering in the Sierra*, p. 92.

23. Ibid., p. 93.

24. John Muir, "The New Sequoia Forests of California," *Harper's New Monthly Magazine* 57 (June 1878): 819.

25. Muir, *Summering in the Sierra*, pp. 99–100.

26. Muir, *South of Yosemite*, p. 38.

27. Badè, *Life and Letters*, II, 54.

28. Muir, *Summering in the Sierra*, p. 127.

29. Ibid., p. 131.

30. Ibid., p. 140.

31. Muir, *South of Yosemite*, p. 181.

32. Muir, *John of the Mountains*, p. 215.

33. Muir, *Summering in the Sierra*, p. 102.

34. Muir, *South of Yosemite*, p. 197.

35. Ibid., p. 183.

36. Muir, *Summering in the Sierra*, p. 102.

37. Muir, *John of the Mountains*, p. 430.

38. Muir, *Summering in the Sierra*, p. 137.

39. Muir, *John of the Mountains*, p. 229.

40. Muir, *Summering in the Sierra*, p. 96.

41. Muir, *John of the Mountains*, p. 229.
42. Muir, *Summering in the Sierra*, pp. 96–97.
43. Ibid., p. 128.
44. Muir, *John of the Mountains*, p. 228.
45. Muir, "New Sequoia Forests," p. 813.
46. Muir, *John of the Mountains*, p. 228.
47. Muir, "New Sequoia Forests," p. 813.
48. Muir, *South of Yosemite*, p. 174.
49. Ibid., p. 175.
50. Ibid., p. 178.
51. Muir, "New Sequoia Forests," pp. 819–821.
52. Muir, *John of the Mountains*, p. 223.
53. Badè, *Life and Letters*, p. 29.
54. Johnson to Muir, August 21, 1889, *John Muir Papers.*
55. Ibid., August 28, 1890, *John Muir Papers.*
56. Muir to Johnson, September 12, 1890, *John Muir Papers.*
57. Johnson to Muir, May 1, 1891, *John Muir Papers.*
58. Muir to Johnson, July 2, 1891, *John Muir Papers.*
59. Johnson to Muir, July 22, 1891, *John Muir Papers.*
60. Muir to Johnson, August 15, 1891, *John Muir Papers.*
61. Robinson, "Yosemite's Rival," p. 8.
62. Muir to Johnson, August 15, 1891, *John Muir Papers.*
63. Johnson to Muir, December 19, 1889, *John Muir Papers;* Muir to Johnson, August 15, 1891, *John Muir Papers.*
64. Muir to Johnson, July 14, 1891, *John Muir Papers.*
65. John Muir, "A Rival of the Yosemite," *Century Illustrated Monthly Magazine* 18 (November 1891), p. 82.
66. Ibid., p. 86.
67. Ibid., p. 90.
68. Ibid., p. 97.

12.
"Fear Nothing"

An Interpretation of John Muir's Writings on Yellowstone

Bruce A. Richardson

In 1885, when John Muir first visited Yellowstone it had been a National Park for eighteen years and he had the opportunity to examine the features it shared with the National Parks in California.[1] This was difficult because Yellowstone was unusual, a "strange region of fire and water" Muir wrote to his wife.[2] The strangeness came, in part, from the comparison with Muir's beloved Yosemite with its mix of sublime and beautiful scenery carved by glaciers and abundantly adorned by trees and plants. Superficially, Yellowstone seemed much different. Indeed many nineteenth-century visitors found its noisy volcanism grotesque, disgusting, and weird. Was it heaven or hell? Many tourists favored the latter but veered back and forth. Almon Gunnison thought the place "fearful in its vast unrelieved weirdness." Rudyard Kipling describes geysers as "miraculous," "wonders," and "terrible creatures." Owen Wister disliked the stench, sound, and violence of the geysers but thought the Canyon was "the most beautiful thing [he had] ever seen."[3] Nathaniel Pitt Langford's influential essays and book about Yellowstone veer between romantic effusions about the scenery and language such as "revolting," "infernal," and "sickening."[4]

Muir's different writings about Yellowstone display a similar complexity. The journal entries and letters articulate his struggle with the park's uniqueness and his effort to find a Yosemite-like order in the landscape. The journal, in fact, was a rehearsal for the ordered vision of an essay published thirteen years later in *The Atlantic Monthly* (April 1898) and in *Our National Parks* (1901).[5] In these public texts Muir assimilated Yellowstone's intimations of the volcanic and catastrophic into his romantic geology. The park, he argued, displays a grand order not immediately apparent in the welter of sensations that assault the visitor. The challenge to Muir the writer is symbolized by the problems, philosophical and physical, that are clear in the private journal and suppressed in the public essay. Nonetheless, traces of the complexities, confusions and contradictions of Muir's primal response to Yellowstone remain a powerful part of the finished essay and give it a particular strength and richness absent in more conventional accounts.

In revising his journal, Muir addressed the myths about Yellowstone. Critic John Sears has recently argued that Yellowstone was not simply an interesting region, but a cultural construction "deliberately produced for Eastern audiences" by "capitalists, explorers, geologists, painters, writers, photographers" who publicized the area and established it as "an important tourist attraction." [6] Also important was the role of road engineers, hotel operators, guidebook authors, and finally, the army, who gave shape to the visitor's experience by designating and, in some cases, inventing attractions, such as the so-called pillar of Hercules near Mammoth.[7] Yellowstone promised, Sears argues, "an exhibition of curiosities, a symbolic access to heaven and hell, a sense of release," and "the restoration of health" associated with fountains and hot springs.[8] In his effort to give Yellowstone linguistic shape, Muir resisted some of these metaphors but employed others. However, his creative reformulation of the stereotypes offered a new myth—one of learning and spiritual rebirth—that he attempted to enact during his brief visit.

By 1885, Yellowstone was well defined, at least as a tourist haven, with roads, hotels, and guidebooks. Visitors could look forward to an intelligible, sequenced tour of designated wonders with some comforts along the way.[9] The major clusters of curiosities were well known, and most featured a hotel or tent camp. The result, as Rudyard Kipling described it, was a mixture of chaos and order:

> The Park is just a howling wilderness of three thousand square miles, full of all imaginable freaks of a fiery nature. An hotel com-

"Fear Nothing"

pany, assisted by the Secretary of State for the Interior, appears
to control it; there are hotels at all the points of interest, guidebooks, stalls for the sale of minerals, and so forth, after the model
of Swiss summer places.[10]

A stage company hauled people from spot to spot, so fast
Muir wrote, that the "multitude of mixed, novel impressions . . .
make only a dreamy, bewildering, swirling blur." [11] He advised
the visitor to take longer and get off the beaten track, where
"Nature's peace will flow into you as sunshine flows into trees." [12]
Though not travelling by stagecoach, Muir stayed mostly on the
beaten track, rushing though the park, seeing the standard sights
and feeling overwhelmed by the volume of sensations. In a letter
to his wife, he worried, "Sorry I can stay so short a time. Afraid
I will not learn much, still I may get some good facts besides the
mere pleasurable mass of wonderment from the spouting steam
and muds and suds." [13] Muir's journal, this author would argue,
stands as the "pleasurable mass of wonderment," whereas the
essay provides the shaping order.

As Muir reported "the park is easy of access." [14] He arrived
on the Northern Pacific Railroad at Livingston, took the spur
to Cinnebar, and a stagecoach to Mammoth where he checked
into the new hotel, which served "abominable" and expensive
meals.[15] The place as well as the hotel was not initially appealing,
as he wrote to his wife Louie:

> The general appearance of the country hereabouts is gray and ashy
> and forbidding—few trees except in hollows and ravines. Gray
> sage hills with here and there rough gray jumpers and two-leaved
> pines, far away removed from the freshness and leafy beauty
> of Yosemite. The piles of salt from the springs hundreds of feet in
> height stained with many colors interblended look like the refuse
> heaps about chemical and dye works.[16]

Muir did not employ this language of wasteland alienation
in the public essay. Rather the terraces are the result of centuries of "beauty work," which he defined with theological and
organic metaphors. At Mammoth is "divine masonry" shaped by

water "as surely guided as the sap of plants streaming into bole and branch, leaf and flower." [17] There is a suggestion of this in the letter to Louie. Muir described walking up the terraces and seeing a "marvellous abundance of beautiful forms and strange colors" though the aesthetic response is immediately undercut. He also described the glare of the hot sun on the white landscape, which made the walk difficult and an hotel lunch, as "bad as possible though costing a dollar." He hiked back up the terraces and vomited. [18]

This episode establishes a matrix of connections that define Muir's complex reaction to Yellowstone. He initially saw the Mammoth terraces as the scene of ugliness and disorder, completely unlike Yosemite and what Muir valued in landscape. He connected its radical otherness with industry—chemical and dye works—pollution, and the tourist culture embodied by the hotel and its bad food. The stomach disorder reflects his dislike of the place. Muir, as it were, took this disturbing land into himself and was hard-pressed to reshape it, himself and his writing into "divine masonry."

Part of the problem was the lack of general information that would help explain this unusual place. At some point during the day he "got some valuable facts relating to geysers and glaciers," possibly from Arnold Hague, of the U. S. Geological Service, who had been working in the park for several years. [19] In his essay, Muir credited Hague for park names, and Muir's account of the area's geology resembles Hague's. [20] In 1896, Muir would travel through Yellowstone with Hague and others on Forestry Commission business. The information provided an essential overview, as did the view of Mammoth from "a mile or two" where it looks like "a broad massive cascade." [21] One might get a similar perspective from nearby Electric Peak, and he recommended to readers of the essay that the weak visitor climb to be "kindly shaken and shocked" though he lacked the time and energy to undertake the ascent. [22]

Honeymooners Mr. and Mrs. Frank Sellers of Chicago invited the weak and still ill Muir to travel with them through the park. They all employed a guide and a cook who did all the camp work. On August 19 the group headed east to Tower Falls instead of taking the main stagecoach route south past Obsidian Cliff and Roaring Mountain to the Norris Geyser Basin. To Muir, Tower Falls were like Vernal in Yosemite but not completely, because, as he wrote in the journal, Tower's "curious mass of pillars" create a "strange setting."[23]

The party turned south and one day, Muir made the fairly easy climb, "a saunter" he reports, up Mount Washburn. In the essay Muir discussed the fine view of the surrounding mountains, forests, Yellowstone Lake, the Grand Canyon, and "puffs of steam . . . indicating geysers and hot springs."[24] At this point on the trip Muir had not seen a geyser, but in retrospect he concluded that mountaintop view is "better than when you are standing beside them, frightened and confused."[25] The overview, in other words, distances and orders the threatening hellish details.

On the third day, a downhill trail took the party to the brink of the Lower Falls and what Muir called "the strange new world of the canyon." The canyon was generally regarded as the scenic climax of any Yellowstone tour, but Muir was skeptical. In the journal he wrote that the scene has "exquisite color," yet is "meadowless treeless . . . half ashes, half stone." The "unstable" and "rotten" lava flows lead Muir to wonder, "a land of dislocation? No only a canyon of dislocation."[26] Glaciers at one time lay on the canyon, but had little to do with its shape, which came from the work of water, the Yellowstone river above and the thermal waters from deep below that decomposed the rhyolite. The result, wrote Muir, is a "weird world crumbling yet forming." In the published essay Muir subsumed his initial response into a conclusion that the canyon is "a kindly, beautiful part of the general harmony," but mainly because of the vegetation on the rims. Otherwise "we imagine a river might be afraid to enter" a place "so novel and awful."[27]

Bruce A. Richardson

The implied identification with the river indicates Muir's discomfort with this natural anomaly that does not fit easily in existing models of canyon building. The canyon seems a scene of destruction and formation with no pattern of steady growth. Muir's alienation from this "meadowless treeless" wasteland represents, as at Mammoth, his confrontation with the horrid other that evokes awe and personal dislocation. Other writers described the canyon in the language of the terrible sublime, but most of them return with delight to the glorious color that redeems the sense of terror and disorder.[28] Muir, though impressed by the color ("All the earth hereabouts seems to be paint"), saw it as a sign of the canyon's otherworldliness and part of the force that might terrify the life-giving river. The canyon is itself a "strange world of fire and water." The river cuts through the walls, which, decomposed by thermal action, "burn in a perfect glory of color."[29] The fiery wasteland threatens but does not destroy the stabilizing vitality of living plants and water.

On the fourth day, the party headed upriver to more comprehensible country, the lush and peaceful Hayden valley and then into the woods, where "much fallen and burnt timber" evoked the threat of destruction. At the outlet of Yellowstone Lake, the party moved along the west shore past the natural bridge, the West Thumb geysers, and some "fine mtn views" across the lake.[30]

Even in that area, nature continued to prove difficult. The lack of a good trail through thick timber made the trip rough that day and the next when they crossed the Continental Divide in rain and hail. After reaching the Upper Geyser Basin at four in the afternoon, Muir was ill from the travel, weather, and awful cooking. Like most tourists, the first geyser he saw was Old Faithful where he experienced an unpleasant moment of cosmic harmony:

> just as the geyser . . . began to play spouting a huge column of boiling water into the sky my organ [stomach] began spouting vast quantities of hot acid water in close accord. How the water got in

"Fear Nothing"

Beehive Geyser, Yellowstone National Park.

my stomach I don't know. Certainly I never drank it & how the sympathy was established between the geysers and organ I don't know but it was all very violent & very painful & very wonderful.[31]

He contemplated giving up the tour and resting in a "house," probably the Upper Basin hotel, but he was able to continue. The hotel had scouts out to check thermal activity and at six in the evening an alarm sounded, and all the visitors rushed across the river to see an eruption of Beehive Geyser that exploded one to two hundred feet out of a narrow cone. Muir reports that

boys played about it throwing hats sticks cans etc. into the cascading column . . . these were tossed to a height of 100 feet or so faster than the eye could see while the current was so compact at the base that one could get close to it without danger and stroke the hard mass.[32]

The relief at being able to stand so close and actually "stroke the hard mass" was lost at night. The party slept out among the geysers that rumbled like earthquakes and that "look like monstrous dancing ghosts." Only the morning dissolved "the seeming chaos of darkness into the varied forms of harmony" by showing that the ordinary work of the world continued.[33] The ordered beautiful, associated with animals and plants, replaced the threat of dissolution. During the day Muir again saw the power in the Upper Basin. There were eruptions of Old Faithful, Fan geyser, many of the small geysers and also Grand, a pool that "throws large bursts of water in ragged jets," then stops for a few minutes before it heaves skyward "with marvellous force," over two hundred feet.[34]

As he traveled the valley Muir was especially impressed by the "steam clouds ever ascending mingling with clouds of sky" suggesting a unity between a peaceful heaven and a violent earth. That the clouds come out of the forest shows the geysers "seeming to be considered one with nature." In a journal discussion probably of the colorful mud pots in the Lower Geyser Basin, Muir wrote that the nearby grasses and trees are

"Fear Nothing"

"all seeming to fear not those marvellous teaching pots of nature as if saying in confidence: you also are one of us strange tho you are." [35]

The text here suggests that Muir has transcended his own alienation and achieved a moment of harmony with the forces of Yellowstone. In the journal Muir's narrative of the trip breaks off and he starts to assemble notes for the projected essay. His problem was how to develop concepts and metaphors to find what he calls "divine government" at work in a land that he initially thought of as bizarre. One strategy was to translate his own epistemological problem into a definition. Historian Michael Cohen argues that, for Muir, "the experience of Yellowstone was educational at center." [36] Muir himself describes the Park as a sort of university with its "teaching pots," "geological library," and "natural laboratories." [37] Here we can study creation in process, he states, and move from confusion to wholeness in our conceptions and in ourselves. Further, he notes that one can study Nature working furiously, as chemist or cook. The passages describing this process have a particular resonance, given Muir's intestinal disorder and complaints about the food in Yellowstone. As at Old Faithful, Muir's inner physiology echoes the outer world. He describes Nature "cooking whole mountains; boiling and steaming flinty rocks to smooth paste and mush" and stirring "pots of sulphurous mush, stringy and lumpy, and pots of broth as black as ink." [38] John Sears, a commentator cited above, finds a carnival quality to this passage; in Muir's Yellowstone, "the forces of creation themselves seem to be on holiday, carrying on not with the solemn dignity of glaciers, but with joyful whimsy." [39] The whimsy, though, does not account for the dislocation and disgust described in Muir's journal and hinted at in the essay, as in the discussion of the mud pots, "sticky, rank smelling masses, with gasping, belching, thudding sounds, plastering the branches of neighboring trees." [40] This is a threatening environment, ugly and chaotic and not measuring up to Muir's Yosemite standard.

How does Muir deal with Yellowstone's most famous feature, the geysers? He attempts to domesticate them with organic metaphors appropriate for Yosemite, but as Cohen points out, "the language of Yosemite" did not translate well to Yellowstone.[41] Geysers are like "inverted waterfalls," with some "as large as sequoias."[42] In a letter to his daughter, the comparison is explicit: "In Yosemite Valley the water falls down out of the sky, & in the Yellowstone Valley the water spouts up out of the ground and into the sky."[43] In the essay, Muir extends the tree conceit. The geysers' sides are "roughened or fluted like the furrowed boles of trees, their tops dissolving in feathery branches." Some lean "as if storm-bent"; some are "broad and round-headed like oaks; others are low and bunchy . . . like bushes; and a few are hollow in the centre like big daisies or water-lilies." We find them "bursting into bloom and vanishing like the frailest flowers,—plants of which Nature raises hundreds or thousands of crops a year with no apparent exhaustion of the fiery soil."[44]

Interestingly, Muir does not sustain these organic metaphors but undercuts them with language more characteristic of the journal. Geysers are "novel and awful," "weird," and "unearthly."[45] Close up they seem to be "lawless cataclysms" that evoke fright and confusion in the viewer. But these are only transitory impressions in a progress from fear to comfort, chaos to order, and the sublime to the beautiful. As an epistemological process it is the move from raw, disconnected detail to theory that orchestrates discrete facts into patterns. Aesthetically it is a shift from viewing ugly chaos to seeing the symmetrical order or beauty. Emotionally it is the move from the discomfort and fear of the unknown to the comfort of the ordered and then a worshipful awe at this order. Textually, it is the growth from the cooking in the journal to the finished form of the essay.

This pattern, characteristic of Muir's writing, occurs elsewhere in the Yellowstone essay. A night among the geysers tests the stoutest faith: "The ground sounds hollow underfoot, and the awful subterranean thunder shakes one's mind as the ground

"Fear Nothing"

is shaken." The geysers look like "monstrous dancing ghosts, and their wild songs and the earthquake thunder replying to the storms overhead seem doubly terrible, as if divine government were at an end." But then the dawn comes, "dissolving the seeming chaos of darkness into varied forms of harmony . . . calming every fear, reducing everything to love."[46] Tourists at a geyser eruption are at first "a little frightened," then enthusiastic and worshipful. All run when "the tremendous outburst begins . . . with awful uproar as if avalanches were falling and storms thundering in the depths . . . all run to a safe distance, and look on, awe-stricken and silent, in devout, worshipping wonder."[47]

Is the fear and confusion resolved by the retreat? And is the disruptive material in the journal subsumed by the metaphors in the essay? Up close Yellowstone's volcanism is messy, but if one retreats, the geysers are beautiful. In fact, one should really pull back. Muir advises, climb a mountain, especially Mount Washburn as he did, for a "general, calming, settling view" and some grand metaphors.[48] From there geysers and hot springs are puffs of steam, "gentle-looking and noiseless as downy clouds, softly hinting the reaction going on between the surface and hot interior." Up close the viewer is "frightened and confused, regarding them as lawless cataclysms" and not what they appear to be from the mountain, one of "the orderly love beats of Nature's heart."[49]

Muir substantiates this airy figure by returning again to water. He knew that within Yellowstone Park were sources for the Snake-Columbia system, the Yellowstone and the Madison and Galletin, two of the three rivers that form the Missouri. Not merely "lawless cataclysms," the geysers are river sources; they dance at the Missouri's head "keeping time with the sea-waves at its mouth."[50] The long passage here provides a rich account of the river's work as source of life along the way to the gulf and suggests that geysers are part of a larger order. The mountaintop meditation attempts, then, to see geysers as part of a living process by focusing on water and not lava. Besides subsuming the geysers in the large spatial system of rivers, Muir places them in the temporal sweep of geological history. He tells the geological story in terms of the petrified trees above the Lamar valley. These giants were buried in a succession of volcanic storms that buried forest on top of forest. He imagines the birds and animals in terror of the volcano and the sympathetic "trembling, rocking, tumultuous waving of these ancient Yellowstone woods" as the sky darkened and the volcano buried them. Then came the glaciers, "fashioning the comparatively featureless lava beds into the beautiful rhythm of hill and dale and ranges of mountains we behold today."[51] Muir sees the glaciers working with the volcanic fires below, which were decomposing the rock while the ice shaped it. He imagines their violent meetings at the surface in the confrontation of ice and enormous geysers. Muir says these forces worked "harmoniously together" though the final result shows the glaciers' power of articulation that left landscapes "incomparably more beautiful than the old volcanic ones were." "In its main telling features," Muir asserts, the Yellowstone landscape "remains distinctly glacial."[52] The key word is "telling." In Muir's cosmology, the volcanic is the powerful, but inarticulate, mess of creation, waiting for the glaciers to organize the lava flows and write the story.

Nonetheless, geysers, not glaciers, dominate Yellowstone's tourist circuit, an elaborate language system in itself. Eighteen eight-five was a crucial year in the development of that system. The Fountain Hotel opened, joining hotels at Mammoth and the Upper Basin that were finished in 1884. Tourist camps and food services were also expanded and Captain Dan Kingman was constructing and reconstructing the roads necessary to handle the increased traffic.[53] The road system, which identified and connected certain special features—especially geyser basins— gave Yellowstone a distinct shape that regulated and structured the tourists' experiences. Muir seems to have recognized that this was an arbitrary system that may have appeared natural since the hotels were attached to the "wonders." After describ-

"Fear Nothing"

Upper Geyser Basin. From a wood carving in James Richardson, *Wonders of the Yellowstone Region* (1874).

ing the park in terms of that sequence of scenic highlights, Muir moves to undercut its authority. The phrase "so-called," which he applies to the "curiosities," "geyser basins," and "points of interest . . . geysers, springs, paint pots, mud volcanoes, etc.," suggests that these provide a false map of Yellowstone.[54] In the essay, Muir revises that map to marginalize the wonders and the artificial construction of the park as a museum of curiosities strung along a road system. Instead, Muir reaches for an ecological-glacial language truer to Yellowstone's essential form as part of natural process and large systems. He advises the traveller to get off the circuit of "the wagon roads and the hotels," climb a mountain to break free of the commercially enforced fragmentation of Yellowstone and see it whole.[55]

That commercial order, though, cannot be understood apart from the emerging American industrial economy and the army that protected it. These concerns emerge in two important

Bruce A. Richardson

metaphors. Muir describes geyser steam "entangled like smoke among the neighboring trees, suggesting the factories of some busy town or the camp fires of an army."[56] The two comparisons are potent images for late nineteenth-century culture. Most tourists compared the geyser basins to factory towns and many wondered at the force expended there and lamented the waste of so much energy.[57] Charles Dudley Warner even speculated that "that there is no doubt energy here enough to outlast our time, and perhaps our nations, there can be little doubt that this region acts as a safety-valve of the continent, which would be shaken with earthquakes if these vents were stopped up."[58]

The army metaphor suggests counterforces that preserve the "wonders" and restrain their seething energy. In 1885, the army had come to Yellowstone and started multiple operations to protect the park, through the control of poaching, vandalism, and fire. Soon outposts were set up and geyser basins were guarded by armed soldiers on patrol; others sought out poachers and loggers and put out fires in the backcountry.[59] By the time Muir returned in 1896, Fort Yellowstone at Mammoth was a large operation and people traveled on a good road system built by army engineers. Muir praises the army, which operates subtly and powerfully, as if it were Nature itself:

> Under this care the forests are flourishing, protected from both axe and fire . . . the so-called curiosities are also preserved and the furred and feathered tribes, many of which, in danger of extinction a short time ago, are now increasing in numbers,—a refreshing thing to see amid the blind, ruthless destruction that is going on in the adjacent regions. In pleasing contrast to the noisy, ever changing management, or mismanagement, of blundering, plundering, money-making vote-sellers who receive their places from boss politicians as purchased goods, the soldiers do their duty so quietly that the traveller is scarce aware of their presence.[60]

On one hand, the army protects the wonders from rampant vandalism, thereby preserving the geysers, Yellowstone's crucial features, and the commercial system emerging in the park. On the other, the army restrains rampant commercialism by stopping poaching and logging. Muir associates the management of resources with protection from capitalism that consumes everything. The problem was not just poachers, but hotel and camp operators who regularly chopped trees and killed game to supply their establishments. Besides stopping human consumption, the army fought forest fires, an act of preservation in Muir's view. He extends the battle metaphor to trees with the lodgepole pine, which dumps its seeds after fire, winning out over Englemann spruce and subalpine silver fur, both poor fire fighters. The lodgepole "not only holds its ground, but extends its conquests after every fire" and "bids fair to obtain possession of nearly all the forest ground in the West."[61] The army, then, acts as a counterforce to this imperial march, controlling fires and promoting greater diversity of trees. Its functions are parallel to the glaciers that overwhelm volcanism, shape the land, and prepare the way for plant life. This work is continued by the rivers. Although water is exempted from controls, fire and heat require human management. Similarly, the forces that drive people to acquire and use up resources demand restraints.

"Fear nothing," Muir tells the would-be Yellowstone visitor.[62] He is writing his essay to encourage visitors to come so he tells them that the bears are no problem, rattlesnakes are few, Indians who would attack you are gone, and the army is keeping order. Muir here ventures into tourist guidebook genre, which allows him to support preservation ideals, but he also finds layered order from Nature, park designers, and the army. We should fear nothing because, at the deepest level, the frightening things are part of divine government. Here the surface management enforces, rather than contradicts, the power of nature.

Muir's rhetoric recalls Thoreau's vision of the railroad cut at Walden Pond, where, as Leo Marx has argued, everything in the world, trains included, can be an organic microcosm of a vital universe.[63] Muir employs his metaphors in a sustained attempt to integrate Yellowstone's apparently cataclysmic volcanism with a uniformitarian, organic model. We have two Muirs here, just as we have two Yellowstones. There is the nauseated Muir of the journal trying to make sense of this "land of dislocation" and struggling, in illness and bad weather, simply to write. The Muir of the essay has subordinated the difficulties into the shape of the organic universe. He also subordinates the volcanism and the commercial structures of the park to his apparently harmonious ecological vision. But at the heart of Yellowstone is the disturbing and potentially apocalyptic force of heat bursting from the earth and expressed in steam-powered industry, all of which must be shaped and controlled. Muir's essay does that work by attempting to contain these complexities as well as the difficulties and confusions of the trip into a sequence of metaphors. Similarly, Yellowstone underwent volcanic cataclysm that was settled and reformulated by the glaciers.

Whereas Muir found universal connections between geysers and the spirit of nature, most people just thought they were unusual and wonderful. Hot pools, mud pots, geysers, the mud volcano, and other Yellowstone thermal features were generally described as strange, hellish, violent, disturbing, smelly, factory-like, ungodly, frightening. All of this language presses against Muir's effort to locate organic form, aesthetic beauty, and divine order in what he initially found to be odd and sometimes distasteful. In Muir's writing the warring dichotomies of Yellowstone play themselves out. His journal and its revisions into essay dramatize the problematics of fire and water and the pressure such a place puts on the rage for order.

NOTES

1. Thanks to Richard Fleck for information on sources and to Jeanne Holland for advice on an early draft of this essay.
2. John Muir to Louie Muir, August 20, 1885, *John Muir Papers*, University of Pacific, Stockton, CA.

"Fear Nothing"

3. Almon Gunnison, *Rambles Overland* (Boston: Universalist Publishing House, 1884), p. 37. Rudyard Kipling, *From Sea to Sea: Letters of Travel* (Boston: Scribner, 1910), reprinted in Paul Schullery, ed., *Old Yellowstone Days* (Boulder: Colorado Associated University Press, 1979), pp. 103, 105, 109; Owen Wister, *Owen Wister Out West: His Journals and Letters*, edited by Fanny Kemble Wister (Chicago: University of Chicago Press, 1958), p. 59.

4. Nathaniel Pitt Langford, *The Discovery of Yellowstone Park: Journal of the Washburn Expedition to the Yellowstone and Firehole Rivers in the Year 1870* (Lincoln: University of Nebraska Press, 1972), p. 24

5. John Muir, *Our National Parks* (Boston: Houghton Mifflin, 1901), reprinted with forward by Richard Fleck (Madison: University of Wisconsin Press, 1981).

6. John F. Sears, *Sacred Spaces: American Tourist Attractions in the Nineteenth Century* (New York: Oxford University Press, 1989), pp. 157–158.

7. See Lee H. Whittlesey, *Yellowstone Place Names* (Helena: Montana Historical Society Press, 1988), p. 122.

8. Sears, *Sacred Spaces*, p. 176.

9. See Richard A. Bartlett, *Yellowstone: A Wilderness Besieged* (Tucson: University of Arizona Press, 1985), pp. 43–72, 113–168 and Aubrey L. Haines, *The Yellowstone Story* (Boulder: Colorado Associated University Press, 1977), vol. 2, pp. 100–159.

10. Kipling, *From Sea to Sea*, pp. 81–89.

11. Muir, *Our National Parks*, p .56.

12. Ibid.

13. Letter, August 20, 1885, *John Muir Papers*.

14. Muir, *Our National Parks*, p. 51.

15. Letter, August 20, 1885, *John Muir Papers*.

16. Ibid.

17. Muir, *Our National Parks*, p. 47.

18. Letter, August 20, 1885, *John Muir Papers*.

19. Ibid.

20. Muir, *Our National Parks*, p. 58. See Arnold Hague, *Geological History of the Yellowstone National Park* (New York: The Institute of Mining Engineers, 1888). Hague's account of the volcanic history of the area resembles Muir's.

21. Muir, *Our National Parks*, p .47.

22. Ibid., p. 59.

23. Muir, Journal, "Trip to Yellowstone Park," (August 15; 19–[24?]), *John Muir Papers*.

24. Muir, *Our National Parks*, p. 70.

25. Ibid.

26. Muir, Journal, "Trip to Yellowstone Park," *John Muir Papers*.

27. Muir, *Our National Parks*, p. 50.

28. Langford, *The Discovery of Yellowstone Park*, pp. 29–37, Cornelius Hedges, "The Great Falls of the Yellowstone," *Helena Herald* (October 15, 1870), p. 1 and James Richardson, *Wonders of the Yellowstone Region* (London: Blackie & Son, 1874), pp. 78–89. Langford's influential account moves from terror and awe to

religious rapture. Hedges described a "feeling of terror that so interrupted the enjoyment of the beauties of the scene. Richardson reprints many accounts generally stressing the canyon's peculiarity as a source of fear. Kipling's vivid account begins with "terror," but ends with the feeling of "floating" amid "blinding color"; reprinted in Schullery, *Old Yellowstone Days*, p. 112.

29. Muir, *Our National Parks*. pp. 49–50.

30. Muir, Journal, "Trip to Yellowstone Park," *John Muir Papers*.

31. Letter, August 30, 1885, *John Muir Papers*.

32. Muir, Journal, "Trip to Yellowstone Park," *John Muir Papers*.

33. Muir, *Our National Parks*, p. 45.

34. Muir, Journal, "Trip to Yellowstone Park," *John Muir Papers*.

35. Ibid.

36. Michael Cohen, *The Pathless Way: John Muir and the American Wilderness* (Madison: University of Wisconsin Press, 1984), p. 252.

37. Muir, *Our National Parks*, pp. 44, 59. Previously, Captain William Jones described the canyon as "God's awful laboratory"; "Report upon the Reconnaissance of Northwestern Wyoming Made in the Summer of 1873," House Executive Document 285, 43d Congress, 1st session, p. 23.

38. Muir, *Our National Parks*, p. 44.

39. Sears, *Sacred Spaces*, p. 174.

40. Muir, *Our National Parks*, p. 45.

41. Cohen, *Pathless Way*, p. 270.

42. Muir, *Our National Parks*, p. 42.

43. Letter, September 9/10, 1885, *John Muir Papers*.

44. Muir, *Our National Parks*, pp. 42–43.

45. Ibid., pp. 47, 48.

46. Ibid., pp. 45–46.

47. Ibid., pp. 53–54.

48. Ibid., p. 66.

49. Ibid., p. 70.

50. Ibid., p. 72.

51. Ibid., p. 64.

52. Ibid., p. 65.

53. Bartlett, *Yellowstone*, pp. 43–72.

54. Muir, *Our National Parks*, pp. 40, 43, 51.

55. Ibid., pp. 51, 66.

56. Ibid., p. 43.

57. See W. W. Wylie, *Yellowstone National Park or the Great American Wonderland* (Kansas City: Ramsey, Millett, & Hudson, 1882), p. 45. Wylie writes that from a distance the geysers basins resemble "a great manufacturing city." Kipling (p. 98) mocks tourists concerned with the " 'dreffel waste of steam-power.' " Owen Wister thought the geyser basin suggested "a manufacturing center in full swing"; "Old Yellowstone Days" *Harper's Magazine* (March 1936), reprinted in Schullery, *Old Yellowstone Days*, p. 71.

"Fear Nothing"

58. Charles Dudley Warner, "Editor's Study," *Harper's* (January 1897), reprinted in Schullery, *Old Yellowstone Days*, p. 163.

59. See George Anderson, "Work of the Cavalry in Protecting Yellowstone National Park," *Journal of the United States Cavalry Association* (March 1897) and Bartlett, *Yellowstone*, pp. 257–280.

60. Muir, *Our National Parks*, p. 40.

61. Ibid., p. 59.

62. Ibid., p. 58.

63. Leo Marx, *The Machine in the Garden: Technology and the Pastoral Ideal in America* (Oxford: Oxford University Press, 1964), pp. 261–262.

13.
John Muir's Travels in Australasia, 1903–1904

Their Significance for Conservation and Environmental Thought

C. Michael Hall

This essay discusses John Muir's travels in Australia and New Zealand in 1903 and 1904, a relatively unknown part of Muir's life that is of interest not only in relation to the history of conservation and environmental thought but is also particularly apt, given the present strength of the conservation movement as a political force in Australasia.[1] Muir traveled constantly throughout his life, often following in the footsteps of explorer-geographers such as Alexander Humboldt. Indeed, much of the significance attached to Muir's influence on environmental thought has been derived from the writings and commentaries of Muir on his travels and walks.[2] However, although much emphasis has been placed on the transcendental character of many of Muir's writings, relatively little attention has been paid to his contributions to botany and natural history. In 1877 he guided the distinguished British naturalist and Director of Kew Gardens, Sir Joseph Dalton Hooker, in the mountains of California in search of *Linnaea* and established a friendship that was to last until Hooker's death in 1911. Muir was a close friend of several members of the influential Harvard Department of Botany including Charles S. Sargent, John Tyndall, James Forbes, and Asa Gray, and he was an early champion of Darwin in the United States. Throughout his life Muir continually "botanised," and he supplied the Harvard School of Natural History with many specimens of fauna and flora.[3]

The "official" biography of Muir by Linnie Marsh Wolfe spent only one page discussing Muir's four months in Australia and New Zealand and paid little attention to the possible significance of this period for the evolution of Muir's ideas on conservation.[4] Similarly, William Frederic Badè's study, *The Life and*

C. Michael Hall

Letters of John Muir, and Wolfe's selection from Muir's unpublished journals paid only cursory attention to Muir's Australasian excursions.[5] Ryan, in a special edition of *The Pacific Historian* on the life and legacy of John Muir, charts Muir's travels to Australia in search of tall trees.[6] However, the article contains several inaccuracies and neglects to place the visit within the broader context of Muir's thought. The present author discussed Muir's visit to Australia in relation to the development of a wilderness ethic, whereas another of his articles examined Muir's travels in New Zealand and their possible significance for conservation thought and the evolution of Muir's own ideas.[7]

Muir visited Australia and New Zealand as part of an extensive world tour in 1903–1904. He had dreamed of coming to Australia and New Zealand since his childhood days in Scotland. "Burrowing like moles we visited France, India, America, Australia, New Zealand, and all the places we had never heard of; our travelling never ending until we fell asleep."[8] Muir's tour took him through Europe, Russia, Manchuria via the Trans-Siberian Railway, Shanghai, Calcutta, Darjeeling, Egypt, and Ceylon (Sri Lanka) before reaching Australia and New Zealand. Muir returned to San Francisco via Timor, the Phillipines, Canton, Japan, and Hawaii. Such a grand tour was remarkable in that day and age. That a rigorous trip by steamer, railroad, and stagecoach, was undertaken by a sixty-five-year-old bears full testimony to Muir's commitment to see "God's glorious wildernesses."[9]

The implications of his overseas travels for the evolution of conservationist thought has not received the attention they deserve. For instance, during his European trip of 1893 Muir met and established firm friendships with such prominent scientists as the Hookers of Kew Gardens and Alfred Wallace. In addition, it may be claimed that his overseas travels helped place the significance of conserving the wilderness areas of the United States in an international context. Indeed, in an interview following his return to California from his world trip, Muir stated,

Travels in Australasia

"when I left here a year ago it was not that I had exhausted North America, or that I was tired of it. I wanted to test a few of the theories evolved during a long term of intimate study." [10] Similar sentiments were also echoed by Muir upon his return to San Francisco from South America and South Africa in 1912.[11]

The record of Muir's four months in Australia and New Zealand is contained in his journals for the trip. Muir recorded his activities and impressions on a daily basis, and it is his diary that provides the main account of Muir's response to the Australasian environment. However, during his stay, he also wrote several letters to family and friends that provide some valuable insights into Muir's thoughts. According to Ryan the primary reason for Muir's world trip was to search for tall trees.[12] Undoubtedly, the examination of official records of tree sizes was an important aspect of his travels.[13] However, to state that tall trees were the primary reason for his visit to Australia would be to take an overly simplistic approach to Muir's writings and actions. Muir appeared extremely anxious to observe forestry management and conservation practices. Indeed, the fact that he was accompanied for a part of the trip by Professor Charles Sprague Sargent of Harvard University, former chairman of the National Forestry Commission and a noted authority on North American trees, suggests that his travels were filled with serious intentions other than the hunt for tall trees.

At the turn of the century, national parks were used to protect nature's monuments.[14] Therefore, establishing the fact that the redwoods were the tallest trees in the world would be a significant weapon in ensuring a degree of federal protection. However, Muir's trip can also be seen as a personal "pilgrimage" to travel in the footsteps of scientists such as Darwin, Hooker, and Wallace and, hence, see for himself the environments of which they were writing and the context within which their ideas of natural history would be developed.

Muir arrived at the port city of Fremantle, Western Australia, on the *S.S. Barbarossa* on December 16, 1903, and wasted no

C. Michael Hall

time in going ashore and visiting the sites that were of most interest to him, the zoological gardens and the Kings Park reserve. At the turn of the century, botanical gardens and zoological gardens were important sources of information on the natural resources of a region and were used to help introduce exotic species that were either regarded as of some economic value or helpful to make the settlers feel "more at home." The gardens were also major scientific institutions and their enthusiasts were the most active campaigners of the day for the establishment of nature reserves in which scientific research could be carried out, particularly in a nation such as Australia with its strong utilitarian approach to the landscape.[15]

Muir was deeply impressed by the Christmas Tree (*Nuytsia floribunda*) and by "the old wild forest" of what is now Kings Park. He was guided by the director of the zoological gardens and spent the evening with Bernard Woodward, director of the West Australian Museum. Muir was obviously warmly welcomed and enjoyed his stay. He wrote in his journal: "Never were strangers more royally [and] kindly entertained I wish I could spend a [year] here."[16] However, of greater significance for the purposes of the present paper was the meeting of Muir and Woodward. At the turn-of-the-century, Woodward was a leading advocate for the preservation of native flora and fauna. Indeed, Woodward was probably the first West Australian scientist to advocate the creation of permanent fauna and flora reserves.[17] Muir's influence on Woodward cannot be specified but there was at least one item of correspondence between Muir and Woodward following Muir's visit to Perth.

After leaving Fremantle, Muir travelled by ship via Adelaide to Melbourne, where he was to spend Christmas. Muir arrived in Melbourne on December 23, spending Christmas Eve at the zoological and botanical gardens where he met the director, William Guilfoyle, an early champion of the conservationist cause in Victoria. Later in the day Muir visited Nicholas Caire, whom Ryan correctly described as "one of Australia's great pioneer nature photographers."[18] Throughout the 1880s and 1890s

290

Caire exhibited and published photographs of Victoria's Eucalypts and temperate rainforests and undertook a crusade for the
preservation of areas of special interest and scenic beauty for
tourists.[19] Caire was undoubtedly an important contact for Muir
in terms of seeking information on the tall trees of Victoria.
The Victorian Crown Lands and Survey publication on the *Giant
Trees of Victoria* indicated the significance of Caire in the tall tree
debate:

> The existence of trees of the Eucalyptus species, some hundreds
> of feet in height had been known for many years prior to the hold-
> ing of the Centennial International Exhibition in Melbourne dur-
> ing 1888. . . . Up to that time, however, no systematic endeavour
> appears to have been made to obtain accurate measurements or
> photographs of these giants of the forest. . . . It would appear that
> Mr. N. J. Caire, Photographer, of Toorak Road, South Yarra was
> the only person who had attempted to obtain negatives of some of
> the well-known specimens.[20]

Caire was a great supporter of conservation-oriented organizations such as the Field Naturalists Club of Victoria, which was
one of the main pressure groups for the reservation of scenic forest areas in Victoria at the turn of the century. Caire's approach
toward his work would have received a sympathetic response
from Muir. According to Caire:

> While making our giant trees a favourite study, I did not do so as
> a botanist, as I have but a superficial knowledge of that branch of
> science. It is my profession as a photographer which has continu-
> ally brought me in contact with them, and, being of an enquiring
> and observant temperament, I have gradually been led to make
> a study of them. If the few facts I have now stated be the means
> of awakening official and public interest in them, and lead to the
> collecting and recording of information for the benefit of future
> generations, then I will consider myself well repaid in the interest
> that has been aroused.[21]

On Christmas Day Muir travelled by train and stagecoach to
the Black Spur Hermitage in the Great Dividing Range seventeen kilometers from Healesville to the east of Melbourne. From

the Hermitage Muir was able to see a vast forest landscape that reminded him of the Appalachian mountains of the eastern United States. The area around the Hermitage was renowned as possessing some of the tallest timber in Australia. Moreover, the owner of the resort, John William Lindt, was a prominent landscape and forest photographer who, being extremely familiar with the Victorian bush, would have been able to clarify some of the information regarding the height of Victoria's Mountain Ash (*Eucalyptus regnans*) forests. Furthermore, Lindt was a contemporary of Alfred Wallace in New Guinea, and it is possible that Muir would have been aware of the work of Lindt on the Eucalypt forests of south-east Australia from information supplied by Wallace. The photography of Lindt and Caire has a special place in the annals of Australian conservation history. The development of picture books of landscape and forest scenery helped to establish the tourist appeal of certain destinations and assisted in the formation of a conservation ethic that had its foundations in the picturesque.[22]

At Healesville Muir went for walks "in the heart of the forest primeval. Where trees are tallest and least changed by man."[23] To his wife, Louie, he wrote that he had, "never imagined a gum forest could be so beautiful, a place after my own heart."[24] The area in which Muir walked is now known as the Narbethong Special Purposes Reserve and it is still possible to see some of the beech trees, Eucalypts and tree ferns that Muir saw.

After sailing up the coast Muir arrived in Sydney and stayed at the Australia Hotel. Here, too, he went to the botanic gardens in order to meet the director, gain some botanic specimens, and gather more information on forestry practices and on *Eucalyptus*. On New Year's Day, 1904, he went by train to Mt. Victoria in the Blue Mountains. At the turn-of-the-century the Blue Mountains were a well-established tourist attraction and Muir was intent on seeing the beauty of the district.[25] Muir went to the Jenolan Caves as one of the three or four thousand tourists that visited the caves each year. He found the caves delightful and was im-

Travels in Australasia

An Australian Eucalyptus. Permission by C. Michael Hall

C. Michael Hall

pressed by the beauty of many of the cave formations. However, he was not so impressed by "the sad sight" of the blackened trees and tree stumps caused by the clearing of land for agriculture in the Blue Mountains and wrote of the "tens of 1000s of dead bleached tree ruins prostrate encumbering the ground or erect gaunt bleached stump with few stubs of main branches stretched to heaven as if for help." [26]

From Mt. Victoria Muir traveled to Katoomba, where he described the scenery in the "gloriously forested" foothills as "very fine," and then returned to Sydney. [27] On January 8 Muir met the director of the Sydney Botanic Gardens, Joseph Henry Maiden, an authority on *Eucalyptus*. [28] According to Muir's diary, Maiden informed Muir that "there were no Eu(calypts) in Australia much if any over 300 ft. in height. That all the stories attributed to Baron Mueller were false or gross exaggerations." [29] It is possible that Maiden's authoritative statement on the subject of tall trees extinguished Muir's desire to visit Tasmania, the site of several magnificent stands of *Eucalyptus regnans*, the tallest hardwoods in the world. However, for the remainder of his travels in Australasia Muir continued to visit botanic gardens and forests. Indeed, as in Victoria, Muir's visit to Maiden was clearly part of a deliberate information-gathering strategy. Maiden was one the foremost conservationists of his time in New South Wales [30] and had been in regular correspondence with Charles Sargent. [31]

The empathy that Muir would have felt for the conservation views of Maiden is well illustrated in Maiden's Presidential Address to the Linnean Society of New South Wales in March 1902, which discussed forestry in New South Wales:

> I brought under notice several aspects of forestry, the importance of which seem to be very imperfectly realised in New South Wales. There is, however, evidence that our people are beginning to understand two things, viz.:
> (1) Forestry is something more than the cutting down of trees and the measurement of logs.
> (2) The forests belong to the whole State, and must be admin-

istered in its interests as a whole, and not merely in that of those citizens resident in the district in which they are situated. The Minister in charge of Forestry is, of course, hampered in his reform work until such time as our people are better educated in regard to the value of our forests, and the proper methods of treating them.[32]

However, research has not, at present, been able to demonstrate an ongoing correspondence or contact between Muir and Maiden although substantial correspondence occurred between Maiden and Sargent in the years following Muir's visit.

John Muir arrived at Auckland, New Zealand, on the *Ventura* from Sydney on January 15, 1904. He traveled to Rotorua the following day and spent several days in the region visiting hot springs, geysers, and the local forests. Muir collected plant specimens and earlier had demonstrated a special interest in the thermal activity, having visited the geysers of Yellowstone National Park. Muir found that the noise of the geysers were comparable to those of Yellowstone and that "they are remarkable for [the] beauty of [the] vegetation around them."[33] However, in a letter to his wife he commented that apart from the Waimangi cauldron, the hot springs were not of the spectacular nature of those of Yellowstone.[34]

From the hot springs region, Muir crossed Lake Taupo for the south of the North Island. He traveled by stagecoach from Tokaanu to Pipiriki on the Wanganui River via Waiouru. This section of the trip had a deep impact on Muir as the volcanic peaks of Mounts Tongariro, Ngauruhoe, and Ruapehu reminded him of Mount Shasta in the Cascade Range of northern California.[35] Such peaks "were isolated temples and seemed to have singular sacred significance" to Muir. "Each mountain was not significant in itself, but in the relationship it bore to the land surrounding it. Each could possibly be a center of the world."[36] According to Muir, Ngauruhoe "showed gloriously against the sky for (hours) pouring forth immense volume of steam wh[ich] immediately circled into glorious (cumulus) visibly rising and rolling away in the wind to enrich the old furniture of the sky."[37]

Muir passed through the then recently established Tongariro National Park and commented that we would never forget the "brown plain . . . with grass in magnificent tussocks which shine in wind."[38] However, despite Muir's enthusiasm for the landscape, he did not mention that a national park existed in the region. This somewhat curious omission may perhaps be explained by a lack of publicity for the national park in contemporary travel guides available to Muir.

The "noble" forest scenery and gorges between Waiouru and Pipiriki were extremely attractive to Muir, surpassing all he had seen elsewhere.[39] Also of great interest to Muir was what he believed to be the "unmistakable traces of glacial action" he observed while steaming down the Wanganui River and on the railroad to Palmerston North.[40] Glaciers played a major role in Muir's natural history researches as they symbolized the importance of geomorphological process on the landscape and its relationship to the nature of mountain ecosystems. In addition, it was his spiritual experiences in the glacial landscape of the Sierra Nevada that led Muir to become such a committed spokesperson for the wilderness.

> I am hopelessly and forever a mountaineer. . . . Civilisation and fever and all the morbidness that has been hooked at me have not dimmed my glacial eye, and I care to live only to entice people to look at nature's loveliness. My own special self is nothing.[41]

When Muir wrote the above passage in 1874, he noted that contact with the mountains had helped him "feel myself again."[42] Given the confessed therapeutic nature of Muir's world tour, it is possible to surmise that contact with the wild mountain landscape of New Zealand assisted with the renewal of Muir's enthusiasm to protect the wilderness.[43] Indeed, a letter to his wife noted that his health and strength were revived and that nature seemed "to hold [and] drive me to work here as in the old Sierra days."[44]

Muir's time in the Sierra undoubtedly came back to him in other ways. On the train to Wellington he noticed the "melancholy remnants of a once glorious forest slowly being burned out of existence" for grazing land,[45] a popular agricultural practice of the period,[46] and a scene undoubtedly reminiscent of the impact of agricultural and grazing activities on his beloved forests of the Sierra Nevada. The clearing of native forests for grazing land was noted several times by Muir during his travels in New Zealand, and clearly grieved him.[47] Indeed, his reaction was similar to that he held toward the effects of grazing by "hoofed locusts" (sheep) on the natural environment of the United States.

As in his Australian travels, Muir hunted for plant specimens in New Zealand's botanical gardens. The gardens of Wellington, "a place unworthy of name," and of Nelson received only brief visits.[48] However, Muir spent several days at the Canterbury Botanical Gardens, where he developed a strong working relationship and friendship with a Mr. Taylor, the director of the Gardens and a former employee of Kew Gardens. In addition to meeting botanical and museum directors, Muir also visited government offices while in New Zealand. However, he unfortunately did not keep a complete record of the people he met.

Prior to visiting Canterbury, Muir had been "botanising" in the delta of the Buller River, where he found "White Rata in great ab[undance] covering stumps, logs, trees dead or alive a charming plant in wealth of bloom [and] glory . . . its influence covering all decay [and] sign of death in (breath) of life."[49] In the Buller Valley the booming rata "made music" to Muir's eye, in conditions very different from that he had experienced in the valley two days before.[50] Traveling from Langford to Westpoint Muir had been caught in a wild storm. The event was significant enough for Wolfe to recount it in her biography of Muir:

> Rain descending in torrents caused most of the stagecoach tourists to be huddled inside. But [Muir] paid extra fare to be allowed to sit on top and feel the rain and wind in his face. His joy was increased by the fact that cataracts poured down from overhanging cliffs, and wet trees and bushes thrashed him and the driver almost off their seats.[51]

C. Michael Hall

Mueller glacier of New Zealand's southern Alps in Mount Cook National Park. Permission by C. Michael Hall.

According to Wolfe the stagecoach ride through the Buller Gorge made Muir feel "wild and elemental once more." [52] Muir's account of the journey is reminiscent of his love of direct contact with nature, which he frequently expressed in his journals and publications. The enjoyment of the ride perhaps provided a foretaste of the happiness that Muir appeared to maintain during his stay on New Zealand's South Island.

Muir's trip from Christchurch to the Mount Cook Hermitage gave him another opportunity to see his beloved glacial landscapes. His admiration of the beauty of the mountains rising out of the plain was tempered by the environmental degradation that he observed.[53] Between Christchurch and Fairlie, Muir noted that, "when the forests are destroyed most of the bottom lands of the country will be lost in gravel floods," [54] an observation that foreshadowed the soil conservation campaigns of the 1930s.[55] Similarly, Muir was highly critical of the New Zealand government's forestry practices he witnessed after passing through the tussock grasslands. "It is interesting to note the efforts of Gov[ernment] to plant forest . . . in this bouldery prairie region while ruthlessly allowing wholesale destruction of native forests where only trees will grow for the sake of sheep pasture." To Muir's conservationist sensibilities such a strategy was equivalent to "selling the country's welfare for a mess of mutton."[56]

Muir enjoyed his brief stay in the Southern Alps and expressed a strong desire to spend more time in the mountains.[57] The nature of the alpine vegetation engaged Muir's botanical curiosity as it was totally unlike anything he had previously experienced. Mueller Glacier also proved attractive to Muir. Despite rain, Muir explored the lower sections of the glacier: "in jumping on the boulder-clad snout I found that my feet had not lost their cunning."[58]

After returning to Christchurch Muir spent more time at the Botanic Gardens "revelling" in the plants.[59] Muir visited the Christchurch gardens some eight times, proof of the interest that he felt in New Zealand's botany and in the friendship that he struck up with the director. On February 18 Muir left Christchurch for Auckland and an opportunity to visit the kauri forest. Arriving in Auckland on February 21, he departed early on the following day for the forest lands around Dargaville and Kaihu.

Muir was undoubtedly influenced in his Australasian journeys by the research of Charles Darwin, Alfred Wallace, and Joseph Dalton Hooker. Muir was a great admirer of Darwin, whereas Asa Gray, Darwin's great champion in the United States, may be regarded as Muir's mentor in botany.[60] Of Darwin, Muir wrote, "This noble character has suffered from silly, ignorant, and unbelieving men who say much about Darwinism without really knowing anything about it. A more devout and indefatigable seeker after truth than Darwin never lived."[61]

Muir recorded in his diary that he was reading Darwin after he left New Zealand.[62] Just as Muir had wanted at an early age to follow in the footsteps of Alexander Humboldt, so it appeared that he wanted to retrace the visit of Darwin to the North

C. Michael Hall

Island.[63] Similarly, Muir also had the works of Hooker with him on his travels or at least wished to read them then, as they are noted on a page of his journal for 1903.[64] Hooker had spent three months at the Bay of Islands in 1841,[65] and it would seem extremely likely that Muir would have discussed New Zealand with Hooker while in Great Britain during the early stages of his world trip.[66] In addition to such talks with Hooker, Muir would also have gained some significant insights and ideas of the natural history of the Australasian region through discussions with Alfred Wallace. Indeed, an examination of the interrelationships and exchanges of ideas between Gray, Hooker, Muir, and Wallace from 1877 onward, may well prove to be a fruitful source of insights into the history of both biogeography and conservation.

Traveling through farmland to Helensville, Muir was led to comment on the destruction of the kauri forest: "not a tree survives. . . . Traces of gum prospectors [and] diggers are to be seen almost everywhere."[67] The account of Muir's walks in the kauri forest around Dargaville and Kaihu reveals that Muir fully appreciated its richness and diversity, although he was clearly saddened by the loss of forest to the ravages of fire and road building and noted that roadbuilders were using "extravagant quantities" of "precious building material."[68] The "glorious" tree fern and palm foliage proved particularly attractive to Muir as he collected specimens during his stay in the region to add to what must have already been a substantial collection of New Zealand flora.[69]

Upon returning to Auckland Muir used the fine weather to dry and study his plant collection. Muir departed Auckland and New Zealand on February 29, 1904, after having spent some six weeks traveling the country. Muir noted that he was happy to have finished his quick visit to New Zealand although he did find it, "absorbingly interesting especially its fast fading forests."[70]

Upon arriving in Sydney on March 4, Muir again spent much time at the Botanic Gardens. Despite the rigors of so much travel his interest in the flora of Australia continued unabated, and he decided to travel to Queensland in order to see the *Araucaria cunnighamii* (Hoop Pine), a tree species that had been of interest to him for many years and that he also sought later during his visit to South America and Africa in 1911–1912.

Muir spent much of his time in Queensland traveling by railway. To Muir this was a valuable exercise as he was able to observe changes in the landscape from the train carriage. He arrived in Rockhampton on March 10 via Maryborough, Bundaberg, and Brisbane. At Rockhampton he visited the botanic gardens and "came away laden" with plant specimens.[71] Heading inland, Muir visited Wondai where he observed the logging of the surrounding woodlands. Here he was able to go for a "grand walk . . . in an Araucaria Forest," something that would undoubtedly have been of a great joy to him given his interest in the species.[72]

Muir returned to Sydney on March 19. For the next eleven days he was to spend his time alternately between the botanic gardens and his hotel room where he dried his plant specimens. Muir also collected information on the forest reservations of New South Wales that he was to take back with him to California. His collection of plant specimens from Australia and New Zealand were a special joy to him, reminding him of the botanizing he carried out in his youth: "nearly every plant to me is novel, many are also very beautiful." The botanic gardens retained a special appeal to Muir. He noted that there was, "always something new for one there, the most interesting garden [I] have seen."[73] His interest was such that he was almost locked in one night, "while absorbed in the native plants was called by one of the guardians of the gardens [and] told the gates were about to be locked for the night [and] I would have to make haste to escape."[74]

Muir departed from Sydney on March 30 for Port Darwin, Timor, the Phillipines and Canton, where he was to catch a ship for San Francisco via Japan and Hawaii. He left Sydney in such rough seas that he could not reach his cabin on the upper deck of the ship "without danger of being washed overboard." [75] However, the storm subsided and he was able to enjoy the passage up the east coast of Australia where he could observe the marine life of the Great Barrier Reef. Muir's last landfall in Australia was at Port Darwin on the April 11. Here he again collected many plant specimens and "found several interesting trees and ferns" in the Darwin Botanic Gardens.[76] The following day Muir left Port Darwin and Australia not only with a large collection of plant specimens but also apparently with many happy memories of his time spent in the "fairly glorious . . . ferny Eucalypt forests." [77]

The recuperative nature of Muir's world trip has already been noted, especially the contact with forests and the glacial landscape of New Zealand. Muir's travels in Australia and New Zealand also signified a renewal of Muir's enthusiasm for natural history. On the ship for Auckland, Muir noted that he was "beginning botany all over again." [78] Further evidence of his appreciation of the "strange and rich vegetation" [79] of Australia and New Zealand was contained in a letter to Henry Fairfield Osborn of the Peabody Museum of Yale University:

> Had perfectly glorious time in . . . Australia and New Zealand. The flora of Australia and New Zealand is so novel and exciting I had to begin my botanical studies over again, working night and day with endless enthusiasm. And what wondrous beasts and birds, too, are there! [80]

The significance of Muir renewing his acquaintance with the wilderness cannot be overstated. Throughout his settled years, Muir felt the need to leave home and see wild country again in order to "recharge" his vision of wilderness and the necessity of its preservation.[81] His travels through Australia and New Zealand may therefore be seen as an essential part of Muir's mental and conceptual preparation for the efforts required to preserve America's wilderness heritage upon his return to the United States. The information that Muir was able to gather on forest conservation and from his search for tall trees provided a valuable new dimension in the campaign for the preservation of the Giant Redwoods of California. In particular, the confirmation, at least to his own satisfaction, that the Redwoods were the world's tallest trees would have assisted in reinforcing the theme of monumentalism so important in gaining government protection of American nature.[82]

Until his death on Christmas Eve of 1914, Muir was continually reviewing his journals in order to provide the material for several books based upon his travels.[83] It appears that Muir was sufficiently absorbed by his experiences in Australia and New Zealand to want to publish them, and his later notebooks refer several times to the state of the Australian and New Zealand forests, especially in comparison with those of South America. However, his leading role within the American conservation movement and the production of other books, journals, and newspaper articles meant that time was not available to him. As Muir noted:

> Nothing I have seen in books gives anything like an adequate description of these noble woods [and] I begin to think I may have to try to write about them myself though there is so much on my hands.[84]

Despite not being able to publish anything from his time spent in Australasia, Muir has still left a valuable legacy for the conservation of the natural resources of both Australia and New Zealand. John Muir, more than any other natural historian of his time, laid the foundation for the present-day perceptions of the role of national parks and the preservation of wild lands. The history of environmental management practices in Australia and New Zealand has been greatly influenced by North American advances in conservation.[85] Although the exact nature of Muir's direct relationship to the development of the national park concept in Australia and New Zealand remains the subject of further research, it is apparent that, at least in the case of Australia, it was of some significance. In addition, current research is focus-

C. Michael Hall

ing on the potential contribution that the work of Hooker and Wallace may have had on the development of Muir's concept of conservation and the development of environmental ideas. Indeed, it is likely that Muir's travels were assisted enormously by the large number of Hooker's Kew Garden appointees in Australasian botanic gardens.

The United States National Park System, which has had such a large influence on the management practices within both Australian and New Zealand National Parks, was created to a large extent through the efforts of John Muir.[86] Similarly, Muir's romantic vision of wilderness areas has had a substantial influence on the directions of conservation movement throughout the world, but particularly in Australia.[87] Muir's account of both the glory and the degradation of the Australian and New Zealand landscapes therefore serves as a timely reminder of the need both to consolidate and extend the gains that have been made in wilderness conservation in the past one hundred years.

NOTES

1. John Muir's journals and letters from his time in Australasia are held in the *John Muir Papers* at the Holt-Atherton Center for Western Studies, University of the Pacific, Stockton, California. Copyright for quotations taken from the John Muir Papers is vested in the Hannah-Muir Trust. The author wishes to acknowledge the invaluable assistance of the Holt-Atherton Center, the ongoing collaborative research with Steve Mark, and the provision of a research grant by the Australian Research Council in making this paper possible.

2. See Anne T. Lynch, "Bibliography of Works by and about John Muir, 1869–1978," *Bulletin of Bibliography* 36.2 (1970): 71–80, 84; Steven Fox, *John Muir and His Legacy: The American Conservation Movement* (Toronto: Little, 1981); Michael P. Cohen, *The Pathless Way: John Muir and the American Wilderness* (Madison: University of Wisconsin Press, 1984); William F. Kimes, and Maymie B. Kimes, *John Muir: A Reading Bibliography* (Fresno, Calif.: Panorama West Books, 1986).

3. Linnie Marsh Wolfe, *Son of the Wilderness: The Life of John Muir* (Boston: Houghton, Mifflin, 1946), p. 190; A. Hunter Dupree, *Asa Gray: American Botanist, Friend of Darwin* (Baltimore and London: The Johns Hopkins University Press), pp. 346–354, 407–408.

4. Wolfe, *Son of Wilderness*, p. 299.

Travels in Australasia

5. William Frederic Badè, *The Life and Letters of John Muir*, 2 vols. (Boston: Houghton, Mifflin, 1924) II; *John of the Mountains: The Unpublished Journals of John Muir* edited by Linnie Marsh Wolfe (Boston: Houghton, Mifflin, 1938).

6. P. J. Ryan, "John Muir and Tall Trees in Australia," *The Pacific Historian* 29 (1985): 125–135.

7. Colin Michael Hall, "John Muir in New Zealand," *New Zealand Geographer* 43 (1987): 99–103; Colin Michael Hall, "John Muir: the Grandfather of National Parks," *Australian Science Magazine* 26.1 (1988): 44–47.

8. John Muir, *The Story of My Boyhood and Youth* (Boston: Houghton, Mifflin, 1913), pp. 22–23.

9. John Muir, letter to William Keith, 28 April, 1904, *John Muir Papers*.

10. "John Muir Ends Year of Journeying in Many Lands," *The San Francisco Call*, 28 May 1904, p. 4.

11. Kimes and Kimes, *John Muir*, pp. 157–159.

12. Ryan, "John Muir and Tall Trees," p. 125.

13. "John Muir Is at Home Again. Noted Scientist Makes a Tour of the World, Collecting Many Botanical Specimens. Crosses Siberia Into Manchuria. Much Impressed With What He Saw in the Himalayas—Spent Some Time in Eucalyptus," *San Francisco Chronicle*, 28 May 1904, p. 9.

14. Alfred Runte, *National Parks: The American Experience* (Lincoln: University of Nebraska Press, 1979); Colin Michael Hall, "The 'Worthless Lands Hypothesis' and Australia's National Parks and Reserves," in Kevin J. Frawley and Noel Semple, eds. *Australia's Ever Changing Forests* (Canberra: Department of Geography and Oceanography, Australian Defence Force Academy, 1989), pp. 441–456.

15. Colin Michael Hall, "The Geography of Hope: The History, Identification and Preservation of Wilderness in Australia" Ph.D. dissertation, University of Western Australia, 1988; Ann Moyal, *"A Bright and Savage Land": Scientists in Colonial Australia* (Sydney: Collins, 1986); Carol Henty, *For the People's Pleasure: Australia's Botanic Gardens* (Richmond: Greenhouse Publications, 1988); Rod Ritchie, *Seeing the Rainforests in 19th-Century Australia* (Sydney: Rainforest Publishing, 1989).

16. John Muir, 1903 Diary, entry for 16 December, 1903, *John Muir Papers*.

17. Bernard H. Woodward, *National Parks and Flora and Fauna Reserves in Australia* (Perth: West Australian Natural Historical Society, 1907).

18. Ryan, "John Muir and Tall Trees, p. 129. Also see Crosbie Morrison, *Melbourne's Garden* (Melbourne: Melbourne University Press, 1955); R. T. M. Pescott, *The Royal Botanic Gardens of Melbourne, A History from 1845–1970* (Melbourne: Oxford University Press, 1982); R. T. M. Pescott, *W. R. Guilfoyle, 1840–1912: Master of Landscaping* (Melbourne: Oxford University Press, 1974); and Joan Law Smith, *The Botanic Gardens, Melbourne* (Melbourne: Maud Gibson Trust in association with the Royal Botanic Gardens Melbourne, 1984).

19. See Ritchie, *Seeing the Rainforests;* Anne Pitkethy and Don Pitkethy, *N. J. Caire Landscape Photographer* (Rosanna: Anne and Don Pitkethy, 1988).

20. Victoria Crown Lands and Survey, *Giant Trees of Victoria* (Melbourne: Victoria Crown Lands and Survey, 1888).

C. Michael Hall

21. Nicholas J. Caire, *The Victorian Naturalist*, 21.9 (1905): 122 reprinted in Pitkethy and Pitkethy, *N. J. Caire*, p. 19.

22. Ritchie, *Seeing the Rainforests*.

23. Muir, 1903 Diary, entry for 25 December, 1903, *John Muir Papers*.

24. John Muir, letter to Louie Muir, 28 December, 1903, *John Muir Papers*.

25. Jim Smith, *From Katoomba to Jenolan Caves: The Six Foot Track, 1884–1984* (Katoomba: Second Back Row Press, 1984); Peter Stanbury, ed., *The Blue Mountains Grand Adventure for All* (Leura: The Macleay Museum and the Second Back Row Press, 1988).

26. John Muir, 1904 Diary, entry for 3 January, 1904, *John Muir Papers*.

27. Muir, 1904 Diary, entry for 6 January, 1904, *John Muir Papers*.

28. See Joseph H. Maiden, *A Critical Revision of the Genus Eucalyptus*, 8 vols. (Sydney: Government Printer, 1909–1933).

29. Muir, 1904 Diary, entry for 8 January, 1904, *John Muir Papers*.

30. Lionel Gilbert, *The Royal Botanic Gardens, Sydney: A History 1816–1985* (Melbourne: Oxford University Press, 1986); Henty, *For the People's Pleasures*.

31. Sydney Botanic Gardens, Letter Registers, held in New South Wales State Archives, Sydney, New South Wales, Australia. At the time of writing no copies of this correspondence have been discovered.

32. Sydney Botanic Gardens and Domains, *Report of Director for the Year 1902* (Sydney: Legislative Assembly of New South Wales, 1903), p. 4.

33. Muir, 1904 Diary, entry for 20 January, 1904, *John Muir Papers*.

34. John Muir, letter to Louie Muir, 27 January, 1904, pp. 1–2, *John Muir Papers*.

35. Muir, 1904 Diary, entry for 23 January, 1904, *John Muir Papers*.

36. Quoted in Cohen, *Pathless Way*, p. 66.

37. Muir, 1904 Diary, entry for 23 January, 1904, *John Muir Papers*.

38. Ibid.

39. Ibid.

40. Ibid., entry for 25 January, 1904, *John Muir Papers*.

41. Badè, II, pp. 28–29.

42. Ibid., p. 29.

43. Wolfe, *Son of Wilderness*, pp. 299ff.

44. John Muir, letter to Louie Muir, 29 February, 1904, *John Muir Papers*.

45. John Muir, 1904 Diary, entry for 26 January, 1904, *John Muir Papers*.

46. Denys Trussell, "History in an Antipodean Garden," *The Ecologist* 12.1 (1982): 34–42.

47. Muir, 1904 Diary, entries for 28 January, 1 February, and 14 February, 1904, *John Muir Papers*.

48. Ibid., entries for 27 January, and 29 January, 1904.

49. Ibid., entry for 31 January, 1904.

50. Ibid.

51. Wolfe, *Son of Wilderness*, p. 299.

52. Ibid.

53. On nineteenth-century timber management practices in New Zealand, see

Travels in Australasia

R. Arnold, "The Virgin Forest Harvest and the Development of Colonial New Zealand," *New Zealand Geographer* 32 (1976): 105–126; Graeme Wynn, "Conservation and Society in Nineteenth-Century New Zealand," *New Zealand Journal of History* 11 (1977): 124–136; Graeme Wynn, "Pioneers, Politicians and the Conservation of Forests in Early New Zealand," *Journal of Historical Geography* 5 (1979): 171–188; Michael M. Roche, "Reactions to Scarcity: The Management of Forest Resources in Nineteenth-Century Canterbury, New Zealand," *Journal of Forest History* 28 (1984): 82–91; and Colin Michael Hall, "Wilderness in New Zealand," *Alternatives: Perspectives on Science, Technology and the Environment* 15.3 (1988): 40–46.

54. Muir, 1904 Diary, entry for 8 February, 1904, *John Muir Papers*.

55. See Kenneth Cumberland, *Landmarks* (Surrey Hills: Reader's Digest, 1981), pp. 202–207.

56. Muir, 1904 Diary, entry for 14 February, 1904, *John Muir Papers*.

57. Ibid., entry for 12 February, 1904.

58. Wolfe, *Son of Wilderness*, p. 299.

59. Muir, 1904 Diary, entry for 17 February, 1904, *John Muir Papers*.

60. Fox, *John Muir*, pp. 81–82.

61. Ibid., p. 82.

62. Muir, 1904 Diary, entry for 3 March, 1904, *John Muir Papers*.

63. Fox, *John Muir*, pp. 47, 49.

64. Muir, 1904 Diary, undated entry, *John Muir Papers*.

65. Leonard Huxley, *Life and Letters of Sir Joseph Dalton Hooker* (London: John Murray, 1918), p. 124.

66. Wolfe, *Son of Wilderness*, pp. 293–294.

67. Muir, 1904 Diary, entry for 22 February, 1904, *John Muir Papers*.

68. Ibid., 23 February, 1904.

69. Ibid., 24 February, 1904.

70. Ibid., 29 February, 1904.

71. Ibid., 8 March, 1904.

72. Ibid., 13 March, 1904.

73. Ibid., 23 March, 1904.

74. Ibid., 26 March, 1904.

75. Ibid., 31 March, 1904.

76. Ibid., 11 April, 1904.

77. John Muir, letter to the Merriams and Baileys, 1 January, 1904, *John Muir Papers*.

78. Wolfe, *Son of Wilderness*, p. 299.

79. John Muir, letter to Louie Muir, 27 January, 1904, *John Muir Papers*.

80. Badè, *Life and Letters*, II, p.360.

81. Cohen, pp. 28–150.

82. See Joseph L. Sax, "America's National Parks: Their Principles, Purposes and Prospects," *Natural History* 85 (1976): 58–88; Runte, *National Parks;* Hall, "History"; Hall, "Worthless."

83. Muir, *John of the Mountains*, p. 428.

84. John Muir, letter to Louie Muir, 2 January, 1904, *John Muir Papers.*

85. See Hall, *History;* Joseph M. Powell, *Environmental Management in Australia 1788–1914: Guardians, Improvers and Profit* (Melbourne: Oxford University Press, 1976); Colin Michael Hall, "National Identity and Outdoor Recreation: A Comparative Analysis of Australia and Canada," *Journal of Canadian Culture* 2 (1987): 25–39.

86. See Hall, *Wasteland,* Chapter 2.

87. Ibid., Chapters 2–5.

John Muir
Chronology

1838 April 21 Born in Dunbar, Scotland, to Daniel and Ann Gilrye Muir
1849 Immigrates to Fountain Lake, Wisconsin
1860 Leaves home; exhibits inventions; meets Mrs. Jeanne C. Carr
1861 Enrolls at University of Wisconsin, Madison
1863 Leaves university
1864 Botanizing and working in Lower Canada
1866–1867 Industrial work in Indianapolis; accident causes temporary blindness
1867 Starts 10,000-mile walk to Gulf of Mexico
1868 First Yosemite visit
1868–1873 Yosemite residence, includes first articles on glaciers for *New York Tribune* and articles for the *Overland Monthly;* meets Asa Gray; decides on career as professional writer
1875 Three-month mule trip to southern Sierra
1876 Gives first public lecture
1879 Announces engagement to Louise Strentzel; first Alaska trip
1880 April 14 Marries Louise Strentzel
1880 Second Alaska trip; adventure with "Stickeen"
1880s Family ranch management
1881 Birth of daughter, Annie Wanda
1886 Birth of daughter, Helen Lillian
1889 Undertakes public campaign to create Yosemite National Park
1890 Undertakes campaign to include Kings Canyon in Sequoia National Park bill
1892 Helps organize the Sierra Club
1892 Louie Muir sells portion of ranch
1893 Visits east coast and western Europe; campaigns to create Mt. Rainier National Park
1898 Travels throughout U. S. and Canada
1899 Participates in Harriman Alaska Expedition

Chronology

1903–1904   One-year trip around the world
1905   Participates in Yosemite recession campaign; wife dies; takes daughters to Arizona for Helen's health
1908   Months-long bout with "la Grippe"; dictates autobiography
1909   Tours Yosemite with President Taft and guides Secretary of Interior Ballinger through Hetch Hetchy
1911–1912 Seven-month trip to South America and Africa
1914   Dec. 24 Dies in Los Angeles

Contributors

Edgar M. Castellini is a Ph.D. candidate and instructor of English at University of California at Davis. He brings to his studies of Muir a background in botany and natural science as well as English studies. His dissertation is entitled "Thoreau's Philosophy of Language."

Dennis R. Dean is a humanist who publishes regularly on the history of geology (both British and American), holds a degree from Stanford and a Ph.D. from the University of Wisconsin at Madison. He has taught in the Department of English and Humanities at the University of Wisconsin at Parkside. He has completed several projects dealing with the history of seismology, and with the influence of geology upon literature.

Arthur W. Ewart did his graduate work in history at Sonoma State University. His interest in the religious underpinnings of American culture and his nearly twenty years of mountaineering led him to John Muir. He has taught classes on Muir at Santa Rosa Junior College.

Richard Fleck holds a B.A. in French from Rutgers and a Ph.D. in English from the University of New Mexico. Currently Dean at the Community College of Denver, Colorado, he has taught at the University of Wyoming since 1965, and was an exchange professor at Osaka University, Japan, and at the State University of New York at Cortland. He is author of *Henry Thoreau and John Muir Among the Indians* (1985), as well as numerous articles on Muir.

C. Michael Hall is with the Department of Tourism and Communication, University of Canberra, Australia. His dissertation

Contributors

was undertaken at the University of Western Australia on the history and preservation of wilderness in Australia. He has published a number of articles on conservation, recreation, and tourism and is the author of a text entitled *Tourism in Australia: From Susceptible to Sustainable Development.*

James D. Heffernan is professor of Philosophy at the University of the Pacific. He has a Ph.D. from Notre Dame and specializes in the philosophy of science. His research and publication fields include environmental ethics, artificial intelligence, and philosophy of mind. An enthusiastic backpacker and hiker, he has explored much of the Sierra Nevada.

Keith K. Kennedy is an M.A. candidate in history at California State University at Hayward. He earned his undergraduate business degree from Indiana University. An avid backpacker, he has been on numerous trips through the Sierra and has combined his love of history and of the outdoors to form an enduring interest in Muir.

Ronald H. Limbaugh joined the faculty of the University of the Pacific in 1966 after completing work for the Ph.D. at the University of Idaho. For over fifteen years he was jointly professor of history and curator of manuscripts at the University of the Pacific. He became the first director of the John Muir Center for Regional Studies when it was organized in 1989. Holder of the Rockwell Hunt Chair of California History, he teaches specialized courses in regional history and currently is working on a book-length manuscript on the origins and writing of Muir's dog story *Stickeen.*

Sally M. Miller is professor of History at the University of the Pacific and holder of a Ph.D. from the University of Toronto. She is the author or editor of six books and many articles in social and cultural history. She has held a visiting professorship

314

Contributors

at the University of Warwick, England, and a Fulbright in New Zealand. She is a former editor of *The Pacific Historian.*

Bruce Richardson is an assistant professor of English at the University of Wyoming in Casper and teaches a wide range of classes. He holds a Ph.D. from the University of California at Los Angeles where he studied the art and literature of late eighteenth-century England, especially the work of William Blake. Currently he is researching representations of the Wyoming landscape, especially in Oregon Trail diaries and writings and art about Yellowstone Park.

Paul D. Sheats teaches English and American literature at the University of California at Los Angeles. He has written and edited books on Wordsworth and Keats, and his interest in John Muir and the Sierra goes back many years.

Nancy M. Slack is a plant ecologist and botanical historian. She is professor of Biology at Russell Sage College, where she teaches ecology, plant geography, and history of science. She holds two degrees from Cornell University and a Ph.D. from the State University of New York at Albany. Her ecological publications involve the vegetation of mountains and bogs. Currently she is engaged in historical research on California botany. Her most recent book is *85 Acres: A Field Guide to the Adirondack Alpine Summits.*

Mark Stoll earned a B.A. at Rice University in history and German. His interest in languages has led him to study nine languages at one time or another; his background in religion led him to study Hinduism in India and Buddhism in Sri Lanka, as well as religion in America; and backpacking led him to the works of John Muir. He has completed a doctoral dissertation in history at the University of Texas at Austin which explored, among other matters, the religious origins of both exploitation and preservation of nature.

Contributors

Dennis Williams presently is on the staff of the Environmental Protection Agency. Having earned a B.A. from Southern Nazarene University and an M.A. from Texas Tech, he is completing the requirements for a Ph.D. in environmental history and an interpretative biography of Muir.

Don Weiss holds a B.A. in History from the University of California at Santa Cruz, and an M.A. in Medieval Studies from the University of York, England. He is a professional photographer and writer specializing in the mountains and deserts of Asia and Africa. As part of the Year of Tibet, 1992, he had an exhibit of photographs in the Roerich Museum in New York. He is completing a book about Muir's wilderness philosophy while living in Japan and photographing mountain temples.

INDEX

Aggassiz, Alexander, 220
Aggassiz, Louis, 69, 175, 183, 223
Alaska, 5, 6, 7, 50, 56–58, 137, 141,
  144–47, 169, 187–90
Alaska Days with John Muir, (Young),
  137
American Association for the Ad-
  vancement of Science, 186–87, 232,
  254
American Journal of Science, 173
American Museum of Natural History,
  221
Animal rights movement, 110
Armes, William D., 238
Atlantic Monthly, 210, 215, 267
Auckland, New Zealand, 299, 300,
  302
Austin, Rebecca Merritt, 221
Austin, Richard Cartwright, 97
Australasia, 287–305
Australia, 287, 288, 289–95, 300–02

Bache, Alexander, 206
Badè, William Frederic, 25, 29,
  287–88
Baird, Spencer, 204
Bancroft Library, University of Cali-
  fornia, Berkeley, 208–9
Barclay, Robert, 86
Beardsley, A. F., 203, 214
Behr, Hans, 207
Bell, John Graham, 203
Bessey, Charles, 223
Bible, 29, 53, 67, 69, 73, 74, 78, 79,
  86, 145
Bierstadt, Albert, 216, 247
Bigelow, John, 204
Blake, W. P., 176
Blake, S. F., 229

Bolander, Henry, 220, 223
Boston Society of Natural History, 171
Botanical explorations, 195–239
Brandegee, Kate Curran, 208, 221–22
Brandegee, Townshend, 221–22, 227
Brewer, William, 195, 196, 197,
  208–20, 225, 237, 249, 251
Bridges, Thomas, 203, 214–15
Brown, Joanna Muir (sister), 19, 22,
  24, 25, 31
Bruce, Mrs. C. C., 221
Buddhism, 87, 119, 128
Burns, Robert, 53
Burroughs, John, 188–89
Byron, George Gordon (Lord), 68

Cairne, Nicholas, 290–91, 292
California Academy of Sciences, 195,
  206–8, 221, 223, 224, 229, 230,
  242n.60, 257
California Geological Survey, 215, 225
California State Legislature, 7, 196,
  208, 219, 220
California State Survey, 195, 208–20
Calvinism, 3, 18, 29, 53, 66, 87, 248
Campbell, Alexander, 66
Campbell, Joseph, 130–31
Campbell, Thomas, 66
Campbellites, 66–67, 73, 80–81n.16
Canada, 4, 26, 27, 29, 33, 69–70, 71
Canby, William, 6
Canterbury Botanical Gardens, 297
Carr, Ezra Slocum, 4, 69, 137, 231–32
Carr, Jeanne, 79, 200, 232; aided
  Muir, 4, 53, 69, 71, 137; correspon-
  dence with Muir, 70, 72, 87, 89,
  119, 120, 122, 123, 129–30, 171,
  172, 231, 249, 252
Centennial Exhibition, 255

317

Index

Century Magazine, 5, 96, 258
Chamisso, Albert von, 201
Channing, William Ellery, 69
Chilwell, Mr., 197, 198
Christchurch, New Zealand, 298, 299
Christianity, 10, 29, 65–68, 69, 71, 73, 76, 83–88, 90–92, 95, 96
Civil War, 4, 10, 28, 69, 224
Clark, Galen, 262
Coast Survey, 206
Coast Survey, Alaska, 207
Cohen, Michael, (*Pathless Way, The*), 84, 148, 153, 156, 275, 276
Conservation, 6, 9, 11, 13n.11, 287, 288, 303
Constance, Lincoln, 223
Contributions to Western Botany, 227
Coulter, Thomas, 201, 227
Conversion experience, 120–22, 127, 128, 139, 164
Cruise of the "Corwin," The, 187
Crystal Palace Exposition, 203
Cuba, 71

Dana, R. H., 202
Dante, Alighieri, 162
Darwin Botanical Gardens, 302
Darwin, Charles, 69, 83, 92, 112, 206, 232, 253, 287, 289, 299
Davis, Jefferson, 206
Dayton, W. A., 229
"Deep ecology," 10, 104, 109, 115, 115n.3
Deikman, Arthur J., 129
Disciples of Christ, 66–67, 73, 80–81n.16
Douglas, David, 201, 202
Dudley, William R., 230, 235
Dudley Herbarium, 230
Dunbar, Scotland, 8, 66
Dupree, Anderson Hunter, 204, 235

Eastwood, Alice, 217, 222–23, 231, 237, 242n.60
Edwards, Jonathan, 87, 121, 122

El Capitan, 177, 180, 252
Elizabethan and Metaphysical Imagery, 148
Emerson, 3, 4, 53, 69, 123, 137, 147, 149, 232, 235
Engelmann, George, 226, 235
Enlightenment, 9, 74
Eschscholtz, Johann Friefrich, 201

Farquhar, Francis, 46
Fay, Jerome, 49–50, 161–62
Finch, Augustus, 203
Florida, 4, 71, 87
Foerster, Norman, 58
Forbes, James, 175, 183, 191, 287
Fox, Stephen, 29, 145
Freemantle, Australia, 289–90

Gaia hypothesis, 92
Galloway, Sarah Muir (sister), 18, 22, 24, 25, 26, 27, 28, 30, 32, 33, 232, 236
General Grant National Park, 6
Geological Survey of California, 45
"A Geologist's Winter Walk," 143
Giant Forest, 253, 261
Gibbons, Henry, 223, 224
God, 19, 20, 28, 29, 30, 33, 36, 53, 59, 65–79, 86, 87, 88, 90, 91, 92, 96, 97n.9, 109, 113, 121, 122, 247
Grand Canyon, 190, 193n.22
Grant Grove, 261
Graustein, Jeanette E., 200
Gray, Asa, 206, 207, 225, 226, 227; and Muir, 4, 127, 231, 232–34, 235, 287, 299, 300
Gray, Jane, 234, 235, 236, 237
Gray Herbarium, 220, 226
Great Basin, 5
Great Chain of Being, 10, 12n.6
Greene, Edward Lee, 224–26, 229
Greeley, Horace, 170, 190n.3
Gulf of Mexico, 4, 19, 33, 83, 84, 206, 277
Gunnison, Almon, 267

Index

Gunsky, Frederic, 245

Hague, Arnold, 270
Half Dome, 143, 180, 249
Hall, James, 219
Hand, Mary Muir (sister), 22, 23, 25, 27, 31
Hanna, Wanda Muir (daughter), 17, 30, 276
Harford, William, 207
Harkness, Harvey Wilson, 224
Harper's Magazine, 254, 255, 256, 257
Harriman Alaska Expedition, 6, 188
Harriman, Edward Henry, 95
Harvard University, 204, 220, 225
Hastings, S. C., 220
Hayden, F. V., 235
Hedges, Cornelius, 283–84n.28
Hetch Hetchy Valley, 7, 9, 73, 106, 238, 248, 261
Hilgard, Eugene, 223
Hill, Thomas, 262
Hillebrand, William, 214
Hoffman, Charles, 212
Hoffmann Glacier, 177, 181–82
Holden, William, 214
Hooker, Sir Joseph Dalton, 127, 231, 235, 236, 287, 288, 289, 299, 300, 304
Horticultural Society of London, 202
Humboldt, Alexander von, 68, 70, 71, 287, 299
Huxley, Thomas Henry, 232

Igjugaijik, 126
Illilouette Glacier, 181–82
Inferno, (Dante), 162
Irving, Washington, 202
Irwin, Benoni, 144, 156, 163

James, William, (*Varieties of Religious Experience, The*), 119, 121, 129
Jeffrey, John, 203
Jenolan Cave, 292
Jepson, Willis L., 221, 229, 239

Jesus Christ, 19, 36, 86, 88, 95
John of the Mountains, 137
John Muir and His Legacy, (Fox), 29
Johnson, Robert Underwood, 5, 96, 251, 258–61
Jones, Marcus, 227–29
Jordan, David Starr, 230, 238
Jung, Carl, 131

Kant, Emmanuel, 12–13n.9
Kaweah River, 246, 253, 255
Keith, William, 144, 155, 156, 163
Kellogg, Albert, 203, 206, 207, 223, 224, 227, 236, 238
Kent, William, 73
Kew Gardens, 287, 288, 297, 304
King, Clarence, 45, 197, 210, 215–18
Kingman, Dan, 278
Kings Canyon, 6, 246, 249, 251, 252, 258, 260, 261
Kings Canyon National Park, 261–62
Kings Park Reserve, 289
Kings River, 246, 249, 255, 258
Kipling, Rudyard, 267, 268–69, 283–84n.28, 284n.57
Kneeland, Samuel, 171
Kobo Daishi. *See* Kukai
Kukai, 120, 121, 129
Kumlien, Thure, 224, 225

Langford, Nathaniel Pitt, 267, 283–84n.28
LaPérouse, Jean-Francois, 201
LeConte, John, 206
LeConte, Joseph, 206, 223, 231, 238
Lemmon Herbarium, 221
Lemmon, John, 221, 227
Leopold, Aldo, 9, 10, 12–13n.9, 103
Lesquereux, Leo, 220
Lewis, I. M., 128
Life and Letters of John Muir, The, 29
Limbaugh, R. H., 29, 97n.2
Lincoln, Abraham, 238
Lindt, John William, 292
"Living Glaciers in California," 173

Index

Lobb, William, 203
Lovelock, James, 92

McIntosh, Robert P., 224
McVaughn, Rogers, 229
Maiden, Joseph Henry, 294–95
Maine Woods, The, (Thoreau) 137
Mammoth, 268, 269, 270, 272, 278, 280
Mariposa Big Tress Grove, 238
Mariposa Trial, 198
Marsh, George, 10
Marshall, James Wilson, 202
Marshall, R. B., 95
Martinez, California, 5, 23, 25, 32, 50, 138
Marx, Leo, 281
Menzies, Archibald, 201
Mexican Boundary Survey, 204
Melbourne, Australia, 290–91
Milton, John, 68
Morrill Act, 220
Mt. Brewer, 218
Mt. Cook, 50
Mt. Cook Hermitage, 298
Mt. Dana, 239
Mt. Katahdin. *See* Mt. Ktaadn
Mt. Ktaadn, 154, 157, 158, 163, 165n.1
Mt. Lyell, 173, 239
Mt. Maclure, 173
Mt. Ranier National Park, 6, 50
Mt. Ritter, 47, 54, 127, 141, 144, 153–60, 161, 162, 163–65
Mt. Shasta, 5, 46, 48–50, 127, 160–63, 164, 165, 217, 295
Mt. Whitney, 45, 46, 47, 54, 144, 223, 246
The Mountains of California, 6, 153–65, 245
Mueller Glacier, 50, 299
Muir, Anne Gilrye (mother), 3, 19, 20, 34, 66
Muir, Annie (sister), 22, 23, 25
Muir, Daniel (father), 3, 18–19, 20, 23, 25, 30, 34, 53, 65, 66–68, 71, 72, 79, 90, 190, 258
Muir, Daniel (brother), 19, 22
Muir, David (brother), 22, 23, 25, 27, 29, 30, 31, 32, 89
Muir, John: birth of, 3; emigration of, 3; and education, 3–4, 22–23, 27, 32, 53, 68, 84, 137, 190n.1; and Emerson 3, 4, 53, 69, 137, 149, 232, 235; and father, 3, 18–19, 34, 71, 72–79; and Thoreau, 3, 53, 69, 127, 165; and Asa Gray, 4, 127, 231, 232–34, 235, 287, 299, 300; and Canada, 4, 26, 29, 33, 69–70, 71; and Civil War, 4, 28, 69; in Indianapolis, 4, 33, 70, 71; and eye accident, 4, 70, 71, 132; and Gulf of Mexico, 4, 33, 71, 83, 84; to California, 4, 196–97; and Sierra Nevada, 4, 46, 47, 51, 52, 71, 89, 93, 95, 137, 138, 143–44, 153–65, 197, 231, 236, 237, 296, 297; and Yosemite residence, 4, 33, 46–47, 71–72, 76, 84, 141, 142, 238, 245, 257, 262; and conservation, 4, 5, 6, 7, 9, 107, 245, 287, 288, 299; and glaciers, 4, 17, 69, 142, 159, 169, 170, 173, 175–89, 214, 223, 239, 246–48, 249, 253, 254, 260, 271, 278, 282, 296; and Jeanne Carr, 4, 53, 69, 70, 71, 72, 79, 89, 119, 120, 122, 123, 129–30, 137, 171, 172, 200, 231, 249, 252; and Alaska trips, 5, 50, 56–58, 137, 141, 144–47, 187–90; and wife, 5, 7, 30, 50, 267, 269, 270, 292, 295, 296; marriage of, 5, 30, 50, 72; daughters of, 5, 6, 17, 30, 50, 276; and Sierra Club, 6, 17, 72, 95, 237, 238, 246; and U.S. Forestry Commission, 6, 220, 270; and Harriman Alaska Expedition, 6; and Harriman, 95; and preservation, 6, 9, 72, 94–96, 104–15, 119, 122, 200, 230, 231, 281, 302–4; and overseas travel, 6, 7, 286–301; death of, 7,

Index

59–60, 72; influence of, 7–11, 303–4; and ecology, 9, 10, 71, 79n.8, 109–15, 198, 199, 200, 231, 238–39, 260, 279, 282; and Christianity, 10, 12n.7, 29–30, 51, 53, 65–79, 79n.8, 83–96, 120, 148, 269–70; and anthropocentrism, 10, 12n.7, 84–85, 86, 238; and "deep ecology," 10, 109–115; and wilderness, 11, 34, 94, 104–15, 119–33, 303; as inventor, 17, 18, 26–27, 32, 68, 70; as botanist, 17, 32–33, 69, 76, 190n.1, 195–201, 215, 231–39, 287; and geology, 17, 33, 159, 169–190, 190n.1, 267; and glaciers, 17, 69, 142, 159, 169, 170, 173, 175–89, 214, 223, 239, 246–48, 249, 253, 254, 260, 271, 278, 282, 296; as naturalist, 17, 169, 287; and mother, 19–20, 34; on God, 20, 28, 29, 30, 33, 53, 69, 70, 71, 74, 86, 87, 88, 90, 91, 92, 96, 97n.9, 109, 113, 114, 121, 143, 149, 252, 288; and generosity, 23–25; and ranching, 25, 30, 31, 32, 50, 72; and Calvinism, 18, 29, 53, 87, 248; and the Bible, 29, 53, 69, 73, 74, 79; and Yosemite, 33, 43, 46, 47, 48, 51, 52, 53, 70, 87, 89, 96, 109, 120, 123, 127, 137, 141, 148, 171, 173–74, 197, 212, 237, 238, 245, 267, 270, 271; and mountaineering, 43–60, 72, 123, 156–63; and pantheism, 30, 51, 71; and transcendentalism, 51, 53, 59, 65, 96, 137–49, 235, 287; journals of, 69, 71, 89, 93, 121, 249, 252, 253, 255, 256, 267, 269, 271, 274–75, 276, 282, 289, 290, 298, 299; as John the Baptist, 73, 94, 120, 128, 257; and Taoism, 80n.8, 83, 87, 96; and Buddhism, 83, 87, 96; and Nature, 30, 84, 93–94, 139–41, 145, 275, 280, 281, 282; and human depravity, 90–91; and original sin, 90–91; religious conversion of, 165;

and the Southern Sierra, 246–62; and Darwin, 69, 83, 92, 232, 253, 287, 289, 299; and Yellowstone, 267–82; and Australasia, 287–304
Muir, Louisa "Louie" Strentzel (wife), 5, 6, 7, 30, 50, 267, 269, 270, 292, 295, 296
Muir Day, 8
Muir Glacier, 145–46, 187, 189
Muir National Historical Site, 23
Muir National Monument, 8
Muir National Scenic Trail, 8
Muir Trail, 123–33
Muir Wilderness, 8, 125
Muir Woods State Park, 8
Murray, William, 203
Munz, Philip A., 231, 241n.49
My First Summer in the Sierra, 7, 141, 199
My Life, 222

Naess, Arne, 104, 115n.3
Nature, 12n.2 and n.3, 30, 71, 74, 84, 91, 93–94, 106, 107, 110, 111–12, 114, 119, 120, 122, 139, 142, 145, 147, 154, 157, 275, 280, 281, 282
"Nature," 123, 139, 144, 147, 149
National Herbarium, 207, 215
National Park Bill, 258
"A Near View of the High Sierra," 153–65
Nevins, Thomas, 207
New Deal, 13n.11
New England, 6
New York Tribune, 65, 170, 171
New Zealand, 287, 288, 296–300
Northern Pacific Railroad, 269
"Notes on the Pacific Coast Glaciers," 188–89
Nuttall, Thomas, 201–02

Old Faithful, 272–73
"On the Glaciation of the Arctic," 187–89

Index

"On the Post-Glacial History of
Sequoia Gigantea," 186
Orsi, Richard, 95
Osborn, Henry Fairfield, 302
Our National Parks, 6, 104, 108, 119,
123, 125, 267
Overland Monthly, 5, 19, 142, 172, 175,
186, 215
Owens Valley, 171, 218, 246

Pacific Historian, The, 288
Panama, 196–97
Parish, Samuel, 227
Park, Mungo, 69
Parry, C. C. (Christopher), 204, 227,
236
Pathless Way, The, (Cohen) 148
Paul (Saint), 88
Peabody Museum, 302
Picturesque California, 5, 31
Pinchot, Gifford, 6, 7, 9, 11, 13n.11,
239
Plummer, Sara, 221
Poe, Edgar Allan, 68
Port Darwin, 302
Preservation, 6, 10–11, 12n.3, 65, 114,
119, 303
Pringle, Cyrus, 227
Progressives, 6, 13n.11
Protestantism, 65, 69, 76, 88, 122

Raker Act, 7
*Rediscovering America: John Muir and
His Times*, (Turner) 17, 149
Reid, John, 24, 25
Reid, Margaret Muir (sister), 21, 22,
23, 24, 25, 31, 93
Richardson, James, 283–84n.28
Robinson, Charles D., 251, 258, 259
Romanticism, 65, 68, 71
Roosevelt, Theodore, 6, 9, 72, 127
Roper, Steve, 60n.10
Rotorua, 295
Rousseau, Jean-Jacques, 9

Royal Society of London, 235
Runkle, John Daniel, 170–71, 172
Runte, Alfred, 95
Ruskin, John, 215
Ryan, P. J., 288, 289, 290

Sacramento, California, 254
Sacramento Union, 254
San Francisco Bulletin, 5, 249, 252,
253, 254, 255, 258, 261
San Francisco Sunday Chronicle, 251
San Joaquin Valley, 108, 210, 245
Sargent, Charles S., 5, 6, 287, 289,
294, 295
Scotland, 3, 8, 66, 288
Scribner's, 5, 254
Sears, John, 268, 275
Second Wave, (Toffler) 11
Sellers, Mr. and Mrs. Frank, 270–71
Senger, J. H., 238
Sequoia National Park, 6, 262
Shakti, 128
Shiva, 128
Sierra Club, 6, 8, 196, 237
Sierra Nevada, 4, 5, 6, 46, 47, 51, 52,
71, 89, 93, 95, 123, 126, 137, 138,
143–44, 145, 153–65, 175, 176, 177,
195, 197, 201, 203, 210, 214, 215,
220, 221, 231, 236, 237, 296, 297
Silent Spring, (Carson) 11
Sisson, Justin, 49, 50
Smith, Michael, 229
Smithsonian Institute, 204
Son of the Wilderness, (Wolfe) 17
South America, 4, 71, 289
South Lyell Glacier, 177, 181–82
Southern Pacific Railroad, 95
Stanford, Jane Lathrop, 230
Stanford, Leland, 220, 230
Stanford University, 195, 196, 230
Steep Trails, 107, 108, 111
Stikeen, 7, 121
Stillman, Jacob, 203
Stockton, California, 211

Index

The Story of My Boyhood and Youth, 7, 28
"Studies in the Formation of Mountains," 186
Studies in the Sierra, 174, 175, 178, 180, 181–86
Sullivant, William, 220
Swett, John, 143
Swett, Mary, 143
Sydney, Australia, 292, 294, 300, 301
Sydney Botanic Gardens, 294, 300, 301

Taft, William Howard, 72
Taoism, 80n.8, 83, 86, 87
Taylor, Mr., 296
Tenaya Glacier, 177, 181–82
Thoreau, Henry David, 142; Muir read, 3, 53, 69, 137, 165; and Muir's writings, 139, 149, 154, 166n.11, n.17, 281; writings of, 157, 158, 159, 162, 163, 164
Thousand Mile Walk, 110
Toffler, Alvin, (*Second Wave*), 11
Tongariro National Park, 296
Torrey, John, 203, 207, 231, 235, 236, 237
Townsend, John, 201
Transcendentalism, 51, 53, 59, 65, 69, 71, 86, 96, 137–49, 235, 287
"Transcendentalist, The," 149
Trask, John B., 203
Travels in Alaska, 145, 187
Tuolumne Meadows, 153, 154, 156, 163
Turner, Fredrick, (*Rediscovering America: John Muir and His Times*), 17, 25, 29, 148
Tuve, Rosemond, 148, 149
Twenty Hill Hollow, 173
"Twenty Gill Hollow," 172–73
Tyndall, John, 175, 183, 232, 287

Uniformitarianism, 172, 180

United States Geological Survey, 215, 270
United States Geological Survey of the Territories, 235
United States National Park Service, 304
University of California, Berkeley, 195, 196, 207, 223–24, 231, 238
University of Wisconsin, 3, 23, 27, 28, 32, 53, 69, 84, 231–32

Varieties of Religious Experience, The, (James), 119, 121

Wallace, Alfred, 222, 237, 288, 292, 299, 300, 304
Warner, Charles Dudley, 280
Watson, Serano, 220
Wawona, 198, 246
Wellington, 296–97
West Australian Museum, 290
White, Lynn, Jr., 83
Whitney, Josiah D., 208, 212, 214, 215, 219, 237; Muir debates, 170, 178–79, 181, 247–49; theories of, 171, 176, 192n.16
Wilderness, 103–15
Wilderness Act, 131
Wilson, Woodrow, 7
Wisconsin, 3, 25, 30, 31, 67, 69, 71
Wisconsin State Agricultural Fair, 18, 32, 68
Wister, Owen, 267
Wolfe, Linnie Marsh, (*Son of the Wilderness*) 17, 239, 287, 288, 298
Woodward, Bernard, 290
Wordsworth, William, 53, 68
Wright, Charles, 204, 205, 232
Wylie, W. W., 284n.57

Yale University, 210, 220, 302
Yellowstone, 119, 267–82, 295
Yellowstone Lake, 271, 272

Index

Yelverton, Therese, (*Zonita: Tale of the Yosemite, A*), 47

The Yosemite, 7

Yosemite Valley, 4, 7, 26, 70, 71, 89, 96, 123, 128, 154, 170, 178–80, 248–61, 271

Yosemite Creek, 43

Yosemite Creek Glacier, 181–82

"Yosemite Glaciers," 65

Yosemite National Park, 6, 7, 237

Yosemite Recession Campaign, 95

"Yosemite Valley in Flood," 172

Young, S. Hall, (*Alaska Days with John Muir*), 56, 137, 144

Young Men's Christian Association, 69, 84

Zonita: A Tale of the Yosemite, (Yelverton), 47

Zen, 128

Zoe, (California Academy of Sciences), 227, 228, 229